"Is It Yourself"?

The life, times and mishaps of an Irishman

by Dermot Kane

The account of my life is as best as I can recall at the time of writing.

For my family and future generations, in particular, my sons, Jonathan, Liam and Jamie, and especially my long-suffering wife, Theresa.

© Dermot Kane 2023

This book is a memoir. It reflects the author's present recollections of experiences over time. Some names and characteristics have been changed, some events have been compressed, and some dialogue has been recreated.

Chapters

Foreword 1

Growing Up In Ireland 3

A New Life In England 37

Marriage And Children 92

Retirement 263

Epilogue 348

Foreword

I only started to write this book due to some pressure but mostly encouragement from my eldest son Jonathan, who thought I should write down and pass on some of these stories for the family and, in particular, for my grandchildren and the following generations of the Kanes, Fords, Kearneys or any other relatives / friends who might care to read it.

As an Irishman, I have always told stories and I think to be honest it's in all Irish people's DNA. However, having never written anything like this in my life before and being a fairly uneducated man, I really didn't know how or where to start writing about my life, but as the Sound of Music song goes 'Let's start at the very beginning' and so it was to be as I started the story with my birth!

I was amazed at how many memories flooded my mind as I started to write about my childhood, and this continued in the same vein right through to the present time. My formative years spent in Ireland with its relative poverty and hardships influenced me immensely and became the template for the rest of my life. I realised slowly that I was also writing about my own interpretation of a bygone era when everyone, generally speaking, seemed to know and care for each other, and society as a whole appeared to be more cohesive as most people relied on each other in order to survive.

Life was quite hard back in the day, and I can recall with great clarity the working and social living conditions for families particularly during the fifties and sixties. The women in my formative years (including my mother, Nellie Darcy and aunties on both the Kane and Kearney sides of the family) were very special to me as despite having their own problems and difficulties, they always showed me love, gave out warmth in abundance and provided some stability in my early difficult years. Their kindness and gift of love had a massive influence on me as they had the ability to make me **feel** loved and cared for.

Their loving influence provided a pathway for me to follow as I grew up and hopefully, I have managed to pass on my own attitude and respect for women to my own boys as they grew up.

With this in mind, as I have made my way through life I have noted and felt that **"people will forget what you said, people will even forget what you did, but people will never ever forget how you made them feel!"**

During the course of writing I also noted that so many of life's clichés which are quoted by learned men and women to be so true during my lifetime, almost every one of them, for example "treat others as you would like to be treated yourself, no man is an island, the love you give is equal to the love you make, live, laugh, love and make the most of each day as who knows what tomorrow may bring, Love is the greatest gift of all etc" (you get the idea reader!).

With some of these clichés in mind, I made a conscious effort not to write too much about the negative aspects of my life and unkind people that I have met along the way albeit strangers, or even family or friends at times. I have only written my own interpretation of things I have experienced and seen during my lifetime, and I sincerely hope that no one is offended by anything I have written. So please folks accept this book in the spirit that I have written it in.

Anyway reader, thanks for picking this book up and I hope that you can find something that may either interest you, make you laugh and perhaps even make you cry. So please take a ride with me through my life and see what you think!

Dermot Kane

November 2023

Growing Up In Ireland

My Arrival

My arrival into this world took place on 26 February 1948 in 67, Rialto Cottages, Dublin, Ireland. Apparently, the winter of 1947/48 was the worst in living memory with twelve-foot snow drifts in places resulting in the whole of Ireland basically coming to a standstill.

My mother told me, later on in life, that my arrival was not without incident either, as my Dad had arranged for a midwife to carry out the delivery at home and had paid up front in person to the midwife concerned for the said task. However, on the night of my arrival into this world, the midwife had turned up drunk and was not capable of carrying out the delivery. Now, as luck would have it, my Dad's sister Teresa (Tessie) had turned up at the cottage to assist in whatever way she could with the birth.

This proved to be very fortunate for both my Mam and me as the birth was very quick and I came into the world with the umbilical cord wrapped around my neck whilst looking decidedly blue due to being strangled by the cord. However, thank goodness Tessie had assisted with previous births and luckily knew what to do.

I was also born with a "caul' over my face, according to my Mam, which is a very thin membrane which covered the whole of my face and is quite a rare thing to see! I was told later in life, that if you were born with a caul over your face, you were considered to be lucky for the rest of your life. Moreover, sailors were known to pay a small fortune for a caul as they felt that this would protect them and keep them safe whilst at sea.

My Mam said that Tessie folded the caul and put it in a safe place at the time. However, it disappeared over the next few years and my Mam thought that it was perhaps my Dad who sold it to a sailor in Dublin Port when he was short of cash to fund his beer drinking and gambling… who knows reader?!

(Tessie - Teresa born 26th March 1913. Married James Jackson 2nd June 1935 and sadly died on 18th August 1951). I never had the chance to get to know her or had the opportunity to thank her for bringing me into the world. However, she had a family of her own (the Jacksons / Caseys) and I have kept touch with them over the years and during drinking sessions with them I have expressed my eternal gratitude to their late mother. I will get back to the Jacksons later in the book!

Drinking with Nellie Darcy

My earliest memory of life in Dublin, was typically Irish in that it was not a memory of any members of my family, but instead it was a memory of going into a pub in Rialto called McCauley's with a lovely kind and gentle old lady called Nellie Darcy.

You see, Nellie (who was probably about 70-80 years of age) used to live in the tenement buildings in the centre of Rialto and would look after me whilst my Mam and Dad were working. Dad was a bus conductor with the CIE Bus Company and my mother was a waitress at Cleary's store in O'Connell Street.

Nellie would take me each dinner time to the pub, and we would sit in a small room called the 'Snug' which was at the front of McCauley's pub (as women generally in those days did not drink in the same bars as men). Nellie was usually joined by several other old ladies from the local area to have a glass or two of stout whilst they had a good old chat. I would sit quietly watching the proceedings and if I was good, I would be given a glass of cherryade which I absolutely loved! I would also have the pleasure of having the attention of all the old ladies who would take turns in patting me on the head or give me a kiss on the cheek whilst telling me what a "good boy" I was!

Having consumed her stout, Nellie would stagger back to her flat in the buildings and put me to bed whilst she had an afternoon snooze to recover from her daily tipple. I remember as if it was only yesterday that she always gave me a clock to go to bed with, which she would wind up, put to my ear to let me hear it ticking and then would tuck me in into bed with a loving gentle kiss on my forehead. My first memories of life were good as I felt very safe and loved by the lovely Nellie.

One of the few pictures I have of myself as a small child, probably aged 18 months.

Granny Kane and the soldier

However, the opposite was true of my Granny Kane who lived just around the corner from us at 23 Rialto Street. Granny Marcella Kane was a very short, overweight, rotund woman with grey hair who always wore glasses and, on the surface, she looked like the perfect Granny. However, she had the ability to be either very kind to those she approved of or very hostile to those to whom she did not. Looking back, I think that she was mainly driven by money and status, of course I could be wrong!

For example, some of my cousins would always be in number 23 and others, such as my brother Frank and I, were rarely allowed into her house. If we were sent around to her house to get something for my Mam or Dad, we would be greeted by her at the door with an angry look on her face whilst asking aggressively in a raspy loud voice that could cut your ears off "what do you want?"

We would always be kept on the doorstep whilst she got whatever we were sent for. I was really frightened of her and never witnessed or felt any kindness or love from her. Sadly, my Granny always made me feel unhappy and unwanted and I really wish that it could have been different.

Granny always appeared to prefer the next-door neighbour's children (Laura and Roy Malone) as their mother and father were in business and were quite rich in comparison to us. Mr Malone

(Victor) owned a barber's shop in Dolphins Barn and his wife was a store manageress in the centre of Dublin. Vic was also my Dad's best man at his wedding. Nevertheless, I think that my Granny felt that my Dad had married below his station and therefore I think that she felt resentment and dislike towards my mother and us - of course once again I could be wrong!

Now then reader! To be fair to my Grandma, her early life must have been tough as she gave birth to 15 children – including my Dad Francis, Patrick, Tony, Violet, Mary, John, Joseph, Angela (who sadly passed away prematurely aged 9), Teresa, Thomas (known as Gerry) and Eileen. Plus, the fact that she lost her husband in 1939 and had to bring the family up on her own which couldn't have been easy.

Having said all that, regardless of my Grandma's previous hardships, I still feel hurt and upset by her total rejection of us and I firmly believe that she was wrong to treat her own flesh and blood in that way.

Nevertheless, my Dad naturally loved his mother and told me stories of her strength and character, including one about the British Army in Rialto.

During the 1916 Rebellion, she always carried a revolver in her knickers (who the gun was for I don't know, I assumed it was for her husband!) and he also stated that she was never frightened of anyone and recalled the incident when the British Army arrived in Rialto to do a search of houses.

Apparently, a soldier entered her house and upon entry pushed one of the boys aside very hard and severely. Granny apparently went to the umbrella stand in the hall and picked up the nearest umbrella and started to beat the soldier about his head with great force. The soldier warned her that he would shoot her if she did not stop. According to my Dad he raised his rifle to do so when an officer who heard the commotion intervened and ordered the soldier to stop. Fair play to her!

I know little of my Grandma or Grandad's previous lives other than they both met whilst working at a hotel in Drogheda where they both lived at the time. My Grandad was a footman and my Grandma a maid. My Grandad Kane later worked for Guinness when they came to Dublin. He was apparently a lovely, kind man, who sadly died in 1939 long before I was born. I know that my Grandma had a sister called Angela who married into the Byrne Family. She had a least fifteen children, but other than this I know very little of her former life.

Grandad Joseph and Grandma Marcella Kane with their children Eileen and Tony circa 1925/30. Grandma Kane is actually smiling on this photo would you believe!

My Mother and the Kearney's

My mother (Eileen Mary Kane - Nee Kearney, born in Ballymahon, County Longford on 11th January 1917, the eldest daughter to James and Ellen) was the most beautiful, kind, innocent and very naive person you could possible meet (she looked stunning in early photographs I have of her). A very slim lady with beautiful long curly hair, smartly dressed who was slightly taller than my Dad at five foot seven. She came from a family of sixteen with five sisters who were all beautiful looking and the rest being males.

My Mam was a silver service waitress in Clery's department store in Dublin (a bit like John Lewis today, but posher!). She worked very hard and received a fair amount of tips which she used to pay her mother 12 shillings per week to look after my brother Frank when he was born. One of my earliest memories of my mother was meeting her with my brother Frank after she had finished work in Clery's and having an ice cream with them both in the American ice cream parlour just past the bridge in O'Connell Street on the North side (it's long since gone though). The ice cream was so delicious, and I remember feeling very safe, comforted and happy at that particular moment in my life.

My obsession with ice cream has stayed with me and I think it stems back directly to that early comforting memory. Moreover, I think, psychology speaking, that even at the age of 75 I am still comforted and happy every time I have an ice cream.

Anyway, I digress so back to the story! My Mam, bless her, kept a spotless home for the family and despite having a fairly poor standard of living, always did her very best for us kids. She loved life in general and was a very good singer and was a member of an amateur operatic society in Rathmines. Mam also loved dancing and going to the theatre when she could afford it.

My mother also went to school with the famous Hollywood actress Maureen O'Hara before she left to live and work in America, a fact that my mother loved and would always tell others of her claim to fame.

My beautiful mother with brother Frank aged approx. 18 months / 2 years.

My mother's father (James (Jim) Kearney born 1884 - died 1962) was a very kindly quiet family man who loved nothing more than to smoke his pipe and read the paper at the fireside. He was a man of few words and stood about five feet eleven tall and of slim build with a moustache. He was a very well-educated man, and his handwriting was beautiful. He married my Grandmother Ellen on 5th April 1911.

His profession was gardening, as indeed was his father and grandfather before him! Most of his sons were gardeners too and they lived in a council house in Crumlin. Grandad Kearney was held in high regard within the gardening world. He was head gardener in Leixlip on the estate of Lady Connell and had eight gardeners working under him. He also worked at several lodges and big estates in Dublin including Farmleigh House in the Phoenix Park and the Dartry Lodge estate.

Grandad Kearney also served in the Irish Citizen Army, with his brother Phillip from 1914 until 1923. Both Phillip and my Grandad are on a famous photograph taken outside Liberty Hall with the banner on top of the building stating that "we serve neither King nor Kaiser but Ireland". I don't know why but I find it very moving and emotional, whilst feeling very proud of both my Grandad and his brother Phillip, whenever I look at that photograph.

Note: Picture taken from the Book "The History of the Irish Citizen Army" by R. M. Fox and available online in the National Library of Ireland.

According to my Grandad: A indicates himself, Grandad Kearney and B indicates his brother, Phillip, front and centre of the picture.

           A   *B*

This colourised, zoomed-in picture, shows James Connolly in attendance, who was commandant of the Dublin Brigade during the 1916 Easter Rising, with Grandad on the left and Phillip in front.

James Connolly was a revolutionary socialist, trade union leader and political activist. He was sentenced to death by firing squad at Kilmainham Gaol for his part in the 1916 Rising. Because of the severity of his wounds from the fighting, he was carried to the prison courtyard on a stretcher, strapped to a chair as he was unable to stand, and then shot. His execution significantly contributed to the mood of the public to seek change and freedom for Ireland.

The fact that my grandparents had fourteen children is amazing in itself: Alphonsus / Alf (I think he was named after an Italian ice cream man as a lot of people in Ireland were in those days), Phillip,

Eileen, Terence, Brian, Vera, Carmel, Danny, James, Shem, Maura, Frank and Gerald. Moreover, the mortality rate for children was very high in those days and a couple of their children (May and Terence and two others unknown) died prematurely, it must have been so hard in those days for parents, particularly mothers!

However, according to Aunt Maura, they had such happy lives with a great sense of freedom to roam the grounds of wherever Grandad was working at the time and they were never short of food as most of it was grown in the grounds. Moreover, they had love and security in abundance from both of their lovely parents.

Back Row Left to right: Danny, Carmel, Brian & Eileen. Centre: Terry, Grandma holding baby Ger. Bottom: Grandad holding Frank.

Another of my earliest memories was attending my Mam's sister Aunt Carmel's funeral. I remember vaguely being with my mother on the day in Carmel's house in Donore Avenue with all the family crying whilst dressed in black attire and a large hearse waiting outside the front door.

Aunt Carmel was born in 1924 and sadly died prematurely aged 28 in 1953 shortly after given birth to her daughter. Bernie survived and I later tracked her and her sister Eileen down in the late 1970s and have kept in touch ever since (I will come back to this later - see Finding my long-lost cousins).

Aunt Carmel (wasn't she a lovely looking woman?) with her eldest daughter Eileen.

Anyway, Aunt Maura always described her Dad as "a bit of an auld ram" hence all the children, however, one thing is clear about my grandparents; it is very obvious that they were completely in love throughout their married life as the family had an abundance of letters written by my grandfather to his beloved Ellen and when you read them it really pulls at your heart strings as he obviously adored her.

Grandma Ellen (Nellie) Josephine Kearney-nee Hickey. Born 1891. Died 1959. Ironically, my grandmother was also from a family of gardeners too, which probably explains why gardening is so prevalent in the Kearney genes. My grandmother was a small quiet gentle woman whose whole purpose in life seemed to be to love and adore her husband and family. Apparently, she was also a great cook and kept a clean and tidy house for all of them. Her main enjoyment was sitting by the fireside reading novels in the company of my Grandad.

Unfortunately, my grandmother had a severe stroke in the early fifties and never recovered. As I grew up, I can remember her, but never had the chance to converse with her due to the loss of her speech (she could only mumble and it was impossible to know what she was trying to say, bless her). Sadly, my grandmother died just a couple of years after we left Ireland.

The blind man's kiosk

Before I talk about my father, I would just like to briefly talk about the blind man's kiosk which originally stood on the large green facing my Kearney grandparents' house in Crumlin at 252, Clonard Road.

The owner (a very small, pleasant man probably about 4 feet six inches tall as I recall) sold sweets, cigarettes, and most of what you would find as essentials in a normal shop. The building itself was square shaped and made of concrete with a flat roof and was very small probably about six foot square, therefore it could only be manned by one person due to the size.

The owner knew all the locals and who could be trusted or not as the case may be, moreover, he was always polite and pleasant in mood and manner. I was totally fascinated by him and his ability to count and recognise every single coin and note that was given to him despite his disability. Moreover, he absolutely knew where every product to be purchased by the public was kept and could put his hand straight on it when required. Many times, I witnessed children and adults testing his sharpness by placing foreign notes or coins on the tray before him.

However, never once did he fail to recognise the difference and politely returned them to the owner telling them that they "must have made a mistake". The kiosk has long since gone along with its owner. I have never encountered a blind man's kiosk since my days in Dublin and I think it's just another example of the Irish race who are quite unique in my opinion.

Francis O'Rahilly Kane

My father, Francis O' Rahilly Kane was born in Dublin on 6th June 1917 (and in case you are wondering, why the O'Rahilly is in his name, it was given to him by his Dad in memory of an Irish patriot who died during the 1916 Rising).

Dad was from a family of thirteen. My father was a very dapper dressed man about five feet six inch tall with a moustache and of medium build and despite his small stature, he was not afraid of any man (I will get to this later).

13

Dad was very bright and intelligent at school and apparently had brains to burn and so he was offered a scholarship at Trinity College Dublin just before he left school. However, his mother put a stop to this as she wanted him to start work in order to add to the family finances - she seemed to have a tight hold of the family and dominated those who were less assertive and my father always resented this for the rest of his life, as he loved to learn and wanted to progress beyond being just a bus conductor and for this, I felt very sorry for him.

Dad and my head punches

Later in his life I experienced Dad's academic frustration and resentment first hand when he sat down with me to help me with homework on several occasions. I was very frightened and froze when I couldn't answer the questions. I remember him punching me several times on the head and calling me "thick". This incident was to haunt me later in life as when I took my training to be a forensic mental health nurse, I nearly had a breakdown for the first and only time in my life (I will get back to this later - see the 'oldest student in the world' and 'childhood memories return to haunt me' chapters).

Anyway, getting back to my story, several of my Dad's brothers did not marry as apparently Grandma would vet each new girlfriend and if they did not live up to her expectations would do her best to prevent any further progress in the relationship. My Dad joined the Irish Army a couple of years after leaving school and rose to the rank of Sergeant.

He told me of an incident whilst in the army when he was cutting turf one summer. He said that after a day's work, he and many others boarded a truck to return to the barracks in the Curragh. On the way back the driver lost control of the truck and left the road and completely overturned the vehicle. According to my Dad, two of the soldiers died that day and several others had serious injuries. However, he recalled that he didn't have a scratch on his body and other than some soreness he was perfectly fine and very lucky to be alive.

Dad also informed me that after coming out of the army, he went to England where he joined the Royal Airforce as a wireless operator, but he did not last long as he deserted after several months and returned to Ireland.

My very young Dad in Irish uniform.

Dad meeting my mother

My father met my mother at the 'Our Lady of Dolours' church in Dolphin's Barn one Sunday morning at mass. According to my Dad, he was in the row behind her and was struck by her beauty. He told me that as she was participating in the mass, he started to blow gently at her hair and ears. She apparently turned and smiled at him which he naturally found encouraging. He waited outside the church for her, and the rest was history as they say!

They married at the same church on 26th December 1942 and first resided in a flat in Harold's Cross where my brother Frank was born in 1944. After this, they moved into 67 Rialto Cottages which was the original home of my Grandad and Grandma Kane and my mother gave birth to me on 26th February 1948. There was to be an eight-year gap between me and my brother Sean who was born on 8th November 1956.

1942. Mam and Dad on their Wedding day with Grandad Kearney on the right.

However, my Mam and Dad's relationship was not always loving, in fact it was, for much of the time, an abusive relationship (particularly when either of them had been drinking). Most nights out could start out fine, but once they returned to the cottage under the influence of the demon drink, it could quickly turn nasty with my mother being pushed, hit or punched by my Dad whenever it became heated.

The rows could vary from financial, interpersonal relationships, or Dad going missing for days or even weeks without any notice and family dynamics, which usually ended up with Mam slagging off Dad's family and my Dad defending his family either verbally or with his fists.

It was quite normal for us to be taken out of bed by my Mam during the early hours of the morning following a big bust up to seek shelter with either of our close Aunties Maura or Eva. Looking back, it was quite traumatic and frightening for us as children and it's no bloody wonder that I became anxious and lacked confidence as I grew to be a man.

My childhood guardian angels!

The women had it very hard in my childhood with the men being the dominant force and the women being our saviours. I'm not wishing to speak ill of past relatives as I have nothing but love and respect for all members of my family. However, I do think it's important for the reader to know how it was in those days for women. Nevertheless, I am not saying this was the case with all men at the time.

To illustrate my point, I can recall Aunt Maura telling me the story of her furniture being sold by her husband Eddie. Apparently, she had come back from shopping and stopped a couple of streets away to talk to a lady she knew. As they were talking, a horse and cart went by, full to the brim with furniture and Aunt Maura mentioned to the lady as it passed saying "that looks a bit like my sofa" followed by "and that looks a bit like my table and chairs" etc... and so it went on and on. To cut a long story short, when Maura arrived home, there was not a stick of furniture left downstairs as Eddie Snr had sold it all! Aunt Maura went on to say it was probably sold for beer money and, bless her, even when she told me this story, she still had the ability to laugh and smile about it!

As for Aunt Eva, Uncle Alf left Ireland and made a new life for himself in England whilst Aunt Eva brought up the children mainly on her own, without ever really complaining. My own mother was to experience the same when my Dad left for England several years later (see 'dad leaving poorer times').

On many occasions we would walk up to stay overnight at my Aunt Maura's in Drimnagh (Maura Kearney born 1930, died 2020 - married Eddy Sutcliffe and had six children - Eddy Jnr, Terry, Carmel, Katherine, James and Michael). Aunt Maura was a kind, loving and generous woman and despite having little in the way of money of food for her own family, she would share whatever she had with us, whilst providing shelter and safety for us all and for this I shall always be grateful.

Footnote: Incidentally skipping forward, Aunt Maura came to live in Leicester in the early sixties with her children and lived with us in Avon Street for a short period of time before finding their own place. She eventually returned to Ireland to live in the late eighties, I believe.

On other occasions it would be Aunt Eva's turn to put us up overnight as she lived in Cashel Road, Crumlin just around the corner from Grandad and Grandma Kearney. Eva (Hannah) Condron was Uncle Alfie's wife, who had five children herself - Irene, Terry, Angela, Mona and Helen.

My Dad would sometimes follow us to either of these addresses and it was not uncommon to hear him banging on the doors of my Aunties houses for long periods whilst shouting loudly and making threats against my mother. This is while we were in bed feeling very frightened and hugging each other for comfort.

Both of my lovely aunties, despite having their own problems, would never turn us away, but welcome us in with love and affection and share whatever little they had in the house with us and for this, I shall be forever grateful! However, I have to point out that this was fairly common with many families at this time in Ireland as males were very dominant and generally sexist and selfish in those days (not all I might add). It was also the general view of males back then that woman should be chained to the sink and children should be seen but never heard.

Our two wonderful guardian angels. Left - Aunt Maura on her bike, always smiling, bless her! Aunt Eva, here on the right leaning on the posh car with Aunt Carmel and her daughter Eileen in the forefront.

Regarding children not being heard, my Uncle Terry always called me "earwig" as a child as I was always listening in and watching what the adults were doing and saying. I make no apology for this whatsoever as it was true. This early trait lasted throughout my life, and I am still interested and fascinated in people and what makes them tick and also in life itself generally.

The Kane family in Rialto

Going back in history as I understand it, the 'Kane Clan' had originated in Derry, Ulster and over the centuries they made their way south and ended up spreading across the world. The original name in Gaelic for Kane was O'Cathain, meaning battle or warrior I believe, however, during the seven hundred years of British rule the name became anglicised to O'Kane initially and eventually just Kane. Anything remotely Irish was frowned upon and discouraged by the English government back in the day.

Nevertheless, I would have loved to have had my proper Gaelic name of Diarmuid O'Cathain and I did seriously think about changing my surname legally as my children were growing up. However, having considered the implications such as my own children going to school one day with the name of Kane and then overnight going back to school with the completely different name of O'Cathain, also my own siblings having a different name to myself and all this to say nothing of what my extended family might make of it all, I decided not to go ahead with the name change.

Anyway, getting back to my family in Rialto, I only saw some of the Kane family on occasions growing up, as they were generally not encouraged to see us by their mother who for whatever reason did not seem to like us. We were actually much closer and saw more of my mother's family, the Kearneys, who lived in a council house (252 Clonard Road, Crumlin) which was roughly about two miles from where we lived in Rialto.

My personal favourites of the Kanes were Uncle Tony, Aunt Eileen and her husband, Uncle Sean Lacey, Uncle Pat, Uncle Gerry and his wife Francis Armstrong. 'Over the wall, Joe' (dads eldest brother) very rarely spoke to us and Uncle John was somewhat similar. We never had presents at Christmas other than a few clothes, apples and oranges in a sock. However, one Christmas, Uncle Tony bought me a Roy Rogers tie and a blackboard. I was over the moon and have never forgot that lovely Christmas feeling.

Aunt Eileen was also generous and would sometimes give you a sixpence or even a shilling if she popped in to see my mother, who she was very fond of, despite her own mother's disapproval. On another occasion, my Uncle Pat turned up at our house in a car and would you believe took us down to his new house in Naas. This was the first time I had ever been in a car as not many people could afford such luxuries in those days. His house was very posh compared to ours as there was lovely furniture and plenty of food. I remember thinking how lucky my cousin Pat Jnr was!!

My Dad's elder brother Pat Kane, Auntie Lydia and Pat Kane Jnr.

Life in Rialto

Rialto was a friendly kind of place where everyone knew each other, and all of the community would look out for one another and step in to help anyone, should the need arise. No one famous ever came out of Rialto other than Gay Byrne, who lived just around the corner from us with his family at number 17 Rialto Street. Gay was a very clever guy who studied at Trinity College and went on to have his own famous television show in Ireland called 'The Late Late Show' (it ran for 37 years and was the world's second longest-running chat show, plus he was the first person to introduce The Beatles on-screen).

I went to the Rialto Boys National School, which I hated as we were taught mainly by teachers as well as Christian Brothers and priests on occasions. The Brothers, especially, were very disciplined and cruel at times, especially if you were not academic like me. You were likely to get a smacking from them if you didn't know your maths timetables, spelling, Catechism, etc. What's that to do with Christianity, I ask? The church in Ireland was very powerful and influential in Irish life and more or less ruled Ireland along with the government at the time. They have a lot to answer for in my opinion!

I couldn't wait for school to finish each day as our dog Spot would be waiting for us (see Spot Kane section) and there was a great sense of freedom due to my mother and father both working. Both Frank and I were left to our own devices to roam wherever we wanted and there were also very happy times when we built our own go karts made up from bits of old prams, wheels from anything or bits of wood nailed together which would eventually end up as some kind of go-kart. We would then have races against each other down the hill from the top of Rialto in the hope that you would become the champion go kart kid of Rialto!!

Rialto Street in 1950. The house on the left looks just like Grandma Kane's house - it could well be actually!

I had a couple of friends that I can remember playing with. The first one was called 'Fid'. I never did know his surname or why he was called such a name, but he was a scruffy lovable urchin who also adored my dog, Spot. The thing I remember most about him was that he constantly picked his nose throughout the day and if he was spotted by myself in the act of mining his nose, he would put his hands behind his back and wipe the contents of his pickings on the back of his trousers or on the nearest wall!

Another friend was Mick O'Brien. Both Mick and I would love to play handball with a tennis ball against the side of the houses at the end of Rialto Cottages where I lived. We would spend hours doing this and I suspect that my love for squash was a direct result of our games together. Mick incidentally went on to represent Ireland at football at under 15 level I recall.

I also had my own hideaway which was at the top of the canal behind the advertising boards at Rialto Bridge. I would go there either alone or in the company of my dog, Spot. It felt like a safe place to be where no one else could find me. I never really minded my own company, but I did prefer Spots company as he always showed me love and loyalty. I was in my own world behind the advertising boards and would let my imagination run wild as I pretended to be a cowboy or a war hero. I still return to this place whenever I go back to Dublin, and it gives me both a sense of comfort and melancholy.

It might seem incredible now, but at the ages of seven and eight, I was sent most Thursdays across the city to Ringsend bus garage to collect some money from my Dad's wages before he spent it. He would always give something reluctantly. However, if he was not around or returned from a trip, I would have to wait around. Now most of the bus conductors knew me and would say hello and sometimes give me a couple of pennies or even sixpence to spend on my favourite sweets, 'Honey Bees'. I remember on several occasions finding my Dad in a good mood after returning from his trip. It was fantastic when he would lift me up and let me sit in the driver's seat and then allow me to punch the bell with my fist which was how you would ring the bell in those days.

Violence was never far from us in one form or another in Rialto as there was an eight-foot wall which ran along the length of all the cottages in Rialto, and on the other side of the wall was Fatima Mansions. This was quite notorious in Dublin as one of the worse estates in the south of the city. I felt this at first hand on several occasions. Once I was shot in my left knee with a pellet gun shot directed from the mansions. It was really painful, but no one seemed to bother about this including my Mam and Dad and I still bear the scar to this day.

On several other occasions, the kids from Fatima would suddenly appear at the top of the wall which separated them from us and would commence to pelt us with anything they could find including bottles, bricks, bits of wood or anything that could cause a person damage. I witnessed quite a few bloody casualties with split heads and wounds but again, no one seemed bothered despite us feeling like we had been to war! You just got on with things in those days and political correctness did not exist!

Footnote: Fatima Mansions were pulled down Circa 2004-07.

36 and 37 Rialto cottages. Mrs. Doherty on the path with Mrs. Nolan in the 1950's. The 'wall' and Fatima Mansions in the background. We lived in the row of cottages in the next street to this, which looks the same as this apart from us having a higher wall.

Back in those days the barges on the canal at the top of Rialto Street (which is now incidentally filled in and part of the tram system) used to be constantly taking barrels into and out of the Guinness factory all day long. Back then, I couldn't swim and I didn't learn until I was 20 years of age, nevertheless we used to jump on the barges when they passed close to us under the Rialto Bridge. We would then get a ride to the next bridge on most occasions if you were lucky enough not to be seen by the captain. However, if seen by the captain he would throw stones or lumps of coal at you. We thought this was exciting as we knew he couldn't leave the tiller of the barge and so we ducked and dived whilst killing ourselves laughing at each stone or lump of coal that was thrown at us. However, on one particular occasion when I was on my own, the captain stopped the engine on the barge and left the tiller as it approached the second bridge. He then managed to catch up with me and proceeded to give me a good kick up the arse before I made my escape off the barge!

Accident Prone

Throughout my life I have always been accident prone (as you will see as my story progresses). I remember my first accident when I was probably about 5-6 years old. It was a hot summer's day in Dublin and Rialto Street had just been resurfaced with tar and chippings. I remember coming out of me Mam's cottage and I spotted a friend on the opposite side of Rialto Street.

Without thinking or indeed looking, I ran straight out into the road, and I was hit full on by a cyclist who was coming down the hill from the top end of Rialto near the canal at high speed. I went flying through the air and landed on the opposite kerb where unfortunately the tar was still fairly hot and unset as it had only been laid about an hour before.

Apart from being bruised and bleeding, I was covered from head to toe in tar and chippings. My clothes were shredded and torn, and the tar was in my hair and all over my body. I was naturally crying for my Mam and the cyclist who was battered and bruised himself picked me up and asked a neighbour who was present as to where I lived.

My mother was getting ready for work as he knocked on the door and I remember the shock on her face as she blessed herself and said, "Jesus Mary and Joseph, look at the state of you". In those days you had to pay for any treatment at your doctors and so my mother took me to the local chemist who cleaned the wounds out and advised my Mam on the best form of treatment. I remember for what seemed like weeks afterwards, my Mam trying to get the tar off my skin with butter and tar out of my hair with a nit comb, which was all very painful!

Spot Kane

My main companion during these times was my dog, Spot Kane, and even though he was actually Frank's dog which he had from a puppy, I nevertheless considered him mine. Every dog in Rialto would be referred to and be given their full official name including the owner's surname.

Spot Kane was a mongrel who was quite small and very slender in build with floppy longish ears and his coat was very dark brown, almost black. I loved that dog with all my heart! He would follow me everywhere and was a constant source of love and faithfulness. Both Frank and I would be greeted by him after school (Rialto Boys National School) every day, with him waiting on the other side of the road with his tail wagging like mad.

He was also there one very windy day when the metal dustbins had just been emptied by the dustmen. I was encouraging him to chase after me when a dustbin flew by me at a speed of knots. I ran for a very short while afterwards before collapsing. It was then I realised the dustbin which had a rusty jagged edge, had ripped a large lump of flesh from my left thigh. It was about two inches deep and the bone was clearly visible.

As you had to pay for health treatment in those days, my Mam took me to the local pharmacist who treated the wound and bandaged it up. I was in bed for nearly two weeks with this and Spot was my constant companion during this time, bless him!

Another story about Spot was not so positive. At the top of Rialto was the canal which ran all the way into Guinness brewery. The canal had a large water rat population which thrived due to having access to food in the grain stores of the brewery. The water rats were tan coloured, very large, long and sleekly and in the summer, they could be seen on the opposite bank of the canal in large numbers bathing in the sunshine, fighting and socialising.

One day I was walking with my brother Frank at the top of the street when a lady from the tenements came running out into the street screaming. She told us that a rat had gone into her flat. As we had Spot with us at the time, my brother Frank gave assurance to the lady and sent our dog in to sort the rat out or so we thought! Within seconds of going in, we heard him yelping having been bitten by the rat only to see him return much quicker than when he went in with his tail tucked between his legs.

Having failed in his mission, a crowd had now gathered to see what was going on and someone suggested that Ace O'Brien, who was incidentally Spots half-brother (same mother, different father) and a much bigger dog, be sent for. Ace entered the flat and in a short time we heard a commotion which resulted in Ace bringing the dead rat out of the property between his teeth. Ace almost smiled as he dropped the rat at the feet of his owner Mick O'Brien. Frank and I felt somewhat shamed by the incident as the locals then began to speak of Spots poor 'ratting skills' and all three of us left quietly with all of our tails tucked between our legs!

Houdini

Spot was also called "Houdini" for a short time. This resulted from his many escapes from our back yard. We first noticed this after locking him in the yard and proceeding down to the bus stop to go into town. As the bus started off, Spot was seen running after the bus and then jumping onto the platform. We got off at the next stop and returned him to the yard feeling perplexed as to how he had escaped.

As we waited for the bus, we spotted him on the corner of Rialto Street. Having returned him to the yard we waited on the corner of our street only to see him coming over the roof of our cottage. It transpired that he was climbing onto his kennel roof, then jumping onto the wall to gain access to the shed roof, before climbing over our cottage roof and freedom.

Spot and the Ice Cream

As I began to write this book, I had a text from Aunt Eileen's daughter Sandra Keller (nee Lacey), who now lives in Paris with her husband, Andre and their three children (Brian, Sean and Aiden). She informed me that her mother used to often talk about Spot and myself and the special relationship that we had between us. She recalled that her mother loved to buy me ice creams as a child, so that she could just sit and watch as Spot and I would share the ice cream together. She remembers her mother saying with a grin on her face that it was "one lick for Dermo and one for Spot, one lick for Dermo and one for Spot, one lick for Dermo" you get the idea! We continued until we finished with great satisfaction and happiness as both Spot and I enjoyed each other's company and the ice cream so much!

Spot had a wonderful life of freedom, and he would roam the local area with other dogs and spend his days sniffing around and doing his doggy things whilst getting stroked and receiving 'tit bits' from our neighbours who nearly all knew and loved him. As I said, he also used to meet myself and my brother Frank out of school every day, so how the bloody hell did he know the time? He would eat the same food as us (if there was any leftovers) as dogs in those days were not pampered as they are today.

He was so loyal and faithful, and it broke all our hearts to leave our beloved Spot behind with my Aunt Maura when we left Ireland. Aunt Maura informed us that he kept going back to Rialto looking for us for a long time after our departure. Bless him! He lived to the ripe old age of nineteen before he was knocked down and instantly killed by a car outside my auntie's house in Drimnagh. What a wonderful dog he was and what lovely memories I have of him!

Frank on the right, holding our wonder dog Spot as a pup, with Mam holding my hand on the left.

Cinema, Cowboys, Stage and Music

Television wasn't broadcasted in Ireland until 1949 and so in the early fifties there was very few televisions as most ordinary people could not afford them and even if you could, the quality of the picture was terrible as it was relayed from Northern Ireland. However, cinema was the main source of entertainment, especially films about cowboys.

We used to go to the Rialto or the Leinster cinemas in Dolphins Barn if you had the money. If no money was available, my brother Frank used to lift me over the wall of a local shop to pass over pop bottles which he would then take back into the shop owner to sell him back his own bottles for half a penny each!

The Rialto cinema was the more expensive of the two so most of the time was spent at the Leinster on a Saturday morning which was called the 'four penny rush'. Hundreds of kids would attend all of whom thought that they were either Roy Rogers, John Wayne, the Cisco Kid or other film heroes of the time. As the gates were opened, they would rush in smacking their backsides as if they were on a horse whilst pretending to shoot other kids at the same time.

During the film they would clap the hero and boo the baddie whenever they appeared on the screen. There would be two or three films and the value for your money was very good. However, it could get rough sometimes when the male usher (I never did know his real name, but we used to call him either Hitler or rat face as he had a very thin pointed nose and moustache) would come around and hit you with a stick if you got too noisy. He would think nothing of hitting you on the head or legs, and again I can never recall any parents getting involved in such matters, even if their children reported it.

The Rialto cinema. Much posher than the Leinster (I think it's a car dealers showroom now!)

Another great memory was the start of rock and roll. We used to listen to the radio daily and I remember one night trying to tune into Radio Luxemburg. The station would oscillate, and you would try constantly to retune the station. This particular night, the voice of Elvis Presley came through the airways singing 'Heartbreak Hotel' and it hit me like a bolt out of the blue. I remember thinking "What the feck is that"! From then on, I was hooked on this new music which was so exciting compared to the old artists such as Crosby or Sinatra. Following this, my brother Frank took me to see 'Rock Around The Clock' and 'The Girl Can't Help It' at the Leinster.

I couldn't believe my eyes and ears as when the music played everybody without exception started singing and bouncing in their seats and before long, they started dancing in the aisles and this included some of the female usherettes who started dancing with male punters. What a sight and experience. It was contagious!

Music became a big part of my life at an early age. My Mam and Dad would regularly have people come back to the cottage follow drinking sessions at local pubs. We would sometimes be kept up to the early hours of the morning hearing them singing rebel songs, ballads, opera or hit songs of that particular time. I really enjoyed these times as I loved all kinds of music, and it was happy for all concerned ...until my Mam and Dad decided to have a row. We couldn't go to bed even if we wanted to as my brother and I slept on a bed settee in the front room which everyone sat on until such time that they had had enough to drink and left to go home to their own beds!

As I already said the radio was our main daily entertainment. I used to listen regularly to a show called 'School Around The Corner' which was hosted by a guy called Paddy Crosby. The show would feature kids from different schools around Ireland who would sing a song, tell a joke or inform the listeners of funny things that had happened to them in their lives. I never thought for one moment that I would appear on the show. I hated school and apart from history and geography, I was hopeless at every other subject. However, one day whilst at school, several people from Radio Eireann entered our classroom.

The teacher then called me out and the guy from the radio station spoke at some length to me before asking me to sing and tell a joke which I did! He then gave me a letter to take home to my Mam and Dad (I hadn't a clue what was going on) but I was apparently funny enough to warrant a place on the show.

The show was recorded at the community hall in Dolphins Barn. My Mam and Auntie Maura took me on the night, and I loved every minute of it particularly when the people clapped - it felt good ...fame at last!

I hated school and could hardly read or write when I left Ireland, but I was very grateful for the part school played on that day in terms of opening my eyes to music and entertainment whilst realising I had some basic talent, which in turn stood me in good stead later in life when I was in the band, Crisp.

Footnote: A recording of my appearance on school around the corner was put on record, however, as we didn't have a record player at the time and the record itself was priced at 14 shillings (a lot of money back then)! Given this, it was not purchased by my parents and 40 years later I tried to get hold of the recording, sadly without any success.

Appearing on radio and the Royal Theatre

A couple of weeks later, the show was broadcast on Radio Eireann and I remember it was a hot day when my Mam put the radio on full blast and opened the window to the front of the cottage so that all the kids assembled outside could hear it. When I came on, the kids all cheered, whistled and shouted "Dermo" over and over. I was over the moon! The kids all patted me on my back when I came out and told me how good I was. I couldn't believe that it was me they were talking about!

Following the show, I was then invited to appear with three other children from around Ireland on the stage version of 'School Around The Corner' at the Royal Theatre in Hawkins Street which was the biggest theatre in Dublin (it was big time for me!) My Mam and Dad took me on the night and before going into the theatre they took me to a pub just around the corner.

The pub was a typical old Dublin Victorian pub with all brass fittings and dark wooden oak panels and from what I remember I think the pub was called Mulligans which I believe is still there in Poolbeg Street. My Dad introduced me to the landlord stating that this is the son appearing on the Royal tonight. I remember feeling very important as the landlord shook my hand and asked me if I would like a cherryade drink. My Mam and Dad had several drinks too before the performance and informed the landlord that they would return following the show.

I loved doing the show and I remember having no feelings of being frightened or overcome by the occasion. I sang the song 'True Love' from the film High Society and spoke about my family life in general with Paddy Crosby. At one point all the kids on stage were asked to build a tower made out of wooden bricks and informed us that the child with the highest tower within a two-minute period would be the winner. All the other kids built theirs on the stage floor, however, I not being the brightest spark built mine on the school desk that each of us children had on the stage for some stupid reason. Mine was actually the biggest prior to the time limit however, as the compare Paddy Crosby walked across the stage to see how I was doing, his footsteps made the wooden stage floor move resulting in my tower collapsing on the stage. The audience started laughing and I thought that this was brilliant. What a night!

Later after the show, we went back to the pub and the landlord gave me free chocolates and drinks and from what my Dad told me years later, my parents also enjoyed their alcohol for the night, 'free gratis' courtesy of the very generous landlord.

Robbing Apples and the Police

I remember that I used to go scrumping a lot with my brother Frank and some of his friends (particularly when we were hungry - which was most of the time). There were some posh houses that used to have orchards which could be easily accessed if you climbed over their back walls which backed onto the canal near the Rialto Bridge. Many times, we used to have belly ache from eating too many green apples.

However, I remember one sunny day when we had just robbed an orchard and we were walking away when a Garda car turned up. The road by the canal was in a very bad state with no particular surface other than rocks, boulders and any substance that would provide some kind of surface. We all started to giggle and run when we spotted the Garda car coming our way and we laughed even more when the police car came to an abrupt halt when one of the front wheels buckled and completely collapsed. The thing I remember most was the guards did not give chase on foot, but instead both of them got out of their car and started to smile, whilst scratching and shaking their heads at their current predicament.

My Brothers

Frank Kane (Francis Joseph Kane, born 23rd May 1944 and died 11th September 2014) was my hero growing up. He was a good-looking boy who was fairly tall for a Kane, standing at approximately five feet ten inches! He enjoyed all sports including hurling for which he represented Dublin at county level. However, with a four-year gap he was, understandably, not always happy to have me around whenever he was with his mates.

I can remember an incident involving my brother Frank. We had been together near the canal and then had walked back towards our house via the main road shops. As we neared Rialto Street, Frank climbed up on a small wall which had some spiked iron railings all around it. Suddenly he slipped and one of the spiked railings went up into his armpit. Strangely, Frank did not utter a sound. I am sure he was in shock looking back. I then noticed some blood dripping down from the spike. With this, I called over to a man who was passing by for help. The man lifted him off the spike and carried him to a neighbour's house who was one of the only few car owners in the street. He ran Frank down to the hospital for treatment. I was really worried about Frank. But my Mam was full of praise for my hand in getting him help and Frank did not seem to suffer too much from his ordeal.

Skipping forward in years, Frank married Barbara Greaves in 1966 and they went on to have two lovely girls, Tara and Louise.

Uncle Terry Kearney holding myself whilst Frank is looking annoyed with his little brother.

My brother Sean was born on 8th November 1956, and I remember it being very sunny when Mam brought him home. I was delighted to have a new baby brother as I would no longer be the youngest. He was a beautiful baby weighing about 7 lbs with lovely blond hair. I remember some of my Mam's sisters and brothers coming to see him including Aunt Maura and Uncle Terry. Dad's mother never turned up to see him to my knowledge, however Uncle Tony and Uncle John did.

Our dog, Spot, really took to Sean and would sit guarding him in his lovely new pram, which Mam bought on the 'never never'! Whenever Mam would put him outside the front door for some fresh air, Spot would protect and guard him and would growl and show his teeth if any strangers approached.

(Moving forward to the 70's, Sean married Jill Gilbert - they had no children and he later married Julie Woolatt and they went on to have two beautiful children, Rhuari and Siobhan).

Sean aged approximately 4 years old with his big brother Dermot.

Dad's leaving / poor times

In the home, things were worse than ever with Mam and Dad constantly arguing about anything and everything. One day out of the blue, Mam informed us that Dad was going to work in London. She went on to say that he would send for us as soon as he found accommodation. I later found out that he had in fact robbed the bus company CIE Union of some of its funds and had to do a runner! My Dad was the treasurer of the union and with his gambling and lifestyle, I assumed it was all too tempting for him, resulting in him having to leave Ireland very quickly.

On one hand things got better in terms of him leaving as there were no longer arguments and we kids no longer lived in fear of his temper or seeing my mother upset or beaten. However, on the other hand, Mam had very little money other than what she earned as a waitress. Dad had promised Mam faithfully to send money regularly. He apparently had got a job as a conductor with London Transport within days of arriving in London and my mother assumed money would be forthcoming. However, this was not the case, as during his period away from us very little came her way.

I remembered being cold and hungry most of the time and relying on our aunties to give us food whenever they could. I recall thinking at the time that Mam would be happier with him away, nevertheless, this was not the case. Mother seemed very preoccupied with my father's life in London, and I remember her talking to Aunt Maura about this, telling her that she had reports of him with other woman, whilst gambling, drinking and generally having a great time with his friends but without his family.

Conversely, things were grim for us as we had little to eat and were cold and hungry most of the time. I remember filling up on bread and milk with sugar sprinkled on the top, most days and also being sent out by Mam to pick up any coal for the fire that had accidentally dropped off the coal wagon as it passed through Rialto. If Mam had a few 'extra bob', she would sometimes cook us cabbage, with bacon and spuds which I really loved.

My cousin Mona, who I adored, lived in 162 Cashel Road, Crumlin which was just around the corner from Grandad Kearney's house. If Mona knew that I was coming up to see her after school, she would save her bottle of milk and a current bun (which she was given every day in school) and bring it back for me which I thought was heaven.

I still keep in touch with Mona and have never forgot her kindness when I was very hungry. Mona and I loved to play bus conductors, with me being the conductor and Mona the passenger. Despite being several years older she always went along with my games without ever complaining and helped to make my life more bearable at the time…. bless her!

As I grew older and thought in depth about my childhood with both the sad and happy times, I realise that it made me the man I am today, stronger in character and more appreciative of life. I also firmly believe, **"that hard times are inevitable, but misery is nearly always an option"**- I just don't do misery!

From what I remember, Mam wrote Dad lots of letters pleading for him to send more money or get us over to London as soon as possible. My Dad kept telling her that he was doing his best to get us over but added that we would have to be patient as accommodation was very hard to find in London. My Mam then decided to sell up and go over to London regardless of what he had said. This must have been very hard for her, as she had never been out of Ireland and was basically an innocent, and without being unkind, a very simplistic girl.

We were very poor and hungry during this period, and I remember having to go most weeks to the pawn brokers in Cork Street with my Mam's fur coat and whatever valuables she had to trade for money. I would wait outside to make sure no neighbours or anyone else who might know me were in the vicinity watching me enter as I felt so embarrassed and ashamed! A week or so later, I would have to go again to collect the items whenever Mam could get money together to get them back out again. I think she lost some of the valuables due to not having the money, however, she always managed to get her fur coat with a fox's head back again. She kept that fur up to her sad death due to Motor Neurone disease in 1974 (I will get to this later).

Over the next few weeks my Mam sold everything in the cottage, including selling the new pram to a policeman when it wasn't even paid for. I recall feeling a mixture of excitement and sadness at the thought of leaving Dublin as this meant leaving friends, family and my beloved dog, Spot. However, Mam went ahead and purchased the tickets for the 'cattle boat' which left Dun Laoghaire and arrived in Holyhead in Wales.

A New Life In England

1957- bound for London

We left Ireland in either January or February in 1957 (I am not sure which) on the night boat crossing. However, I do remember that the voyage was horrendous. The boat comprised of four decks with the three decks being for the cattle and the one deck for passengers. The Irish Sea was as rough as hell once we left Dun Laoghaire and with the swell and the listing of the ship (no stabilisers in those days), most of the passengers started being seasick particularly those who had been drinking prior and during the early part of the voyage.

Halfway across, our deck was swimming in vomit, and I remember both Frank and I laughing at some of the passengers who slipped on the vomit and landed heavily on their arses, moreover, the toilets were like a battle zone and the smell of sick and urine was overbearing. None of us were actually sick during the voyage as I recall but my mother was very frightened.

A kind priest helped my Mam look after us on the journey and he gave lots of reassurance to us all throughout the terrible voyage. He not only helped us on the boat, but throughout the journey and onto the train going into London. I remember thinking what a nice man he was compared with most other priests I had met previously - most of them only seemed interested in your attendance in church, if you learnt the Catechism, putting money on the collection plate and beating any children who did not comply with the teachings of the 'Mother Church'.

We arrived early morning in London feeling very tired. We had no pram for Sean and so my Mam or Frank took turns in carrying Sean who was only about a year old. Mam did not know how to use the London underground and so we either walked or caught buses. I remember being amazed and overwhelmed by the sights and sounds of London with people running everywhere, red buses, red phone boxes, red post boxes, whilst at the same time seeing female bus conductresses. This was unusual and fascinating for me as I remembered my Dad telling me in Ireland that they allowed female clippies in England, unlike Ireland.

I also recall my brother Frank walking into a lamp post, cutting his eye and virtually knocking himself out, as he was naturally too busy looking at his new surroundings rather than where he was going. We eventually got to Hanwell where my Dad was supposed to be residing with Mam's brother Brian and his wife, Dorothy (known as Cissy). Cissy actually answered the door and appeared very surprised to see us. She told us that there was no room for us (to be fair this was probably true as she had my Dad, her elderly mother, Kenny the lodger (who was Cissy's brother), my cousin Raymond and both herself and Brian living there). However, she told my Mam that she would inform Dad of our arrival and get him to make contact somehow.

Uncle Shem and his kindness

With this, we turned around and made our way back across London to my Mam's brother Shem (James Vincent Kearney, born 18th February 1922 and sadly died in 1959) who lived in Hornsey, north London. Once again, we walked a lot of the way as Mam hadn't a clue quite where she was going. She kept stopping people and asking directions and we eventually ended up at my Uncle Shem's flat (Crouch Hill Court, Hanley Road, Hornsey). Despite having five children (four girls and one boy – Anne, Joan, Audrey, Carmel and Kevin) himself and living in a three-bedroom flat, Uncle Shem and his wife Lil took us in and put us up for the following six weeks.

It was a little cramped to say the least, but we were never made to feel unwelcome by either of them. I loved and was actually fascinated by Uncle Shem who, despite losing one of his arms in an industrial accident, managed to play the guitar with the one good arm to hold down the cords whilst strumming the instrument with his false arm. He did this whilst also playing a harmonica which was strapped around his neck in a frame, and all this was prior to Bob Dylan doing the same in the mid-sixties - it was amazing!

I really wished that I had the chance to get to know Uncle Shem in later years as he sadly died age 36 in 1959. Despite this, the Kearney family did not really keep in touch or support his widow Lil or his children, that is apart from my lovely Uncle Danny Kearney who apparently did send them money and clothes whenever he could. I personally feel that this was shameful as the family desperately needed support at the time.

However, skipping forward many years, Danny's wife, Rose showed me a Christmas card with an address and contact details, which turned out to be from Shem's son, Kevin. I rang him up and arranged for his mother and sisters to have a reunion with all the family members in Leicester. I only wished that this had happened years before. However, I still keep in touch with his son, Kevin, and have had many good get-togethers and drinking sessions with him over the years.

Uncle Shem on a trip to Boulogne with Uncle Alf. According to his son Kevin, Shem gave this French boy all of his spare money before they left. You can actually see the boy holding it in his hand!

After the six weeks were up, my parents found a flat in Arthur Road just off the Seven Sisters Road and so we moved out. It was a two-bedroom flat on the top floor of the building which had a small balcony (I used to take Sean onto the balcony when I was left alone to look after him). My Mam found a job as a waitress at a nearby store called Beale's and my brother Frank, despite being only 13 years old at the time, lied about his age and started work as an apprentice cabinet maker. He loved the job and with having a few bob in his pocket, he grew up quickly and started going out drinking with his cousins Ray and Terry Kearney and, generally speaking, had a great time.

I started at the local school and I remember on the first day that most of the kids could not understand me due to my thick Dublin accent. My name, Dermot, also caused problems in that nobody could pronounce it and I was called everything from 'Dermont' to 'Dermonk' and other names besides!

Now then, one boy suggested that I be called Dave as it was easier to pronounce and this appeared to satisfy all the rest, as the name quickly stuck. I also remember that I decided to try and talk in a cockney / London accent. I did this, not because I was ashamed or in any denial of my proud Irish heritage, but only because I wanted to communicate, to be accepted and understood as I felt very much the outsider and lonely during this time in the 'big smoke'.

No Blacks, no dogs, no Irish

Talking of feeling lonely and an outsider, I do recall that during the eighteen months spent in London, that I saw two signs - one of them in the front window of a house in Archway which was advertising a 'room to let' and another on a board outside a property in our own area advertising a ground floor flat to let. Both of these advertisements bore the criteria as above, 'No Blacks, No dogs, No Irish'!

In those days' reader, it was not illegal to blatantly vent such discrimination openly in public. I remember feeling quite scared as it just heightened my fear of being an outsider and therefore added to my loneliness away from my homeland.

Sadly, even today, discrimination is still very prevalent in the world, and I remind myself very often that people have more in common than that which divides us. I also have a saying that I pass on to others in the hope of neutralising discrimination which is that every person on this planet has the same red colour blood running through their veins and that in itself makes us all part of the same family. The whole world bleeds red without exception!

However, life wasn't all gloom and doom as sometimes the kindness of people shone through as in the following case. We had a lovely Maltese family (the Pantelli family was their name, I think) living in the flat below us and so the lady looked after Sean whilst I went to school. However, when I got home from school letting myself in with my own keys provided by Mam, I would look after

Sean until my mother came home which was normally around 11/12pm. I used to be starving as my Mam was working and, therefore, she did not cook for us that often, however, on occasions my Mam would leave money for me to get chips from the chippy and I would have beans with the chips.

The Maltese lady was also very kind and I remember her cooking pasta for me. It was the first time I had tasted pasta and the added taste of overwhelming garlic proved too much for me to take (to this day I feel guilty about not eating it) as she had three children of her own and they appeared to be as poor as us.

Looking back, I also think that she took pity on us as she knew that my Mam, Dad or brother where not in very often in and so she would call for us to come down to her flat on occasions where she would cuddle Sean whilst trying to give me assurance and support as I am sure she recognised my insecurity and loneliness. I had a picture of me taken at my school in London during this time and on the picture you can clearly see a piece of twine with the keys to the front door strapped to my right wrist - children in those days were known as "latch key kids" as they had to let themselves in and take care of themselves if their parents were working, and I was definitely one of them!

Dermot the 'latch-key kid; note the key twine on right hand

I saw very little of my parents or Frank during the period that we lived in London and I used to spend many hours on the small balcony at the top of our flat looking out for them and wishing them to come home as I felt so lonely whilst I looked after my baby brother, Sean. It was a completely different life to the one I had known in Ireland surrounded by family and friends.

I think that we stayed in London for approximately two years. During this time, I made several friends including some Polish and Irish friends. Two of the Polish boys were brothers and were a couple of years older than me, however I can't remember their names. Nevertheless, I do recall that there was 24 of them! Yes, 24 of them, all living in two Victorian houses joined together to accommodate them all.

One day the two brothers called for me and took me up to the Finsbury Park area. Somehow, we ended up via an old metal fire escape on the roof top of an old cinema. After a short period of time someone must have reported us as two policemen arrived on the top of the roof. They questioned us and then took us to the local police station.

Having given them details of where I lived and where my parents worked, my Dad appeared several hours later, and I can tell you he wasn't looking very happy! He managed to keep his temper under control whilst at the station, but it did come out when we arrived home. Basically, he gave me a good beating and looking back he was probably right as we could have been killed had we fallen off the roof. I didn't have much to do with the Polish lads after this as my Dad made it clear that if he found out that I had been with them, that I could expect another hiding.

During most evenings when the rest of the family were out, I would listen to the radio (mainly Radio Luxemburg). I loved the more modern singers of the day including Terry Dene, Tommy Steele and Charlie Gracie who had hits sounding more like early rock and roll, although they were nothing to the likes of the Americans such as Elvis, Fats Domino or Little Richard, etc, who I thought were the 'dogs bollocks'.

My brother Frank shared my love of music and one day he informed me that Charlie Gracie was going to appear at the Finsbury Park Empire and asked if I would like to go. I naturally said I would and got very excited at the prospect. On the night of the concert, our cousins Terry Kearney (who was nicknamed Flip as he never swore but would say flip instead) turned up to go with us.

However, when we got to the Empire it was apparently not Charlie Gracie appearing, but a nude show! I, of course didn't know this, but I can recall both Terry and Frank whispering together trying to sort the matter out. Believe it or not, they explained to me that it was not Charlie appearing but some lovely ladies which struck me as very odd.

They managed to get me in; being so small I went under the ticket office window! The seats were in the upper circle and therefore the stage was very distant, and I don't recall seeing too much of the female form. I remember getting fed up after a short period but Frank assured me that it would get better and so we saw the complete show, much to my disappointment as it didn't get any better for me despite his assurance!

First girlfriend of sorts!

This incident most have awoken my interests in females as shortly afterwards I encountered my very first girlfriend ...of sorts! She lived just around the corner in a big house with a garden. She was in the year above me at school (I think her name was Joan). We initially became friends in the playground and one day after school, she was waiting for me. To my surprise, she took me by the hand and told me she was going to take me back to her house to meet her parents would you believe! She seemed very confident, whilst I was the opposite being only ten years old very shy and unconfident.

Despite my protests she somehow dragged me there and, lo and behold, both her fairly elderly parents greeted me with a friendly welcoming handshake. It actually appeared that they were expecting me, as on the table was an array of cakes and sandwiches. I was delighted to be offered the goodies and quickly took advantage of the situation by getting down as many as I could during my time at the house. I was a bit shocked when she took me home and gave me a kiss on the lips at the front gate.

I don't remember seeing her much after this incident apart from the odd time at school in the playground as at this point in my life I was not really interested in girls, however, I would have gone back with her should there have been cakes on offer!

Before leaving London, I remember visiting my cousin Moira Jackson several times with my mother and brother Frank at her home in McKenzie Road, Islington. It was great to see at least one of the Jacksons again and Moira always made us welcome whilst catching up with family news with my mother. It was to be many years later that we caught up again with the whole Jackson family (see Brian Higgs 60th Birthday Party in Luton - more of this later!)

Moving to Leicester!

It was about this time that my Dad and Mam announced that we were going to move and live in Leicester. I was excited by this news as I never liked London and I knew that we had a fairly large family living in the East Midlands and therefore, I would likely have more contact with family as I really missed family members since leaving Ireland.

We arrived in Leicester by coach from London and spent the next 6-8 weeks living at my Aunt Vera's (my mothers' sister) in the New Parks area. Vera and Uncle Joe had five children (Helen, Joe, Mick, Sheila and June) of their own and therefore it was definitely a tight squeeze. I really enjoyed the company of my cousins especially Joe boy who was a couple of years older than myself. We subsequently became very close as the years went by, and I would always look him up in Dublin whenever I was visiting there (See chapter 'Joe boy and the horses').

A picture taken while we lived with Aunt Vera and family. From left to right, back row - my mother, Mick, Joe boy, myself and Aunt Vera. Front row – my brother, Sean, Sheila and June.

I remembered Joe boy took me down to some local fields in Glenfield which contained several cows. Whilst living in Dublin I saw very little of cows and therefore I was naturally cautious around them.

We walked around the edge of the field which had, unbeknown to me, an electric fence surrounding it. As we left the field, Joe boy asked me to hold the fence up so that he could get under it. I naturally obliged and immediately felt this very unusual sense of pain. However, being Irish and for some strange reason, I did not let go as the current continued to cause me a lot of discomfort and pain. Joe and his siblings were in fits of laughter as I tried to look as manly as possible before having to let go of the wire as my hair stood on end!

Shortly afterwards, my Aunt Vera found a rented flat for us in the Highfield area of the city. The flat was situated above a restaurant called the L'Aperitif in Highfields Street. I attended Medway Street Junior School whilst Frank started a job as an assistant drayman. My Dad joined the Midland Red Bus Company as a conductor and Mam resumed her job as a waitress in a town centre café. I think that we lived there for approximately one year. I hated the place as Mam, Dad and Frank always seemed to be out. Moreover, the flat was cold, dark and dingy. I also thought that it was haunted and spent many nights with my brother Sean huddled together as I was petrified when I heard any noise coming from the empty rooms and attic above.

I can't remember having a friend or think of anything of note whilst we lived there other than an incident which took place one Saturday morning. My Mam and Dad became embroiled in an argument (no idea what it was about) However, the argument became violent with both of them shoving each other whilst making threats. My Dad's temper got the better of him and grabbed my Mam around the throat and raised his fist to hit her. I began crying and shouted at him to leave my Mam alone whilst at the same time looking for anything to hit him with. The nearest thing was a large pot with a plant in it. Despite shitting myself with fright, I threw the pot at his head. Lucky for him, he moved at the last moment and the pot smashed against the wall.

My Dad turned around in complete surprise and stood looking at me. I wasted no time and ran out of the house as fast as I could. I stayed out all day until the light faded when I sneaked back in. Dad must have been at work and so I went straight to bed. I was really worried that I would get a good hiding in the morning, but to my surprise he never mentioned anything about the incident.... thank God!

Moving again

Following this we were on the move again and moved to 96 Stretton Road, in the Hinckley Road area of the city as it was a much better ground floor flat with an indoor toilet. I remember feeling much happier here as I quickly found friends whilst attending Doveland's Junior School. I also made friends with our milkman (the milk was delivered by horse and cart in those days) who would let me stroke and fuss his horse and also let me sit on the driver's seat on occasions. I would go to the local park to play football with my mates at weekends if my Mam wasn't working as normally I would be looking after my brother Sean. Having reached the ripe old age of eleven, I then took and failed my 11+ exam which was not too surprising!

Mum and me in Stretton Road, Leicester – posh backyard!

I started senior school at Wycliffe Comprehensive, and it was here that I met my lifelong friend, Ian Parkinson. Neither Ian nor I can remember our first meeting, but I do recall that I used to play football every day at dinner time with other school friends and Ian, who was not the least bit interested in it, would watch us play from the sidelines. However, somehow we found something in common (mainly girls and music) and we quickly became great pals and still are after 60 odd years. Ian was very posh compared to me and lived in a great big Victorian house with a large front and back garden in Gimson Road.

I could never understand why he wanted to be friends with me considering the background he came from. Nevertheless, I was always made welcome by his mother who would sometimes feed me with sandwiches and goodies, however, his father rarely spoke as he was always in the front room reading his paper whenever I called, and he would only make a grunt or nod whenever I said hello to him. I loved his house as it always seemed calm, warm and relatively happy compared to my own.

Ian and I started to knock around together after school and were joined by another lifelong friend, Stan Wyatt, who was a couple of years older than ourselves - ironically Stan went on to work with my Dad in later years with the Midland Red Bus Company (what a small world it is)! I recall we used to go to Fosse Park together to meet up with girls and attempt to have a snog, a grope and a grapple. Ian was even shyer than me and therefore I felt that I had to lead the way. I quickly took great interest in the female gender and had several short-lived girlfriends in the area.

Another interest of ours was the stable for the Co-Op horses near the Fosse cinema (Mantle Road). Ian, myself and a few other mates used to sneak up to the hay loft and watch all the activities from above. It was very clear that the horses were loved by the masters as they took great care and attention with them.

We would also go to the Fosse cinema on a Saturday morning to watch the latest films. There was an A Film and a B film. Apart from this, you would have weekly episodes of Flash Gordon, The Lone Ranger or even the Cisco Kid. These weekly episodes would always end with a dramatic cliff-hanger which was designed to encourage you to attend the following week to see what happened.

I loved the cinema as it was an escape from what was, generally-speaking, an unhappy home that I came from. Nevertheless, I loved all my family and always hoped that things would get better and more stable like most other families.

I also remember on one sad occasion, two fellow school friends in the year above me were playing with a shotgun in the loft at the back of a local butchers in Henton Road. The shotgun went off accidently as they apparently did not realise in was loaded and resulted in one of them having their head blown off (the story made headlines in the Leicester Mercury). I can't recall their names, but I remember that the headmaster (Mr. Moute was his name and ironically, he was later jailed for sexual abuse as I recall) called us into assembly several months after the incident and asked us all to be sensitive to the survivor of the incident when he returned to school the following week. Rough as the school was, I think that all the pupils were very sympathetic, understanding and respectful towards him.

More dog tales

Another incident that made headlines in the Leicester Mercury newspaper, was a car crash in Fosse Road. The driver of the car had leg injuries, but he was more distressed by his dog, "Hinnie" leaving the scene of the crash in a frightened state. The dog appeared in the entry of our house in a very frightened state following the accident and Mam took him into the house and tried to give him assurance and comfort. We had no idea who owned him, and I wanted to keep him as I still missed my dog, Spot, back in Ireland.

However, two days later in the Leicester Mercury paper was an article written about the owner stating that he was heartbroken by the loss of the dog and was offering a reward for his safe return. My Dad got in touch with him and the following day he turned up for the dog. I think my Dad was hoping for a cash reward, however, he was disappointed as the man produced a puppy and basket as the said reward, much to my Dad's disappointment. Sadly, the pup's life was very short, as several weeks later the back gate was left open by someone and the pup ran out under a car and was killed instantly.

Uncle Gerry comes to Leicester

In the summer of 1960, Uncle Gerry (dad's younger brother) came to live with us in Stretton Road as apparently work was very scarce for him back in Dublin and he needed a job to keep the family going. However, there was plenty of employment in Leicester at the time and so within a week Uncle Gerry found a job at a textile dyeing company in Fosse Road. It was really nice having him stay with us as I think he was the first Kane to have face to face contact with us since leaving Ireland.

Anyway, the work was very hard and long for Gerry and especially hot in the summertime. I remember on a couple of occasions my Mam asking me to take some sandwiches down to him at his factory as he had forgotten them. As I approached the factory, the large doors at the side of the building were fully open in an attempt to cool the premises down and help keep the workers from 'melting' from the heat of the large boiling dyeing vats. When Uncle Gerry spotted me at the door, he came over and I can remember vividly as sweat was running down his forehead like a river. His shirt was also covered in sweat, changing much of the fabric to a darker colour. I can never remember him complaining or making a fuss, he just got on with it.

However, after approximately six months he announced that he was going back to Dublin. I recall asking him why he was leaving, and he told me simply that "he was missing his family". I have nothing but fond memories of my Uncle Gerry as I remember him as being a kind, gentle and a very easy-going gentleman!

Sean, the toilet and beetroot

My brother Sean was always getting himself into trouble and mischief as a child and I remember one occasion when my mother had taken both Sean and me on the bus to visit Uncle Frank and Aunt Etna (I think her real name was Esther) in Coventry. Uncle Frank lived in a run-down and poor area in Coventry called Red Lane. In those days none of our families had any money especially Uncle Frank. Nevertheless, whenever visitors came, he would beg steal or borrow to take the grown-ups out for a drink as is the Irish way!!

Whilst the grown-ups were at the pub, Sean spent his time investigating his surroundings and after doing so went to the outside toilet which was shared with the next-door neighbours. Sean was probably five years old at the time. I can recall that upon finishing his ablutions, he attempted to pull the chain, but unfortunately, he was too small and couldn't reach. With this, he stood on the rim of the toilet to reach the chain, but whatever happened, the rim gave way resulting in Sean's leg being ripped open by the jagged edge of the bowl as he fell to the ground. Sean was rushed off to hospital where he had the back of his leg treated and stitched.

We all stayed overnight, and the following day Aunt Etna told Sean she had something special for him for being so brave following the toilet incident. Sean was naturally very excited at the prospect of perhaps receiving chocolate, cakes or some kind of sweet treat.

I can remember his face when Aunt Etna placed a single beetroot on a plate in front of him (Aunt Etna, bless her, had probably got nothing else to give him, as money was so tight), Sean looked up at Aunt Etna with total bewilderment as if to say, "what's this?". Sean had never seen a beetroot before and therefore didn't know what to say or do. He simply picked up the object, smelt it, prodded it and politely declined the offer saying that he was not really hungry!

On another occasion, Sean put several stones up his nose for some unknown reason and had to attend hospital to have them removed by a doctor, as they were firmly stuck at the back of his nose. Why would you do that I ask? Well folks, my brother Sean was always impulsive and unpredictable throughout his life, but nevertheless I loved him just the same.

The only picture I have of Aunt Etna pictured here in the middle. Left to right: Unknown, Uncle Alf looking over her shoulder, Eddie Sutcliffe, Uncle Frank and Uncle Shem.

A very tender moment with Dad

My Dad was not a sentimental or emotional man by nature; however, I remember one incident that really blew me away. I think I was about ten years old, and we were in a garden or park together somewhere (I can't really remember where) when he called me over and asked me to take a really close look at a flower he was holding. He started to dissect the flower by pulling away the top flowers whilst starting to reveal the inner of the pod inside. He showed me this perfect symmetric shape of the pod and the seeds all aligned around the middle in perfect dimensions. He then informed me that "man can send rockets into space but could not create anything as beautiful as this".

It was a beautiful moment which I wanted to last forever and I shall always cherish the memory as I was so amazed that my Dad could appreciate nature in this way. This little incident was to influence myself as I went through life with regard to my love of nature and this wonderful planet that we live on. As I started to write this book, I realised just how much my Dad had actually influenced my life, either for good or for bad!

I can also recall other occasions in Dublin as a child when my Dad would tell me stories of his life in the army (see 'My Dad Francis O'Rahilly Kane') and also recall stories of Dublin characters of old including Bang Bang, Forty Coats and Lugs Branigan.

Bang Bang, who was apparently in his forties or fifties as my Dad recalled, would dress up in a full cowboy outfit with two toy guns in his side holster. Dad said he would wait on corners for buses to pass by and as they had to slow down to negotiate the corners slowly, he would jump onto the platform take out the two toy guns and shout at the top of his voice "Bang Bang, you're dead" to each of the passengers he had shot. Having carried out his elimination of the passengers he would wait for the bus to slow down before jumping off and galloping away into the sunset. slapping his arse to indicate he was riding his horse. Dad said that nobody took offence - in fact the opposite as he was loved by all Dubliners and apparently became famous as articles were written about him in the papers and his fame spread over the rest of Ireland.

Another character was Forty Coats who was a tramp in his late forties. He didn't actually wear 40 coats (despite the name) but probably 4-5 coats at a time to keep warm. Again, Dad said that people loved him as he was a gentleman with great pride and self-respect despite his lowly position in society and most people who came across him would give him a 'few bob' if they had it or give him food to keep him going.

Lugs Branigan was a Dublin policeman who, prior to becoming part of the force, was apparently a boxer. Dad said that he was afraid of no man and was renowned for breaking up fights on many occasions all alone, and according to Dad sometimes took on 4 to 5 men at a time and would always be the last one standing. He was loved and respected by all as he was a very fair-minded policeman who always tried to help others and only resorted to violence as a last resort. Apparently, when all three of these great characters died, the population of Dublin came out in their droves at their funerals to pay their respects.

Moving yet again!

After approximately two years in Stretton Road, I was told that we were moving back to a house, would you believe, in the Highfields area again (34 Avon Street). I was sad to be leaving as I would miss my best friend, Ian. However, I need not have worried as Ian took it upon himself to visit us on his bike all the way from the other part of the city.

34 Avon Street was a typical three bedroomed Victorian terraced house with no inside toilet and a staircase so steep that you felt you were climbing Everest whenever you had to go upstairs (they really were unbelievably steep!). If you needed the toilet, which, incidentally, we shared with our next-door neighbour Mrs Pawley, you had to go to the bottom of the garden and enter the small building with no lighting or heating of any kind. There was many an occasion when I would rush down to use the toilet only to find Mrs Pawley sitting on her throne with her under garments around her ankles - not a pretty sight I might add - it was a shock for both of us, I can tell you!!

Ian and the full chamber pot

However, back to my house. I do remember a very funny incident when Ian cycled up to our house one Saturday morning. Mam and Dad were out at the time and Ian and I decided to play a game of hide and seek. He went upstairs to hide and got under mine and my brother Franks bed.

All of a sudden, I heard the sound of our chamber pot (the posh name for a piss pot as we shared an outside toilet with our neighbours) being knocked over. Ian could not understand what was happening as he had two indoor toilets in his own home and therefore never needed any sanitary items placed under his bed! He then found himself immersed in a large flood of urine which soaked him to the skin and then began to run down the steep stairs and into the lounge area. I was in fits of laughter and Ian, bless him, also began laughing. Despite his first introduction to our bedtime ablutions, he never mentioned the incident or made reference to our poor background or the lack of sanitary facilities!

Dad toilets and hats

Talking of toilets, I have to tell a few stories about my Dad and his use of toilet facilities, particularly when he was under the influence of alcohol. Now then, younger readers wouldn't know this but prior to central heating, most homes had open coal fires in each room of the house. Around each fire would be what they called a coal scuttle fender to keep the coal in, with one being placed on each corner of the fireplace. This would have a posh brass fender running across between the two scuttles to make the object appear to be pleasing to the owner's eye.

My Dad on occasions when he was basically pissed, would get out of bed during the night for a pee and took to opening up one side of the scuttle and peeing away to his hearts content. Unfortunately, the urine ran from one side to the other via the fender which made things worse as the other scuttle had a large hole in the metal resulting in his urine running out of the hole and all onto the lino floor, wetting his bare feet. This would awake him from his stupor making him swear with anger as he danced about the room on the very 'slippy' floor. Mam would then naturally wake up to the commotion and a row would ensue – it was bloody chaos!

Another habit he developed for a short while was of a similar nature as he woke up in the middle of the night for a wee and without thinking, he would open Mam's wardrobe, climb into it and then, would you believe, close the door behind him! He would then commence to urinate all over Mam's precious hats which she treasured! Mam would go mad, pulling him out of the wardrobe whilst calling him a drunken "bas……d" and any other name she could get her tongue around. Ah, it was bliss in our house and the winter nights just flew by!

Just to finish off Dad's toilet stories, I remember one morning in mid-winter with frost on the ground, I ventured down to our toilet at the bottom of our garden for an early morning pee and upon opening the door gently (in case Mrs Pawley was in there), I found my Dad fast asleep and snoring on the toilet with his pants and trousers around his ankles. He had been there all night following a few too many jars at the Catholic club. It's a bloody wonder he didn't die of hypothermia!

Dad climbing Everest and broken clocks

Remember I told you about the very steep stairs in our house, well Dad really did have problems getting up the stairs particularly when he had a lot of the demon drink. We would normally be in bed when he returned from the club and, from our bedroom, you could hear him winding the clock ready for work the following morning.

Many a time he would try to climb the stairs with three steps up and three steps back, five steps up and four steps back (you get the idea). This would go on for some time with him murmuring under his breath some undiscernible language as he made each attempt to get to the top. Most times he would make it but on a few occasions he didn't, resulting in him falling to the bottom.

Ironically, he was never really badly hurt probably due to being relaxed with so much alcohol in his body. Anyway, we would all rush out of our beds to see if he was hurt and upon finding him looking up at us and swearing, we would all return to our beds to get some sleep. Having recovered, he continued to over-wind his clock whilst continuing to swear and call us blind. On some occasions he would sleep downstairs in the armchair if he was unable to make the climb. Over the years, Dad (not surprisingly) got through loads of clocks due to his aggressive over-winding!

School for delinquents

I attended Dale Secondary School on Melbourne Road, which was as rough as a badger's arse! It was more like a school for delinquents and how I never ended up in trouble with the law I will never know. I remember meeting some of my schoolmate's mates on occasions before we went to school, and we decided there and then to spend the rest of the day off at an older bloke's house (can't remember his name) where we would listen to records all day long and those who smoked would have their fill of roll-up cigarettes! We would occasionally sign in at school and then after the first lesson bunk off for the day, it's no wonder that I was poorly educated!

After school I would knock about with Dick Plimmer and 'Big Nose' Williamson (don't know why he was called big nose as his nose was normal as I recall). They both had a love of music like myself, and we used to go to big nose Williamson's house as he had a piano and could actually play it. We would take turns singing lead on songs of the day and try out harmonies on each other.

Another time, in the 4th Year, we were in the woodwork room when a guy called Eric Gibbons had had enough of the teacher when he did no more than jump up on the workbench, then launched himself at the teacher (Mr Burdette) and head-butted him, which knocked the teacher to the floor, before he casually walked out of the room. Needless to say, Eric was expelled! I also recall that we used to have fights with the boys from the nearest school to us which was called Moat Boys. When it was snowing, we would also go to their school as they came out of school, 15 minutes after our school was closed. We would make loads of snowballs and subject them to a barrage of snowballs as the came out of the school gates… very happy days!

As part of the school football team, I used to play most Saturday mornings. I was never any good at football although I really loved playing it. The fact that I could only kick with my right foot made me a bit of a liability for the team and I think I was only picked for the school team because we nearly always got beaten and the school could never get a full team to turn up for each match. Ironically, one of my teammates was a lad called Barry (Baz) Newcombe. Now moving forward in years folks, to when I had children of my own, my son Liam, and Barry's son Simon, both made the final selection for the England youth team at the National Centre Of Excellence at Lilleshall, and both went on to sign full-time with Leicester City FC. I felt so proud of both of them, and it was great for Baz and I to catch up after all those years (isn't life strange as you never know who or what will turn up)!

Dovedale and my first and only fag

In the summer of 1962, Jeff Smith, Rocco, Sam White and myself, decided to go camping for a few days to Dovedale in Derbyshire as the weather was so nice at the time. None of us had a tent or equipment and so we managed to borrow these from another mate called Richard Stroud who was much posher than us. Not only did he lend the equipment to us, but his Dad, who had a car (a V8 Pilot, a real beast of a car with a dashboard full of lovely dark veneer as I recall), kindly took us to and from Dovedale and refused any petrol money – bless him.

It was my first real holiday ever and I remember the excitement of seeing Thorpe Cloud and the surrounding hills for the first time as his Dad drove us up to the campsite which was at the farm at the bottom of Thorpe Cloud. My sensory system went into overload and I was blown away by the scenery, as it looked like a miniature Switzerland with the lovely River Dove nearby running through the valley below Thorpe Cloud - it was perfect and beyond my expectations and I fell in love with the place right there and then (a love that would stay with me for the rest of my life).

The following two days it pissed it down with rain! But despite this we were all in great spirits as it felt like a real adventure, and it certainly beat being in Highfields by a mile. Nevertheless, with hindsight, we were ill equipped for the trip and really did not have a clue as to what the hell we were doing. We would go to the farm early in the morning to get fresh eggs and milk straight from the cows for our breakfast. I think Jeff did the cooking and he was a great hand at cooking our main meal for the two days which consisted of beans, sausages, and potatoes, all in one pot which we scoffed down with delight between slices of bread.

We did manage a walk through the Dove Valley later that day, but we had to turn back halfway through, due to the torrential rain and our lack of appropriate clothing - we were like drowned rats and shivering with the cold as we returned to our site. We couldn't even dry ourselves by a fire as it was impossible to light a fire! I think we spent the rest of the day huddled together in the small tent telling jokes and stories of our lust for females whilst seeing who could fart the longest and loudest!

I remember that on the second day the rain had not stopped for the whole 48 hours and so we were naturally pissed off and fed up to the back teeth. I can't remember who, but someone started to hand out cigarettes. I had never smoked in my life but after some encouragement and pressure from Jeff Smith and the rest of the gang who were puffing away, I decided to give it a try.

After a couple of drags I began coughing and spluttering to the amusement of all the others and I remember saying to them all "why the fuc...in hell would anyone want to do this"? It was bloody horrible! I was never one to run with the pack and despite a barrage of abuse and piss-taking from the gang, I stood my ground and have never smoked from that day to this. Anyway, I was so glad that I had never started smoking on that day as it probably would have stunted my growth!

The following day it was still raining as we were picked up by Mr Stroud and returned to Leicester. However, the trip had opened my eyes to nature and my love for the countryside. I still get that same first feeling of excitement seeing Thorpe Cloud and the surrounding hills whenever I return to Dovedale with Theresa or my family, which has been on numerous occasions over the years, and it takes me back every time to that first holiday adventure with the lads.

1962. Dale School with my fellow delinquents! That's me in the back row, third from left with the cross above my head.

Another nice memory is of the late Leicester and England goalkeeper, Gordon Banks (probably the greatest goalkeeper in history). I started to follow the fortunes of City and heard of a new goalkeeper who had just been transferred from Chesterfield in 1959/60 (at this stage he did not have any caps for England). I decided to cut the clipping out of the paper and go down to the training ground and seek his autograph.

Now, would you believe, in those days there was no training ground but the car park at the side of the stadium, made of cinders, was also used for training (can you imagine any keeper today diving on cinders?). When I arrived, I watched them play for a while and then asked Gordon for his autograph. He did this with great pleasure and then took the time to ask me if I played football, what school I went to, and he was generally interested in my background. I remember him ruffling my hair as I said goodbye and he wished me well. What a lovely man and gentleman... R.I.P Gordon Banks.

A couple of years later, I took a job as a paper boy at Sharp's newsagents on London Road and my round was Highfield Street and Mill Hill areas of Highfields, in the evenings after finishing school. I think it was about seven shillings and six pence a week wages. I was as grateful for the job as it helped my Mam out in terms of her not having to buy any clothes for me from that week onwards. I also used to save up to buy records, particularly The Beatles, who had just come onto the scene in 1962.

I used to deliver the evening paper to another first team City player called Mike Stringfellow, who lived in a modest house in the Highfields area of the city. Many times, I would see him on my round and he would be friendly and talkative to me about the goings on at City and I would usually ask him about the last game he had and how the team might fare in their next match.

We also went to church on a Sunday morning at St. Peters on King Richards Road and saw both Frank McLintock (Scotland and Leicester - who went on to do the double with Arsenal) and Jimmy Walsh (Celtic and Leicester captain) who attended the services regularly. Once again, both of them were very down to earth and normal for a better word as footballers generally in those days were not 'divas', unlike today!

It was around this time that I started to knock about in Mill Hill and it was there that I met Dave Williams, who was to become a lifelong friend. We hit it off from the first meeting and I introduced him to another lifelong friend, Rocco Ambrico (I will tell you more about Dave and Rocco later in the book).

1963 - Leaving School and work

Looking back, I couldn't have been too bad at school, as to my surprise, in my fourth year, the headmaster (Mr Grimley) called me into his office and informed me that I was being made a prefect. I was gobsmacked as I had never achieved anything in life so far and this was, as far as I was concerned, some kind of honour I think! I felt quite proud wearing my prefect badge (which incidentally I still have).

The last term went very quickly and it was not long after this that I was due to leave school and so the employment officer came to the school to advise us all on future employment. Prior to this, my Dad had assured me that a job was waiting for me in engineering at Pollards through a friend of his called Tim Maloney, who Dad told me was the works doctor? This sounded very strange to me, however, being my Dad, I accepted this as a done job! I told the employment officer of the plan and assured him that there was no need of his input.

Two weeks prior to leaving, despite assurances from my Dad there was nothing in the way of written or verbal word from Pollards. I decided to go down to Pollards factory myself and get some kind of confirmation one way or the other. I went to the office and told my story, and a person from management came out to see me. He was kind, sympathetic and sensitive as he informed me that that all the posts for apprentices had been filled and my name was definitely not on it! He also asked who had arranged it. When I informed him of the name, he said that he was definitely not a doctor but was in fact a first aid man with the firm!

I felt very embarrassed and a little ashamed by the whole incident. I told both my Mam and Dad of the findings of the meeting when I got home, and my Dad uttered something about Tim being a good mate and would not lie but made no attempt to assure me that all would be well or offer to help find me a job.

The following week I took myself down to the labour exchange and by this time most of the jobs for school leavers were taken. I was given a short list of what was left mainly manual jobs, but there was one for a tailor. To cut a long story short, I went down to the said tailors, Eric Birr, who had a small room above a shop owned by another tailor named Mr Coleman, in Bond Street, Leicester. Eric offered me the job starting at two pounds, seventeen shillings and sixpence old money.

Playing Football on Victoria Park

Anyway, back to my story, having left school at 15 years of age in 1963, my first year of working with Eric Birr was so badly paid (£2 17s 6d), that I also took a morning paper round prior to going to work, in order to supplement my wages. After finishing work, I would rush home for a quick dinner before running up to Victoria Park to play football with my mates. I played football on and off from the age of 15 up to the age of 18.

A few of my mates were very good at football, unlike myself, including Jim Turner and Bone. Bill Garner went on to play for Southend and Chelsea and was one of the first £100,000 transferred footballers. Jimmy Johnson (who was the best footballer of them all in my opinion) played for Coventry and ended up with Kettering Town, as did Sam White and last, but not least, my friend Rocco Ambrico, who tried his hand at professional football 'down under.' (See later chapter Meeting Rocco again).

Most times I was late after work and so I would just join in when I got there. However, if I was there from the start, they would have two captains who would pick sides, I always seemed to be the last one to be picked (I really couldn't understand why)!

Another pal who played with us was Pat Moran. He went on to do very well in the music business as producer / engineer with the likes of Robert Plant from Led Zeppelin, Queen, The Searchers, Foreigner and John Miles to name but a few. Sadly, Pat passed away in 2014.

First engagement ring

It was whilst working with Eric Birr that romance started to bloom between myself and a second-generation Irish girl named Yvonne Morgan. I knew Yvonne prior to starting work as she lived quite close to us in Highfields and she also went to the same school as myself.

As we worked in the same premises but on different floors, we would meet occasionally in the shared kitchen to make tea etc. As I say, romance bloomed and we started courting (as the old expression goes). I think I was about 17/18 years old at the time, and I remember Yvonne suggesting that we get engaged to be married. To be honest, I was far too immature to even consider this but I went along with it as I thought at the time that I loved her. Yvonne and I started to save for marriage and we had a small engagement party at her parents' house. Yvonne's mother was particularly nice and I found the Morgan family to be far more stable overall than my own, which felt good.

Looking back at the whole affair, which was fairly short-lived, I think that both having a life outside my own home and having another family in my life was probably the get-out card I needed at the time. However, it ended in tears for myself as, embarrassingly, Yvonne informed me, as she handed back the engagement ring to me, that we need to part as I "don't think you will ever amount to anything!" She was probably right, as with hindsight, I had no real ambition or drive to speak of, as I just lived from day-to-day and this was probably too mundane for Yvonne. Nevertheless reader, my pride had been severely dented and I was gutted and heartbroken at the time. I sold the engagement ring a couple of days later for £10 and went out on the beer!

Getting back to being a tailor, I hated that job but nevertheless I stayed in tailoring for the next 28 years, would you believe, whilst working for three Birr brothers (the first being Eric, second Reginald and finally Harold, who was the owner of Birrs Sportswear) at different times over this period. Looking back, I think I should have got out of the job but didn't, because I lacked confidence and had little self-belief and therefore, I was too scared to try another trade.

Talking of Birrs Sportswear and skipping forward, I ended up buying the business after working for Mr Harold Birr for approximately 20 years and went into partnership with another worker, Mick Woodfield. We became joint partners / Directors in the business of Birrs Sportswear Ltd and this, I might add, was to be a decision I would sadly regret.

My main job was cutting and designing. I particularly enjoyed the freedom in being given a free hand in designing for the shows such as 'Les Miserables'. We employed 36 people whilst making costumes for many films and shows, such as all of the productions of Les Miserables across the world. 'Out Of Africa' with Meryl Streep (we made her 32 pairs of jodhpurs for the Oscar winning film), 'Revolution' with Al Pacino, and most of the early James Bond films, TV shows such as 'Allo Allo', dozens and dozens of Teddy boy drain pipe trousers for the seventies hit-making group Showwaddywaddy from Leicester, as well as the hunting fraternity and lastly but not least, the Royal family, including the Queen, Prince Charles and all the rest of my least favourite family (I am not a royalist), which resulted in our firm being granted the royal warranty via the Royal Palace.

Ironically, the worst payers were the Royal Family. They usually took up to two years to pay, as I am sure they thought it was an honour to make for them and therefore they should not have to pay us. However, my biggest disappointment whilst working in tailoring was the partnership with the late Michael Woodfield, and his greed and lack of empathy to my situation and the financial struggles with bringing up my young family (See 1990 the closing of Birrs Sportswear).

On my arse again!

However, there was some funny moments whilst working in Birrs Sportswear. I remember that I purchased five music albums from a lady we nicknamed "Mush" (don't ask me why she was named so), who ran a club book so you could pay weekly for your purchased goods. Delighted with the albums, I left work and went to the car park to put them in my car. However, in order to get my keys out of my pocket, I placed the albums on the car roof. I then got into the car and drove off forgetting about the goods on the roof and distributed the albums all across Leicester on my way home.

Another time, at the same car park, the owners had recently put a small chain around the perimeter to improve the appearance of the site. As I cut across the car park to go to the local shops at dinner time, I noticed three lovely looking girls in summer frocks coming in my direction. I broke into a macho trot trying to look cool but, in my vanity, forgot about the small chain and went flying head-first into the gravel filled car park ground. There was gravel up my nose, my cheek was bleeding, my trousers were ripped, and my dignity was completely gone as the girls broke into spontaneous laughter. What a plonker!

Rocco's home and the music

I used to love going to Rocco Ambrico's house at 1 Guildford Street, as the family were so warm and kind and there was always Italian music playing constantly, which I loved, as it provided a very happy background and atmosphere. I remember mostly hearing Dean Martin records being played (Dean singing 'Return To Me', which was one of my favourites) with him singing in English and Italian, and other Italian stars records such as Domenico Muddugno, who had a hit with the international song 'Volare', which he wrote.

'Marina' was sung by Rocco Granata and this was another one of my favourites, and I can still recall the tune even after all these years. I remember it being played over and over again in the Ambrico household with everyone singing along to it. I also thought the world of his family and in particular his lovely kind mum, brother Joe and sister Angela. To me, their house, as I said before, was always full of warmth and love and provided an escape for me on so many occasions from the tense atmosphere of my own home. Happy memories, I loved going there!

Jeff Smith, our tandem and park keeper

In 1964, a friend of mine called Jeff Smith told me about a tandem that was going very cheap and asked if I would like to go halves with him to buy it. Having been working for the past year, I had a few shillings spare and happily I agreed (can't remember how much we paid, but it wasn't much). Anyway, having purchased it, we cleaned, polished, and oiled it up. We were delighted with the machine and decided to give it a spin around Victoria Park. We set off at a pace and all went well as we completed a couple of laps around the outer perimeter of the park in order to get used to our new prized possession.

We increased our speed as we felt more confident and were unaware of just how fast we were moving. Jeff Smith was doing the driving and having done the circuits, he drove towards the pavilion.

Unbeknown to us the park keeper must have been watching us or maybe a member of the public had reported us, it could have been either! Anyway, as we went around the pavilion, the park keeper must have decided to head us off from the opposite direction, as when we took one of the corners at speed, we encountered him coming towards us. I can see his face even now, as we hit him full on in his 'Crown Jewels', resulting in the poor man being completely floored and flattened by the impact and our pace. We both came off the tandem too and decided to run for it.

We headed towards the Old Horse Inn on London Road opposite the park and hid behind a car to watch the repercussions of our reckless driving. The keeper was helped to his feet by members of the public and shortly afterwards a police van turned up. The keeper seemed to have recovered as he helped the police put our 'dream machine' in the back of the van. We could only watch with utter disappointment as we only had it for one day. We had considered going over and holding our hands up to the accident in the hope we would get our tandem back but neither of us had the bottle! (I will get back to Jeff Smith again later - see chapter, Life changing events).

The allotment

Ian and I decided for some stupid reason to get an allotment. We found one near Evington village and worked very hard at getting it dug over during the winter. Ian, bless him, used to cycle over from his house with all manners of gardening tools strapped to his body as well as the bike frame. Having done all the hard work for about 18 months we decided that we had had enough of being 'Percy Thrower's and gave the allotment to a local Church Group who were delighted to have a readymade allotment for instant use. What prats we were!

At this point in time, Ian and I lost touch over the next couple of years as he went into the Army (Tank Regiment) and served abroad in Germany. I wrote to him several times and felt sure that we would always be friends and keep in contact which proved to be the case.

George May

At the age of 16, I started drinking alcohol. I remember that I used to go to a local pub in Highfields called the Barley Mow on Sunday dinner times with my new mate George May, who I knew from school and would go on to form a group with. I started drinking Mann's Brown initially and usually got pissed after having about 2-3 small bottles.

However, going back to George! He was looking at starting a band at the time and some mates of mine told him that I was music-mad and was always singing harmonies on street corners with two other mates, Dick Plimmer and Big Nose Williamson. Anyway, with this in mind, George approached me and asked if we could meet and see how we got on.

Harmony at the Jolly Angler

We went to a pub called the Jolly Angler in Conduit Street. George asked me what music I liked, and I said The Beatles, The Everly Brothers and other bands of the 60's and George suggested 'Cathy's Clown' by The Everly Brothers as a starter. As we started up the session, I sang the melody and George sang the 3rd harmony automatically. It was like we had always sang together as the blend of our two voices was almost perfect!

We just looked at each other with a big grin on our faces and sang that song over and over again, as if to confirm that it was not a fluke! I always wanted to make my living in music, and I saw this as the start of my ambition. We practised mainly in the front room at George's house in Clipston Street and then after we had perfected our songs, we began singing together in pubs for money by passing the hat around after we had done our bit.

At one pub in the Nether Hall area that we played at, things were about to change when a guy called Tommo (Robert Bob Thompson), who was a real wild character, approached us and asked if he could join us. After a practice a few days later, Tommo joined us as he was a very capable musician and likeable character. We were then a trio, which was soon added to with a drummer and bass player (I can't remember either of their names) and we decided for some reason to call the band The Kremlins. The band commenced playing the club circuit on odd occasions and we were managed by a guy called Brian Walker. Now then reader, I never did get on with Brian, due to a gut feeling I had about him - basically I didn't trust him and so the bands life was fairly short-lived, and we packed it in about nine months later.

However, George and I were very close and he was more like a brother to me at the time and so we decided to continue playing regularly as a duo, calling ourselves firstly The Kane Brothers and then 'Studio Two' for several years after this and eventually, in 1972, we formed another band called Crisp.

The Mays make a move

Well folks, having told you about practising in the front room at George's house at 67 Clipston Street, I must tell you a couple of funny stories regarding George and the May family.

George's parents, Hilda and Harry May, who were both likable Liverpudlians, had ten children between them (seven boys and three girls) during their marriage and so you can appreciate that living in a typical Victorian Terrace house with only three bedrooms and an outside toilet, overcrowding in their home was a really big issue.

Now then, one Sunday morning as I recall, I called around to his house and upon entering I heard a commotion coming down from the bedrooms upstairs. I asked George what all the noise was about, and he replied with a grin "follow me and you can see for yourself". As we got to the top of the stairs, I couldn't believe my eyes as I saw that his brothers had smashed their way through their bedroom wall with a sledgehammer into the adjoining bedroom of the empty house next door (it's absolutely true readers). Moreover, his younger siblings had already put new mattresses in their new bedroom floor and were jumping for joy on the new beds wallowing in their newly found space – it was bloody amazing and a very funny sight that I shall never forget!

George went on to explain in a matter-of-fact way, that not only could they have a bedroom each now, but they also had another toilet in the yard. It made total sense to them all as in one stroke they had found the solution to their overcrowding problem!

However, I have to explain the reason why they had broken through to their neighbouring house. You see, the area the Mays lived in had been targeted by the Leicester City Council for demolition in order to make way for new housing as the area itself was even more run down and dilapidated than that of our own. And so, the Mays, being the last ones to move out and their next-door neighbour's house being empty, they had taken full advantage of the situation and made very practical use of the opportunity. The Mays lived for a couple of months in their new extended accommodation before being moved to a larger house in the Braunstone Estate area of the city known as 'Dodge City' but that's another story folks.

The half bog door

Another time I called around to his house, and after knocking a few times at the door without having a reply, I decided to go around the back passing the outside toilet without noticing anything different. As I knocked on the back door a voice came out of nowhere saying "He's not in!". I looked around wondering where the voice was coming from - was it from the upstairs window - no it wasn't! So, where the hell was it coming from?

I then made my way back towards the toilet in case the voice was coming from there and as I approached the toilet the voice spoke again saying "Hi Dave". I then found Georges younger brother Derek sitting on the toilet reading a comic with his pants and trousers around his ankles.

The reason why I could see him immediately was that the top half of the toilet door had been completely cut off, which gave Derek a perfect view of the outside world and helped to dispel any odours as he carried out his ablutions! Derek carried on talking to me as if this kind of thing was quite normal stating that he didn't know where his brother had gone and what time he might possibly be coming home etc. I didn't blink an eyelid as I continued to converse with him as I didn't want to embarrass him or myself for that matter. The whole meeting was very bizarre and quite surreal. Anyway, I then said goodbye to Derek and left him on the bog as if nothing unusual had happened whatsoever.

Now then reader, looking back I think that both of these stories are very funny, and I think that there is nothing funnier than people and life itself!

Footnote: Later George told me that the missing half of the door had been used for firewood and apparently there was enough left over to make a small chair for one of the children. This was how life was in those days as life was really tough for the working class.

"Was it himself you're wanting"?

Now reader, do you remember how I told you earlier in the book about how I came to be called Dave whilst living in London and how subsequently this had stuck with me via my mates as I went through life? Well, as I started to write this book I got in touch with George, and he reminded me of the story about coming to my house for the first time.

Having knocked on the door my Dad answered, and he asked George what he wanted. George naturally said innocently "is Dave in?" as this was the only name he actually knew me by. Dad blew a fuse and went into a rage and told George firmly and in no uncertain terms (but to be fair without actually swearing and losing complete control) that **"there's no Dave who lives here! There's a Dermot, but there's no Dave! Now then, was it himself that your wanting?"**.

Poor old George, it couldn't have been pleasant being on the end of my Dad's temper (as I knew myself what his temper was like), but he weathered the storm and never forgot to ask for me with my proper name whenever he called around to my house following this incident. However, I couldn't really blame my Dad for this as after all, it was me who accepted the name of Dave all those years ago and it was my Dad that gave me the name of Dermot at birth!

Mods, Rockers, Bikes and Mockers

Apart from not knowing which name I was to be called by - Dave or Dermot - as a 16-17 year old I was also unsure if I wanted to be a Mod or Rocker, as on one hand I loved the Mods for their very smart and trendy sense of fashion, with their velvet jackets, flared brightly coloured trousers and shirts with extremely long collars, that were either round or star shaped. I also loved the Mod music at the time, including The Who, Faces and Kinks, etc.

Conversely, I loved the Rockers who stemmed from the 1950's, with their love of Elvis, Fats Domino, Little Richard, The Everly Brothers and other greats of that era. The leather jackets and denim look combined with flying boots also appealed to me. However, as I couldn't afford a flying jacket, which were very expensive, I decided to be a Mod for most of the time as it was more affordable! As my foot was in both camps at times, I suppose I was really a 'Mocker'.

I used to frequent a café on Mere Road with my Rocker mates which had an American jukebox, and we would put on all the old rock records as well as the modern records of the time, including my very favourite band of all time, The Beatles. I used to put the Beatles on as often as I could afford it (incidentally, I was lucky to see the Beatles live in 1963 at De Monfort Hall. You couldn't hear a lot of them due to girls and some boys screaming. However, I do remember a male jumping from one of the side private boxes, onto the stage, trying to give Macca a hug before being removed by the bouncers).

Nevertheless, back to the Café. I also loved some of the records of the time and one I remember playing was by Johnny Kidd And The Pirates called "I'll Never Get Over You" which I played over and over again.

Dermot at full throttle!

I was desperate to have a motor bike but could never afford one and so I decided to get (I know it sounds daft) a Honda 50 would you believe! It was at least practical to get me to work and visit relations and friends. Naturally, all of my Rocker mates took the piss initially. However, I would go out with them at weekends riding around the roads and lanes of Leicestershire with me always at the back trying to keep up, with the Honda 50 at full throttle all the time!

I remember one time we went to Groby and stopped at a pub for several drinks. We all came out a bit worse for the drink and decided to go to another pub on the opposite side of town. As we set off the rain began to pour and as we went around the ABC island in the centre of Leicester (Charles Street) the majority of the gang skidded and landed at the side of the road unhurt but with some superficial damage to their bikes.

As I was always lagging behind, I was surprised to see them all on the ground pissing themselves laughing with the drink in them and as I approached, I started laughing too and feeling cocky I put two fingers up to them whilst shouting "who's behind now?!" Nevertheless, as I took the next corner feeling somewhat superior, I came off too! I landed on the deck and the plastic windshield completely buckled but, to my surprise, as I picked it up, it flew back into its original position.

My Honda 50 was the only bike not to be damaged that day! We all had a great laugh and thankfully no-one was injured, however, sadly several of these mates died very prematurely in motor bike accidents over the next two years.

The singing competition

In the summer of 1968, Studio Two entered a singing contest that was held at the Granby Halls in Leicester, which has long since been pulled down which is very sad because it was a great venue for top bands like The Rolling Stones and The Who, as well as acting as a roller-skating rink for myself and others most Saturday mornings. Talking of Granby Halls, I loved skating around it whilst doing my best to impress the girls with my roller skating moves / abilities which were quite poor actually, as music from The Beatles and other groups of the day blasted out from the massive speakers - happy days, I loved it! Anyway, I digress, so back to the story, George and I made it through the first two rounds and into the final, singing The Everly Brothers songs during each heat.

The panel in the final included Bill Maynard the actor (from the Heartbeat series), Lady Isobel Barnet and the TV celebrity, musician and composer, Steve Race. To cut a long story short, I hated and still do hate singing competitions, however we came second in the final and at least we didn't embarrass ourselves. The one thing I do remember that was nice was when Steve Race came over to us at the end of the final and shook our hands, stating we were very close to winning and added that we sounded very much like The Everly's. For me, this was a real compliment from a professional musician and composer, and I thought at the time we were heading in the right direction musically.

Driving test cock up

In late 1967/8, I passed my driving test first time which was more luck than judgement! As I recall, I had about 10 - 11 lessons before the test and on the day of the actual test, disaster struck, as my driving instructor turned up in a hired car, as his regular car had broken down and needed repair in a garage.

I was totally unfamiliar with the new car and only had one lesson to get used to it before the test. To add to my problems, half-way through the test, it started to piss it down and the windscreen started to mist up. I pushed every button in sight to try and clear it, without success. It was obvious to the tester that I didn't know the car and by this time I could hardly see the road for mist.

I made a bold decision, thinking that I was going to fail anyway if I didn't do something. I indicated to pull in and followed procedures in pulling the handbrake on, switching off the engine and opening the window to get air in. I then began wiping the windscreen with all my might until I had a clear screen.

Having completed the test I felt sure I had failed, but to my surprise, the test instructor handed me a pass certificate and informed me that although my driving wasn't great, I had shown common sense by pulling over to clear the windscreen and proceeded to drive safely. I was gobsmacked as it was probably the first and only time in my life that I had ever shown common sense!

Isle of Wight with the boys

Later that year, I had my first holiday ever when Dave Williams, Steve Miller, Terry Mason, Mick Wilkes and I headed off in a camper van to tour Devon and Cornwall and finished up in the Isle Of Wight.

Cornwall 1968. Left to right. Dave Williams, Steve Miller, Mick Wilkes and myself.

I had just met Theresa at this point, and she had gone on holiday with her sister Kate to Jersey and although I had a great time with the boys on holiday, I was really looking forward to seeing Theresa again as I felt I had met someone special (see meeting Theresa and the Fords).

Theresa in Jersey 1968. Wow, is it any wonder I wanted to get back from holiday to see her!

1968. Meeting Theresa and the Fords

In 1968, my life changed forever as I met the love of my life, future wife and mother of my three wonderful children. (Theresa Margaret Kane - nee Ford. Born 24th November 1951. Parents Eric and Gertrude Ford. Siblings: Kathleen, eldest sister, Kelvin ('Old Bean', the quiet one), Barry and Trevor.

All of her family welcomed me from the very start, and I became closer to Theresa's siblings than my own brothers as the years passed by, and I do consider them to be my own brothers and sister.

I recall going to Theresa's house for my first Sunday meal with the family. Uncle Syd, who was Eric Ford's brother (Sydney John Ford born 1936-died 2021, married Maureen Grewcock in 1971) was one of the nicest men you will ever meet and was present, as he was every Sunday in those days, and just before the meal was dished up, he leaned over and whispered into my ear, "you better get in quick as you might get a fork in your hand when the food comes out, as its every man for himself!". He wasn't joking, bless him, as the Fords all have enormous appetites as I found out to my cost that day!

Theresa and her siblings - from left to right. Trevor, Barry, Kelvin, Theresa & Kathleen.

Anyway, back to my story, on the night of our first meeting, I was out on the town with several of my mates including Dave Williams, Jeff Smith and Terry Mason. At the end of the night, we decided to go for a steak at the Town and Country Steak Restaurant in Granby Street.

As we walked in, I noticed this young beautiful looking waitress whizzing around and serving customers at a rate of knots, she was all of 5ft nothing and a lovely brunette (I think it was love at first sight for me, as I felt in my gut that this was someone very special entering my life). As we sat down, she came by again and I winked at her, however, she did not acknowledge my gesture and made no attempt to give any encouragement whatsoever!

I told my pals that I was determined to get a date with her before we left. Jeff Smith started to laugh at me whilst telling me that she was out of my league, and I had no chance at all. I then bet him five shillings that I would get the date. I took the opportunity when she brought some of our meals to the table and asked her would she come out with me. She informed me that she already had a boyfriend and was not interested! I was gutted and disappointed as I really did feel she was something special. Jeff Smith started to laugh and had "told me so!"

One of the other waitresses called Marjorie (Marg) must have overheard the whole thing and came over to talk to me. She informed me that she did not have a current boyfriend and therefore I should try again. She made some excuse with Theresa that she should collect our plates as she was too busy to do it herself. When Theresa came to our table, I asked her again for a date and informed her that I knew she did not have a boyfriend. This time she reluctantly said yes!

However, I never did get my five bob from Jeff Smith but it was worth it as I knew that she was something special. Later, I went home and told my Mam that I had met this lovely girl (which was something I never did with previous dates). Many years later, Theresa and I bumped into Jeff Smith again at his brother Des' 60th birthday party. He still refused to give me the five bob, insisting that Theresa had married the wrong man as it should have been him!

Anyway, I arranged to meet Theresa on the following Monday at Lewis's store near the Clock Tower (this is where most couples met in those days). However, on the night in question, I could not remember exactly what she looked like, and Theresa informed me later that she was in the same predicament. Having looked at several other girls who turned up for dates on the night, I decided that it must have been the gorgeous pretty little one as all the others were much taller.

We shyly introduced ourselves to each other and I decided to take her for a drink as I thought that she was about the same age as myself. As I drove her towards the pub in Houghton on The Hill, I naturally asked her about her family and herself etc. I nearly crashed the car when she told me that she was only 16 years old and still at school! As I was 20 years old at this point in time, I was worried about the age gap as perhaps people would call me a paedophile (my son Liam made reference to this on many occasions later in my life - well he would, wouldn't he)!

I think we fell in love very quickly (I know I did) and couldn't wait to see each other whenever we were apart. I also loved Theresa's family from the start as they all appeared to be so happy and comfortable in each other's company. Their home, unlike ours, always appeared to be calm, warm and loving with no underlying tension. Moreover, the food was always great and plentiful. They had an indoor bath, and the house was very posh compared to ours.

Theresa's parents were very strict though and to this day I am still unsure if her Dad Eric actually approved of me, as he initially refused my request to get engaged to Theresa, although I can honestly say that I thought the world of him (see section Engagement and marriage).

One of the rules was that I would have to have Theresa back home by 10.30pm if we went out and so we would come up with plans such as taking back food from chip shops or Chinese takeaway's and tell them that we had to wait as there was a queue or it took a long time to cook etc. (anything to spend more time in each other's company as we were very much in love!). Theresa's parents soon cottoned-on to our schemes and asked us not to bring back any food as they were bursting at the seams and were fed up with the same food every time anyway!

Farting in the Row Boat

Having courted Theresa for several weeks, I had the opportunity to take her out for the day to help me deliver a consignment of garments to Burberry's factory near Basingstoke. It was a bright sunny day as we departed in the works minivan from Leicester, and we soon arrived in Basingstoke to deliver the goods. Following this, as it was a beautiful day, I decided to drive down to the nearby river, to hire a rowboat and make the most of the day. We soon found a boat hiring firm and having paid for a couple of hours rent we set out on the craft.

Having rowed before several times, I felt fairly confident that I could impress Theresa with my wonderful rowing ability! Initially all went well with me pulling away with strong deep strokes into the water which propelled us headway up the river. Thinking in my mind that I was some kind of macho man by now, I pulled even harder and stronger than before to impress her with my strength, however, after several successful strokes going deeper into the water, resulting in the craft gliding along the water at some pace. However, by now I was totally over-confident with a big smile on my face and as I attempted the following stroke (which I put all my strength and very being into) to prove to Theresa that I was more or less up to Olympic standard or so I thought!!

Wrong! Despite my beliefs, I somehow managed not to drop the oars into the water this time, but instead completely skimmed the top of the water with both oars resulting in myself falling backwards from my seat into the bow of the boat, all this whilst letting go of the oars and producing the biggest fart through all my exertions which nearly blew Theresa out of the back of the boat! To Theresa's credit, she was in bits, laughing at my antics and never made any reference to my poor seamanship or indeed the aroma. However, looking back, I often wonder what she must have thought of me during these early days, and she must have wondered what she was letting herself in for! To be fair, I never took her on a rowboat again during our marriage.

1969. One of the saddest days in my life!

Whilst I was working in tailoring, I had to deliver garments to shops in the Leicester area every Saturday morning. It was in August 1969 that I was on my way to deliver some garments to "Scotneys" clothing shop on Blackbird Road. I can recall with great clarity that it was a beautiful sunny day as I drove up towards the traffic lights in Slater Street, but I had to stop short of the lights and await in a queue of traffic for the light to turn green again before I turned right into Frog Island.

As I waited in in the queue, I had this strange, unsettling feeling in my stomach that something was about to happen (I really can't explain why to this day). I then spotted two children, one boy aged approximately 6 years and a girl probably about 10 years of age, near the traffic lights.

As they approached the lights, they began to play tick and chase. As I watched the children the world seemed to slow down in real-time as the horror of the scene unfolded. Just then a huge dustbin lorry slowed down to a crawl, in order to turn hard left into Slater

Street which is very narrow. I then watched in disbelief as the boy 'ticked' his sister and, without looking, ran straight out into the road and only stopped when he noticed in bewilderment and shock, that he was in between the front and back wheels of the huge lorry.

Time stood still as I looked at the boy putting his hands up to protect himself from the massive wheels as they drove over his little body. I jumped out of my car to try and stop what was happening, but it was too late as the driver didn't even notice the slight bump as he drove further down the street.

At this stage, the boy was lying in the middle of the road as the traffic, would you believe, drove around him without stopping. I picked up the boy and took him to the side pavement and put my coat under his head. He just looked up at me with a half-smile and without speaking a word passed away peacefully. I couldn't believe that he wasn't crying or complaining of pain, and he just looked serene. He did not appear to have major injuries other than some blood coming out of each ear.

A passing ambulance then pulled in and the crew tried in vain to resuscitate him, but it was obvious the little mite had sadly died. I gave the police my details before I got back into my car completely shocked and dazed, and then, on automatic pilot, completed my deliveries before going back home to share my grief with Theresa, who was waiting for me at my Mam's. I later received a letter from the court telling me that I did not have to attend as the driver had been completely exonerated by other witnesses at the scene and the verdict was a complete accident as ruled by the Judge. It's a day I will never forget until the day I die!

Mam / the pee bucket and Theresa

Sometimes Theresa was allowed by her parents to stop over at my house. However, there were rules to be applied. Theresa would have to sleep with my mother under supervision, just in case someone would slip in! Theresa recalls that one night she awoke to what she thought was running water. She was not far wrong, as she spotted my Mam at the bottom of the bed, sitting on a bucket with a big smile on her face! Mam gave her a little wave and then continued to relieve herself whilst giving Theresa advice regarding her nightwear, telling her that she would get her "death of cold" wearing those flimsy night dresses. Theresa took the whole incident in her stride as she loved my mother and did not judge us by our poor sanitation situation or lack of amenities.

Mam was also very naive when it came to any talk about sex or any other embarrassing subjects, particularly if males were present. One day I came into the room as Mam was telling Theresa about a girl that we knew becoming pregnant. She clamped up as I entered the room but continued to make gestures behind my back with her hands by gesticulating about the girl having a swollen belly, her bosoms becoming much bigger etc, whilst giving Theresa silent lip service about not mentioning any of this to me as her innocent son! Later, Theresa and I discussed the event and laughed at her lovely innocent ways and naivety.

Mam and the human ash tray

My Mam also had a great sense of humour, and I can remember on a few occasions when she was smoking in the company of my Dad, she used to let the ash on the end of her cigarette get longer and longer as she smoked so that it got cold on the end whilst it hung on by a thread.

My Mam, with a mischievous grin, would then go behind my Dad's back and point to the bald patch at the back of his head, before she proceeded to tap the fag with her index finger, which deposited the ash like a feather on her designated target. Dad never even noticed as she tried to control her muted laughter behind his back whilst she crossed her legs in an attempt to stop wetting herself! I remember going out of the room just in case he saw me trying to suppress my own bloody laughter.

Another example of my Mam's humour was the following picture taken on a trip to Derbyshire with Uncle Danny & Aunt Rose. Mum and Dad had clearly had an argument on the day, as they didn't speak to each other for the whole of the trip. When my mum got the pictures developed at the chemists several weeks later (as people did back then), my mum had cut our Dad's head from the picture in anger!

And here's the proof! Front row, Theresa and myself. Back row, 'guess who???, mum and Aunt Rose. What a loving family!!!

First Christmas at the Fords

My first Christmas at the Ford household was joyous! Mainly because there was peace, contentment and happiness, combined with excitement in their home, as Christmas drew near. However, I stopped overnight on Christmas Eve and after attending midnight mass we returned to their home for a quick drink and to help Eric and Gertrude put the abundance of presents into sacks ready for the children the next morning (Trevor was only six years old when I met Theresa). I was totally surprised that whilst putting presents in the sacks, when I saw a sack with my own name tag on it, containing wrapped up Christmas presents (in proper Christmas paper). I was very excited at seeing this, for as I grew up, we rarely had presents of any kind and if we did, they were never wrapped in proper Christmas paper (it would either be in an old sock or wrapped in newspaper).

Having gone to bed, I tossed and turned as I couldn't sleep for the thought of the presents waiting for me downstairs the following morning. Eventually I did drop off and was awoken by Theresa's brother, Trevor asking his mother if he could go down to see if Santa had been yet. As it was very early in the morning she initially refused. However, by now I was peppering to go downstairs and used Trevor as my leverage by sending him back into his mother, time-and-time again, to ask for permission to go downstairs.

Gertrude reluctantly agreed, eventually due to bombardment for her son, and with this I jumped out of bed with the intention of being the first to open my presents. As I entered the landing the rest of the family were also waiting for permission and were starting to make their way downstairs, but being so excited myself I pushed my way through knocking poor old Trevor to one side as I made my way to the front of the queue then running and sliding onto the lounge on my belly whilst making a last desperate grab for my sack. I then shouted with a grin "I did it" as I took hold of my Christmas goodies.

Looking back, the family must have thought I was mad, and they all started laughing at the sight of this excitable plonker acting like a little kid! This was to be the first of many times spent in the company of the Ford family at Christmas and I have to say that each one has been just as joyous as the first.

Courting, Uncle Danny and his pranks

Moving on, Theresa and I began saving hard, as we wanted to get married at some point in the future and therefore did not go out often. However, being really close to my Uncle Danny and Aunt Rose, we decided to visit them weekly, as we always had a laugh with them and could catch up with family events, etc, and we did this for the next couple of years.

Daniel Patrick Kearney born 1925, died 1973 and Auntie Rose (Rose Agnes Kearney - nee Read, born January 19th 1921, died 29th October 2012.) They married on 27th October 1951 and went on to have three children (Mick and John, twins born 1952) and daughter (Susan born 1959).

Uncle Danny pictured here in British uniform. Danny served in the British army during World War II in the Royal Artillery North African Corp.

Uncle Danny was the kindest man I ever met, and he was a tall man, standing about six feet tall and of slim build, with very dark hair and dark skin. He actually looked a bit foreign, as did some of his brothers, with large Jewish-type noses. I remember saying to him that we must have some Jewish blood in the family for a laugh. However, this appears to be true as my eldest son Jonathan's DNA was analysed in 2018 and he had 1.3% Ashkenazi Jewish, 1.5% North African and 14% Iberian and the rest Celtic in his DNA which might explain my observations of my relatives?

Anyway, back to Uncle Danny. He always had a twinkle in his eye and loved laughing and joking, playing pranks on people and generally getting into mischief. Auntie Rose on the other hand, was a small woman of about five feet three inches, with slim build and a very thick Leicester accent, she also seemed to spend her whole time laughing at anything and everything that was in the slightest bit funny. The pair of them were always laughing and joking with each other and it was always a pleasure to be in their company.

Each Sunday we really looked forward to seeing both of them as I felt that Danny was the Dad that I never had, as he was kind, gentle and funny with a heart of gold and Aunt Rose always made us very welcome. Each Sunday, Danny would tell us of the previous week's events particularly when he saw my Mam and Dad or Vera.

He would also organise games for us each week; this might be mini golf or tennis played in his large back beautiful garden (Uncle Danny was a gardener by trade), with teams trying to beat each other and have Uncle Danny declare the winner with a big grin. Danny and Rose were so close that their love for each other was infectious.

Both Theresa and I hoped that we might replicate their marriage when we got married. Rose would make cheese sandwiches each and every week and Danny would make the same statement each week informing her that we would all turn into mice unless she provided some other kind of sustenance! It sounds corny, but we would laugh, as it was the way he said it and the faces he pulled behind Aunt Roses back! Listed below are just some of the stories and tales involving Uncle Danny…

Rose and the Bacon and Egg

One such story was them having a night out with my Mam and Dad and also Aunt Vera and Uncle Joe McLoughlin. Apparently, the night started well, with them all going to St. Patricks Club in town and having a good old drink. Mam and Dad suggested that they all come back to our house in Avon Street and finish the night with further drinks. Upon returning, Mam rustled up bacon and egg for all concerned. I was there at the time, and all seemed to be going well. However, something was said between my Mam and Dad which altered the whole night proceedings, and a full-blown slanging match took place between both of my parents.

Vera, who could be quite fiery, then began to have a go at my Dad. Dad told Vera in no uncertain terms to mind her own business and with this Vera did no more than pick up the plate of freshly cooked bacon and egg and slung it with some force towards my Dad. However, she was not the best shot as it missed my Dad and hit Auntie Rose on her forehead, bless her.

The egg yolk broke and started to run down her face and over her rather large nose (which incidentally Uncle Danny always referred to for a laugh as massive!) and down her cheek. Typically, Aunt Rose did not get angry or upset as anyone else would, instead she began to laugh with all her might and could do nothing as the tears rolled down her face. The get-together finished rather abruptly at this stage, and I could still hear Auntie Rose laughing as they all left through our front door.

Danny and bingo callers

Another story involved Danny playing bingo at the St. Patricks Club. The normal callers were absent and therefore two incompetent men gave it a go. One of the men accidently knocked over the metal container which held the balls and was worked by turning a handle (not electric in those days)! They put back the balls which they felt had not been pulled out yet and so continued to play. Uncle Danny was fed up by this time as the game was taking so long to complete. He quickly marked each of the numbers left on his card and shouted very loudly "House". They half-heartedly pretended to check the numbers as they knew they had made a balls-up and quickly declared him a winner! It can only happen with the Irish!!!

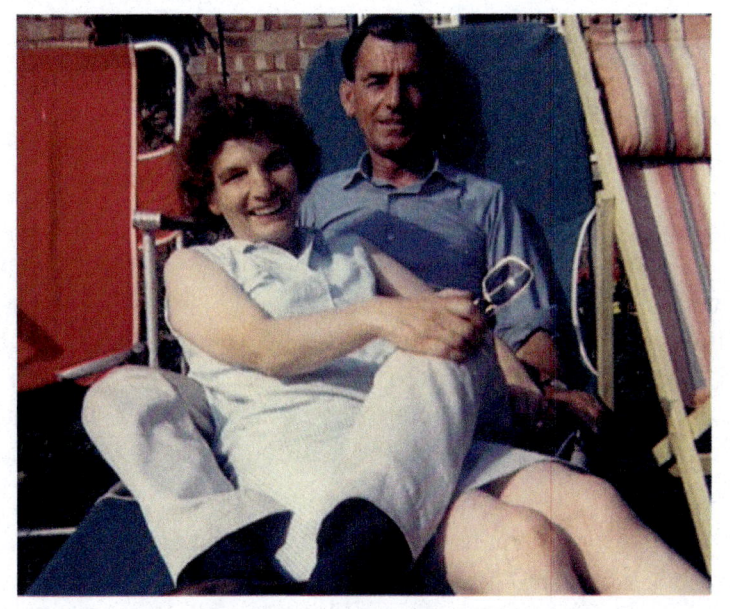

The loving couple Danny and Rose.

Danny and the new contraceptive

The best story Danny ever told me was when he received a letter from his brother, Uncle Ger (Gerard Kearney born 1933, died 1998) from Ireland, asking for his help in obtaining contraceptives for him as there were no contraceptives available in Ireland at that time. I think Uncle Ger had six children at this time and went on to have three more after this story!

Now, Uncle Danny was more than willing to oblige and so he sent a letter back to Ger, in which he told him that there was a new contraceptive on the market in the form of a tablet and enclosed several of the said white tablets, with full instructions on how to use them. The instructions advised him to tell his wife Maura to 'insert' said tablets and wait for half an hour before any 'action' could take place.

Anyway, Uncle Danny heard nothing for five months and then received a letter back from Uncle Ger in which he thanked Uncle Danny for sending the contraceptives and went on to say that although he had followed the instructions to the letter and had used all the enclosed tablets, his wife was now pregnant again! Moreover, he said that whenever the action had taken place, there was a lot of 'foaming' coming from the area of the action!

Uncle Danny went on to explain to me, whilst killing himself laughing, that the contraceptive tablets he enclosed were actually Trebor mints taken out of their packaging!

Danny and the wrong address

Uncle Danny went on his scooter to Coventry, to see his brother Frank. It was pissing it down with rain on the day and Danny was cold, wet and dying for a cup of tea when he arrived at the house. He knocked at the door, which was opened by who he thought was one of Frank's kids. He asked the boy to put the kettle on and enquired if he had any biscuits to go with the cup of tea. The boy put the biscuits on the table whilst Danny took off all of his biking clothing.

Eventually, the boy made the tea and brought it to Danny at the table. After having a few slurps and eating several biscuits, Danny inquired where Frank and other siblings were? The boy looked at Danny perplexed and told him he didn't have a Dad named Frank nor did he have any other siblings. Slowly, it hit Danny that he had gone into the wrong house, as they all looked very similar on that estate. Danny left feeling very embarrassed but also laughing at the situation at the same time, but not before he finished his cup of tea!

The plant switching scam

Uncle Danny was always telling me stories about his brothers and the scams they got up to, particularly later in their lives when most of them were involved in gardening. I remember one such story about Uncle Alfie. Apparently, Uncle Alf had lots of Jewish clients and many of the wealthiest resided in the big posh houses in The Bishops Avenue. Uncle Alf had his son Terry and also Uncle Frank working for him during this period.

Alf being the mastermind, would recommend annually to his clients that they should consider changing the large flower beds in order to brighten up and enhance their garden each spring. His advice was usually taken and so he would arrange to have that particular flower bed dug-up and the bulbs removed, whilst telling his clients that he would return within a couple of days with new bulbs.

Having loaded them into his car, he would take them to the garden's that either Terry or Uncle Frank were working in. By the time he arrived at either garden, the owners would have already agreed to have their particular garden bed dug up and the bulbs removed. When Uncle Alf arrived, all they had to do was put the previous neighbours' bulbs into the flower bed and take the bulbs from this site onto the next unsuspecting neighbour at the next location.

In essence, each neighbour was providing bulbs for each other every spring, with Uncle Alf being the provider of the service for cash payments. Danny said that Uncle Alf told him that there was never a problem with this very profitable scam and there was never any comeback or suspicion from his very happy costumers. Who says the Irish are thick!

By 1972/73, Uncle Danny's health took a turn for the worst as he had several heart attacks. He spent some time in hospital and I went to visit him. Despite feeling very ill he still managed to have a laugh and a joke. At this stage I was only 24 years old and still thought that everyone I loved would live forever and so I continued to work, play in the band and get on with life generally. With hindsight, I wished that I had seen much more of him at that time. He was then discharged back to his home in Thurnby Lodge where he later suffered another heart attack and sadly died in 1973.

In between this period, our beautiful son Jonathan was born in June 1972 and to show you how much I thought of my Uncle Danny, my mother and father were not the first to see him, as Theresa and I took him straight from the hospital to Danny and Rose's house. I remember Danny having a cuddle with him and remarking that we had produced a "beautiful child" in a soft and loving voice.

A few weeks later I received a lovely letter from Uncle Danny (I still treasure this letter) in which he thanked us for the visit and again remarked on Jonathan's beauty and went on to advise me to take care of my health as I was working too hard both in full-time employment and also with the band. I think he knew that he was a very ill man and his time was short, as he finished off by saying "take care and look after each other". This was typical of Uncle Danny, even when very ill and in his last months of his life he was still putting and thinking of others before himself.

Uncle Danny was perhaps the most generous man I have ever known, as despite having very little income himself throughout his life, he was always sending money, clothes, and gifts to others less fortunate than himself, particularly family members who I am sure will have their own tales of his kindness to tell.

What a wonderful man he was and what a great role model for myself. I loved both my Uncle Danny and Aunt Rose and they will always hold a special place in my heart.

In October 1971, Studio Two had their first exciting visit to a recording studio in Kettering to record 'Ebony Eyes' and a song I wrote called 'Flowers'. The two other musicians on the recording were my friend Tony Wilkinson and his little brother Nigel on the drums. Nigel was later to join The Real Thing from Liverpool as their drummer and they went on to record a number one with "You To Me Are Everything" as well as several other top ten hits.

Refused Second Engagement

After 18 months of courting, Theresa suggested that we should get engaged to be married! I agreed and we went back to tell her parents. Theresa's Mam Gertie seemed very pleased, however when I asked her Dad Eric for his daughter's hand in marriage during a washing up session later that evening, he replied, without even a blink or looking at me; "**No**"!

I was shocked and devastated and upon announcing this to Theresa and her Mam, an argument ensued between both of her parents. They went upstairs to their bedroom and left Theresa in a flood of tears (I think she was desperate for me!). Theresa was then summoned up to their bedroom and her mother asked her in front of Eric if I had asked Theresa to marry me (technically speaking I never actually asked Theresa, or indeed my first fiancé Yvonne Morgan for that matter, to marry me) nevertheless Theresa declared that I had. With this, her Mam informed Eric in no uncertain terms that we were engaged to be married whether he liked it or not!

As Eric never seemed to win any arguments with Gertie, he reluctantly agreed, as he knew he was beaten. However, he stated that we should not have a long engagement, as he felt a date should be set as a focus for the wedding. Shortly after this, we had a great engagement party at the Heathcote Arms in Croft with all those present whom we loved.

Eric and Gertie: I snapped this picture at Jonathan's 21st Birthday bash. It's my favourite picture of them!

We then started saving in earnest, hardly ever going out and spending most of our time together in my Mam's front room listening to records. My Mam always seemed to be on shotgun watch, as she would come into the room every half an hour to pump up the cushions and tidy up unnecessarily.

We managed to save up enough for a deposit of £600 on a house over the 18 months and, through a lovely lady called Doreen Bland, who worked with me at Birrs Sportswear, found a property in Wilnicott Road, which was on the market for £2,800. The property was newly decorated in each room, however, it did need to have a small extension built on the back of the house, for another £250! I often look back and wonder why Theresa married me and I have come to the conclusion that it was the £12.50 that I had in the TSB bank at the time we first met which made me a real catch!

Studio Two and the hanging

I remember with clarity one funny incident with Studio Two. It was the very night before our wedding and we were playing at our local club, the Braunstone Working Men's club (W.M.C.) Now, in those days (before radio mikes) we had long leads on the microphones and so as I was singing, the lead must have dropped over the edge of the stage and landed, unbeknown to me, over the head of a person sitting on a table directly below the stage.

Now, as I walked to the other side of the stage, I felt a tug on the mike lead, and I assumed that someone was taking the piss out of me. I was determined not to give him the satisfaction of looking down and so I started to tug back. It then became a tugging session for the next few minutes, with me and him pulling to and fro, with neither of us seemingly willing to give in.

Within minutes the audience were in tears and both George and the organist stopped playing as they were helpless with laughter. Being thick, I couldn't understand what was happening! However, when I eventually looked down, the poor bugger below was trying to get the lead off from around his neck as it was actually strangling him!

Ironically, the organist that night was Theresa's old music teacher from Lutterworth Grammar School whose name was Cecil. He loved seeing Theresa again and wished us both every happiness for our forthcoming marriage.

"Studio Two" - George May and myself with Choc Kershaw - (a lovely man and our manager).

Marriage And Children

Honeymoon on a budget

Our happy marriage started on the 12 April 1971 at the Catholic church in Narborough (Pope Pius X) and the service was conducted by the late Father Nolan. After the service, as we were having the photos taken, Father Nolan went over to my Uncle Alf and said "you are Alf Kearney aren't you?" Apparently, they had both attended Synge Street School in Dublin together 50 odd years ago and would you believe they still recognised each other after all those years - isn't life amazing and you never know who or what will turn up do you?

(See more about Father Nolan later in the book - Father Nolan takes a tumble).

Anyway, it was a joyous occasion, we were so happy and excited at the prospect of starting our life together and our wedding picture was on the front page of the Leicester Chronicle (can you believe such fame! They must have been short of news…).

1971 on the front page of The Leicester Chronicle

It was a wonderful day with everybody half-cut at the end of it, that is apart from myself, who had to drive to our honeymoon in Mundesley-On-Sea (such an exotic place!). We left the celebrations with £11 in our pockets to cover the trip, including petrol and 2 nights at the guesthouse.

I remember it was a hot day and halfway there, I stopped at a layby to take off my shirt and jacket and change into lighter ones. Everyone passing could see we were newlyweds as the car was covered from front to back with streamers, lots of foam with written congratulations from guests and well-wishers and tin cans tied to the bumper. As I stripped off in a layby to change from my wedding suit, all the passing cars blew their horns and shouted congratulations, we felt so young and happy to be alive and together in marriage.

1971. Left to right. Mam and Dad Kane, the little groom, my gorgeous new wife, Mam and Dad Ford.

When we arrived in Mundesley, it was dark, and we initially could not find the B & B, so we stopped and asked a chap who was passing by. He leant against our car to give us directions, not knowing that the car was covered in foam. As we thanked him and drove away, we could see that the whole of his top and trousers were covered completely in foam. It looked so funny, and we were both in stiches laughing at the incident.

We drove into Ingleside Guesthouse and were greeted by the two old lady owners, who seemed so delighted and happy to have newlyweds stopping with them. By now it was fairly late at night and so they showed us up to our bedroom, whilst telling us on the way that we only had to ask, and they would get us whatever we wanted. Without going into any details of our first night on our honeymoon, other than telling you that the lady had put on the electric blanket several hours earlier and I can tell you it was definitely **not** required!

To be honest, we couldn't wait to get back to our new home as we felt so excited to see the finished work on the house, including the new lean-to £250 kitchen. When we arrived back home, the front of the house was decorated by Theresa's sister Kate and her friend Christine, with buntings, balloons and a 'welcome home newlyweds' sign.

We both felt so lucky as we entered the house, however, as I picked Theresa up trying to look macho by carrying her over the threshold, I bumped her head on the door frame as we entered, and I am sure she thought what a prat he is and she must have wondered what the hell she had let herself in for! Despite this, we were excited at the prospect of our new life together and although we had very little in the house, other than second hand furniture, we felt like it was our castle and our heaven.

Our wedding in 1971. Nearest on the end of each line-my brothers Frank (left) and Sean (right).

Milkman not paid and the patter of tiny feet

We soon settled into married life and rarely saw the milkman for the first year of our marriage as I was very busy!

I was back at work the following week and we were paid weekly in those days with a sealed wage packet. Remembering how my mother never knew how much my Dad ever earned, also my mother being left short or indeed not left any money on some occasions by my father, I told Theresa that when we wed that I would give her every penny I earned to support her and our family. I never did open my wage packet from that first week until I finally retired from work on 28th February 2014.

Anyway, back to the story, we cracked on so well that 14 months later our first child Jonathan Paul Kane was born on 3rd June 1972 (I would have loved him to have the other middle name of George as I wanted my son to have a Beatles connection in his name). Theresa had a difficult time during the birth, which lasted two days and she was only the second lady in Leicestershire to be given the new 'epidural injection' for the pain.

I remember the consultant, a big chap of about 6ft 3, asking me to sign the permission for the epidural. I hadn't a clue what I was signing for and was very worried that something bad was happening to Theresa and our child as they would not let me into the room. I saw lots of activity with staff rushing in and out to her and I was really scared. However, all was well in the end, and I was told I had a baby boy.

I remember going in to see them both, Theresa was out for the count and so I went over to the nurse who put the little chap in my arms, He was so beautiful and perfect and as soon as I saw him floods of tears, filled my face and I cried tears of joy. It was one of the most wonderful experiences that I ever had, and I have subsequently experienced those same feelings with each of the births of my children. It's a miracle every time!

As for Jon, he became known as 'Prof' in the family as he grew up, due to being very sensible, intelligent, and responsible. He saved my bacon on many occasions (more of this later in the book) as he grew up, whilst giving sound advice and direction whenever I was about to make cock-ups or indeed made cock-ups and needed bailing out! He is a great son, and we are so proud of him. He is a man of principle and honour along with the capacity for being a great human being.

Skipping forward, Jon married Lilian Thomson in 2009 and exactly a year later they had their first child, a beautiful girl named Imogen Erica Stewart Kane (Erica after Theresa's Dad, Stewart as is the Scottish tradition of taking the grandmother's maiden name). Five years later, they had their second child Alfred Mark Kane - named after myself, as my second name is Alfred, and Mark, after Lilian's late father. We both feel that we are blessed to have such wonderful grandchildren.

Jonathan pictured here with his family. Left to right - Jonathan, Alfie, Lilian & Immy

Anyway, as I was saying, the news of our new arrival was difficult to communicate as there were no mobiles in those days and so it had to be done on the old landlines. I telephoned Theresa's parent's house first and Kelvin took the call. Having given him the details, I reiterated that he needed him to pass this on to his parents. Later in the day he just happened to mention this to them, they apparently danced around together in the kitchen with pure joy.

That evening, I was playing the King Richards Road Club, and both sets of parents attended and a great night was had by all. I also spent a lot of time wetting the baby's head with friends and family over the next couple of weeks. Theresa left me in charge of the finances whilst she spent time in hospital recovering, and she had always told me of her struggle to make ends meet on my very low wages. I saw none of this and continued to celebrate the birth of our son.

A couple of days later I told Theresa of my recent 'financial management', stating that I still had several pounds left after my spree and suggested to her that I might as well take over the finances permanently! She said that was fine, and then asked me if I had put away the weekly £12 to cover the mortgage and bills including gas, electricity, etc. My jaw hit the ground, as I had spent nearly all of our money on celebrating over the past two weeks. Needless to say, I have never done the finances from that day to this!

Life moved very quickly and the following year we had our second child, Liam Barry Daniel, who was born on 18th November 1973. Theresa's brother Barry was also born on 18th November and so Liam was also named after him and my late favourite Uncle Danny Kearney. Theresa was in hospital awaiting the arrival and I was both working and playing in the band in the evenings. Theresa was a long time in labour and every night I would ring the hospital before going to bed to see if I needed to go in as I wanted to be present at the birth this time.

I rang the ward about 11.30pm and was told by the nurse that there was no chance of Theresa giving birth that night and therefore advised me to get a good night's sleep. I asked if they would ring if there was any change in circumstances and she assured me they would.

The next morning, I awoke to a banging on the front door. I opened the door to find my brother-in-law Kelvin who said in his own inimitable style, and without any explanation whatsoever, "you need to ring the hospital". Apparently, the hospital staff had tried to ring me during the night (I am not so sure) however, unable to rouse me they let Theresa's Mam know of the birth. Liam came out backwards down the birth canal and I think this was a sign of things to come! It never ceases to amaze me how much humans have the capacity to love, as because with each of your own children or grandchildren we have been lucky to have, you love them all just as much as each other. I was so proud to have two beautiful boys to carry on the Kane name.

As for Liam himself, he is one of the funniest and most generous guys you could ever meet, and I always have a laugh whenever I am in his company. However, as a child he was a terror. He was always into mischief and had a catalogue of accidents to his name with broken arms, split heads to say nothing of him constantly annoying his siblings and causing uproar in the household.

Theresa and I - very proud parents with Jonathan and baby Liam. Left- Frank in the background looking like George Best and Sean & his ex-wife Jill, on the right.

Skipping forward, Liam married Donna Bartlett in 2011 and the ceremony was presided over by the most attractive vicar you have ever clapped eyes on, namely the lovely Reverend Lynsey Collins. Liam and Donna went on to produce two wonderful grandchildren for us, Addison and Dawson. Liam is a great dad to both of them. It's hard to believe but Liam ended up as a schoolteacher and a fine one at that! He is a very funny guy and a great human being and once again, we are so proud of him.

Liam pictured here with his family. Left to right - Addison, Dawson, Liam & Donna.

Jamie and Doctor Dermot

It was to be nearly four years later that we had our next child, Jamie Stuart, who was born on 12th July 1977. I was determined to see this child born and I have to say that the experience was unbelievable and fantastic, and I would also go so far as to say that I played a major part in his birth.

On this occasion, I was there from start to finish and as Theresa started having contractions I was brought in by a nurse and the doctor instructed me not to let Theresa have too much gas and air, should they not be present due to looking after other mothers about to give birth. I took my role very seriously as I dressed up in my gown and mask (I looked like a real doctor). Every time that Theresa asked for more gas and air, I reminded her of my new role as her supervisor and therefore restricted her amount of intake, which Theresa was not too happy about, however, I did give her encouragement and comfort by kissing and stroking her forehead as she did her bit.

Now as the birth got nearer, I was invited down to the 'business end' where it was all happening, by the nurse. What followed was like a scene from Frank Spencer, with me shouting "come on Theresa, you can do it" and then relaying a blow-by-blow account of movement like "I can see hair" and "the head is coming out" and eventually the actual arrival of Jamie into the world.

Theresa told me that at one stage I was partly climbing up on the same bed whilst shouting out the instructions. She went on to say that she really did not require the gas and air, as she was high on laughing at me.

Once again, I had a beautiful child, and the tears ran down my face as I put him in his mother's arms. I felt so lucky to have three wonderful boys who were to become not only my boys, but my best friends for life. However, there was one drawback to Jamie being born on 12th July as this was Orange Day for the people of Northern Ireland. When I gave the news of the birth to my Dad, he was really pleased but straight away made reference to the fact that he was born on the 12th July.

Dad pleaded with me to register Jamie's birth on the 13th and not the 12th as this was only a day later and therefore would not have consequences for Jamie and the family as Catholics. Having told him that legally I couldn't do it, he reluctantly resigned himself to having a grandson born on Orange Day!

As for Jamie as a child, he was a beautiful little man but generally very shy and quiet in mood and manner and could easily spend the day playing contentedly on his own in his 'office' which was on the floor in between the settee and chair in the lounge.

I remember Theresa telling me (as I was at work) that on his first morning at his infant school she couldn't find him in the house. After a lengthy search he was found hiding in the washing machine, would you believe, as he didn't want to go to school! When Theresa told him he had to go to regardless, as she would get into trouble with the authorities, he replied that he "wouldn't tell anyone if she didn't"!

As he grew up, he always loved music and I remember teaching him his first three chords on the guitar when he was probably about ten years old. He went on to become a great musician and surpassed his Dad by miles. Jamie married Claire Brown in 2002 and they produced our first grandchild, Dylan Francis Kane (Francis after my Dad) followed shortly by the birth of Evan Charlie, which started the ball rolling for Jamie's brothers to follow suit.

Years later, Jamie had a new partner, Fleur Stanford, and they produced our last but not least grandson, Danny James Dermot Kane (James after Fleur's late father and Dermot after myself). Jamie is a great human being and a wonderful dad to his three sons. We are so proud of him and his brothers and their respective wives and partners!

Jamie pictured here with his family. Left to Right: Dylan, Fleur, Danny, Jamie & Evan

Hand Tennis / "The Flying Flea"

Over the next few years, we had lots of fun in our home with parties and visits from friends and family, including Uncle Tony and Auntie Violet from Ireland, who would usually come over for the Christmas period. My mate Ian would visit most Thursdays and we would play our guitars and have a sing -song, with the kids sometimes joining in.

Moreover, when Theresa would go to work night shifts, I would drop her off at the hospital and following this, if I had enough money, I would treat the kids to a 10p Brucie choc ice, which they loved, before heading back to the house to play 'hand tennis' in the front room over the coffee table. Many a time we got over-excited in the game, resulting in broken ornaments in various parts of the room.

Another game was rough and tumble with the boys. This would involve me play fighting with the two eldest boys on the floor, whilst their younger brother Jamie ('The Flying Flea'), who on occasions would have a tea towel around his shoulders for a cloak like superman, would be waiting on the settee to rescue his elder siblings from their Dad.

The boys would call for his help when needed, shouting "bring on The Flying Flea" and he would have great delight in jumping onto my stomach and pulverising me. We used to have so much fun and laughter during these simple games and even though we didn't have much money, all of our boys to this day speak about their childhood as happy, secure and being full of love. Both Theresa and I couldn't ask for more as this is what we hopefully set out to achieve when we got married.

The spoon with the smiley face

Looking back over the years, I think that Theresa and I had a great marriage partnership between us as parents, as the balance was just right in terms of having to discipline the children or having fun with them. For example, Theresa was the major disciplinary force in our marriage as she naturally spent the most time in our home with the children, and I, on the other hand, was the clown in our marriage. However, I always backed Theresa up if ever she had to discipline them, even if I disagreed with her on a particular matter, I would never say so in front of the kids and would discuss it with Theresa later in the evening when the children were in bed.

However, on one occasion Theresa sent me upstairs to sort out the children. I took a wooden spoon from the kitchen and made my way upstairs, assuring her that I would "sort it out" with a good smack on their arses. Now to be honest, this was one of those occasions when I disagreed with her on a matter, as I felt it was fairly trivial. As I got to the top of the stairs, there was complete silence in the kids' bedroom, as Theresa had previously warned them that their Dad would be up when he got home from work.

Now then, I didn't have the heart or the will to punish them over what I thought was a trivial matter and so I decided to go to my bedroom and draw a picture of a smiley face on the spoon. Having done so, I went to their bedroom, opened the door, and slowly put the smiley faced spoon around the door before I entered, to make them laugh and allay any anxieties they may have had. It did the trick as when I entered the room the three of them had beaming smiles on their faces.

I then told them that I had to pretend to punish them with the spoon as I had promised their Mam and asked if when I whacked the spoon very hard on the bed, if they could cry out in pain to assist my plan. And so it was that I pretended to punish all three of them in turn, by whacking the bed with the smiley spoon, with them shouting out loud, and as I did so "don't do that again" and other warnings of punishment if they misbehaved in the future, whilst the kids cried out with "ah uh don't Daddy no no no ah uh" while crying from the bottom of their hearts with promises of not misbehaving in the future.

With this I left their room, with them all pretending to cry, whilst I shouted out like an assertive father as I walked downstairs, "now get to sleep; I don't want to hear another peep from any of you!"

As I entered the room downstairs, Theresa was standing with her arms folded and a smile on her face whilst shaking her head in disbelief stating, "that was bloody pathetic!" How did she know, I ask?

The spoon with the smiley face was kept in the kitchen drawer for a long time as a powerful deterrent, 'just in case'…

Our beautiful boys. Left to right. Jamie, Jonathan and Liam.

1974. My lovely mother

My mother sadly passed away prematurely at the age of 57 on 5th November 1974 after being diagnosed with Motor Neurone Disease. I loved her so much and this left a hole in my life which would never be filled. She died within six months of diagnosis; from being a healthy woman who enjoyed weekly dances, she started to trip and have mobility problems, her speech began to slur and eventually had problems swallowing. I was only 26 years of age at the time and looking back, I think that I was in denial at the time as, to my shame, I carried on with the group and family life in general, instead of spending more time with my mum as I should have done.

I remember on the night of her passing that I was practising with the group. When I returned home, I was informed by Theresa of the news. I was in total shock and disbelief. I felt lots of emotions, such as resentment, sadness and anger, certainly towards my father in particular, who I blamed for her poor quality of life and the violence in their marriage. With hindsight, I was very wrong, as who was I to judge anyone, and what did I know of life at the age of 26?

I think I was definitely in denial at the time and couldn't face the thought of my mother dying, as I recall with shame that I didn't go over to see her in the hospital as often as I should have at the time and, for this, I still regret my actions and bear a heavy conscience.

There aren't many days that I don't think about my mother, even to this day, and looking back I recall the words of the John Lennon song 'Beautiful Boy' in which the line **"Life is what happens to you while you're busy making other plans"** appears. My heart still sinks every time I hear that song as it is so profound and apt regarding this and subsequent sad events in my long life.

I remember going over to St. Marys Hospital on the night of her passing, with my brothers and Dad, but could take little in of the night, due to being completely distraught and crying continuously with grief and raw emotions. However, I wrongly took my anger out on my Dad, telling him that I didn't want to see him anymore, whilst blaming him generally for my Mam's demise. However, this was all said in anger and was to be short lived, as following her passing in November, I invited my Dad up to spend Christmas at my house.

Dad taking on Goliath

On Christmas morning 1974, I heard the taxi pull up outside my house and within a couple of seconds an argument ensued between my Dad and the taxi driver. The driver was young, perhaps in his late twenties, and he was huge, probably about 6ft 2 inches in height and weighing approximately 20 stone, as he seemed to have difficulty fitting behind the wheel!

My Dad was afraid of no man and so he was shouting and threatening the driver over what he felt was an overpriced journey. I quickly went outside and asked my Dad to pay the driver, as the price reflected the higher cost over the festive period. After a standoff between the two of them, my father reluctantly agreed to pay, and he threw the money at the driver through the window, whilst continuing to verbally abuse him.

I brought my Dad into my house and told him in no uncertain terms that he was always welcome in our home, but he had to respect us all. I laid my cards on the table stating that he was not to turn up drunk or bring any kind of anger or hostility to my home, as I wanted my family to always feel safe and secure. My Dad did not argue, and I can honestly say that from that day until his death in 1986, he became the best father and grandfather to myself and my family. We had turned a very negative period in my life into a very positive one. I was so pleased to have shared the last twelve years of his life (find below more stories of my Dad).

Dad and his bus tales / A few jars for the road

My Dad was a bus conductor with the Midland Red bus company and most of their routes covered the County of Leicestershire, rather than the city, which was the domain of Leicester City Transport. He told me it was quite common for the driver and himself to cover outlying villages such as Tilton and Houghton on the Hill.

Things were much less 'politically-correct' or 'health and safety' conscious in those days as my Dad recalled. The buses on these routes would only run every two hours or so. And so, once they had reached the outwards destination, they naturally had some time to kill before the return journey. He told me that for the two-hour wait they would both pop into the local pub for a few jars! He went on to say that the driver and he would consume 4-5 pints of Guinness normally, before both of them got back onto the bus for the return trip to Leicester! He went on to say that neither the landlords nor passengers ever reported them, despite knowing about their little tipples.

The dog on the long lead

Dad was on the bus one day when a lady passenger got on. He was giving out a ticket to another passenger further down the bus and was not really concentrating on the woman or the long lead that she was holding, as he rang the bell for the driver to move on to the next stop. Unfortunately, at the other end of the lead, unbeknown to my Dad, was a small dog. However, upon hearing the bell, the driver closed the doors, trapping the lead, and leaving the dog outside the bus as he set off towards the next stop.

Dad was in stiches recalling that the lady concerned was speechless as the bus took off and the little dog started running like the clappers for his life, he said the dog must have been like "one of those little gerbils on a wheel but with sparks flying out of his paws" as it tried to keep up with the bus! However, another passenger spotted what was happening and rang the bell to halt the bus before further damage could be inflicted on the poor dog.

Dad meeting Theresa before me

Ironically, as I met Theresa's grandmother before I actually met Theresa (see Fred Tapping story), my Dad actually met Theresa before I did (isn't life very strange at times!). This came about as my Dad was often on the route which passed by the Ford family home in Trinity Road.

The Ford family would get on his bus on occasions and be taken to mass in the nearby village of Narborough. Anyway, Theresa's mother had actually reported my Dad to his company when apparently, he turned a boy off his bus for not having enough fare for the ride, this was despite Theresa's mum offering to pay the boys fare for him - but Dad refused her offer for some strange reason!

After this incident the Ford family called him 'Little Hitler'. Now when Theresa first met my Dad at my house, she was naturally shocked to see 'Hitler' again, as they both recognised each other, with Dad pointing and stating "you're one of the Fords" and Theresa replying "you're the bus conductor". Theresa couldn't wait to tell her Mam about the meeting when she got back home saying "you will never guess who Dermot's Dad is Mam?" Despite the past history, Dad got on well with the Fords as they both respected each other and there was never any animosity between them.

1974 IRA bombing in Birmingham

Life was quite tough for any Irish person living in Britain in 1974, as on 21st November, the IRA planted two individual bombs at separate public houses in Birmingham, resulting in the deaths of 21 innocent people, with several hundred others being severely injured. This cowardly act by the IRA naturally had a massive impact on the British public who were quite rightly appalled by the bombings. This led to resentment towards the Irish communities throughout the country and in Leicester, being so close to Birmingham itself, felt the anger of the British people.

I remember with great clarity ,the hostile and distrust looks of people who I worked with and previously called friends. I also recall that at that time, being a member of a working men's club called The Knighton, I would go most Sunday mornings to have a few beers with my Dad and brother Frank. Most of the members who knew us (not all I might add) suddenly gave us the cold shoulder. There was also a friend of ours who was born in England but was brought up in Dublin, put some distance between us and himself. He turned up on the first Sunday after the bombing with his birth certificate waving it in the air as he told club members "look, here's the proof - I was born in England".

Now reader, laying my cards on the table, I could perfectly understand the feelings of the British public at the time and my heart and sympathy went with them. Nevertheless, as an Irishman I would honestly love to see a united Ireland as there are good people both North and South of the border (in fact I believe that most people in the world are good). However, unlike the original IRA who were fighting for freedom and independence in their own country, this indiscriminate bombing of the public in Britain, appalled me as I hate violence of any kind and I could never understand why they targeted innocent members of the public. However, these were difficult times and we had to ride them out without ever denying our proud Irish heritage.

Regarding the above Birmingham bombing, six completely innocent Irishmen were arrested and each sentenced to life imprisonment in 1975, following false convictions by the police. Sixteen years later, following several appeals through the courts, their convictions were quashed. The six Irishmen were released in March 1991 and their case remains one of the biggest miscarriages of justice in Britain to this day.

The Catholic Club, "Is It Yourself?" and other tales

The Catholic Club was our main link with the Irish community in Leicester and there are many stories to tell about the times spent in the company of the characters that frequented that wonderful place, which sadly is long gone (please find below just a couple of these stories).

Drinking in the bar of the Catholic Club on St. Patrick's Day with my Dad and brothers. From left to right; Me (I look a bit worse for wear with the demon drink!), Frank, Dad and Sean on the right.

One day Dad, his friend Joe Riley and I, were sitting in the lounge in the Catholic Club when this big fellow came in and ordered a pint at the bar. Dad and I initially took no notice but after a while, we noticed that Joe was studying this fellow as you could practically see the cogs turning in Joe's brain.

After a lengthy period, Joe got up from his chair and walked over to the man and unbelievably asked him "**was it YOURSELF or your brother that died last year**"?

The man instantly replied, "ah no, it was my brother Seamus!" Joe (or indeed the man in question for that matter), having no insight to what they had just actually said, offered his sympathy to the man before returning to join us. Dad and I just looked at each other without speaking as we were lost for words in the circumstances - it was so typically Irish!

Later, when Joe was in the toilets, we spoke about what he had said to the man, Dad smiled a slight grin before saying "Ah sure it could have been any one of us". Joe himself was also a big drinker and would often ride on his bicycle all the way from Evington to have the odd nine pints of Guinness or so on a night. Many a time, the club members would have to take the bike off him and lock it up when he attempted to ride home, due to him being completely pissed!

I remember one story Dad told me when Joe retaliated against all those who tried to stop him by putting up his fists and offering to take them all outside and knock them senseless! Basically, he was a lovely gentle man and that was not how he normally acted. Joe and my Dad have long since gone and I often wonder if they sit together at the big bar in the sky discussing the events at the Catholic Club.

To this day, I love greeting my close friends and relatives with the saying "**Is it yourself?**" as it reminds me of that very funny incident so long ago (hence the title of my book!).

The Lawn-mowing goat

At the back of the club there was a large concrete area that was of little use to anyone, and so a member of the committee had the bright idea of ripping it up and making in into a grassed area for children to play whilst the parents had a few beers. The project was undertaken and completed for the following spring. However, as the grass grew and became longer it became almost impossible for the children to play on it due to the length. And so, the committee held another meeting to discuss the matter.

A mower was sensibly suggested by one of the members. However, when the price of the mower that would be able to cope and cut such a large area, and who would carry out said task on a regular basis (and would therefore affect valuable drinking time) was discussed, the suggestion was naturally quashed.

Nevertheless, one member of the committee said that he had a friend who had some goats and would ask him if it was possible to have one over the Spring / Summer period, in order to keep the grass down. His suggestion was seconded and passed by all the committee members and so from that year until the club closed in 1996, the goat had his annual holiday at the club, and would be given the odd pint of Guinness in a bowl by members to keep him going whilst he munched the grass (don't you just love Irish logic!).

1982 - Dad's retirement / Trevor Ford and the punch up

Dad's retirement was a hoot! We had arranged to have a surprise party for him upstairs at the Catholic Club. Theresa's brother Trevor, who was about 20 years old at the time, was assigned to keep Dad occupied with drink in the lounge downstairs, whilst we prepared things upstairs. Trevor started drinking with Dad at around 6.30pm and was lashing down the drink (despite being told to pace himself) whilst my Dad was drinking the Guinness at a very steady pace.

By 8pm, Trevor was completely pissed by the time proceedings had started and he had to be assisted by my Dad and me upstairs to the party. The night continued with everyone drinking copious amounts of alcohol and my Dad being presented with bottles of whiskey left right and centre by his fellow Irishmen. By now, Trevor was fast asleep with his head on a table!

At around 10.30pm, several Scotsmen appeared and (I think there was about four or five of them) asked if they could join the party (where they came from, I don't know). However, we invited them in as they seemed fine and were very polite at this stage. All went well until the end of the night when the Irish National anthem was played. Everyone stood up and respected the flag apart, from the Scotsmen who started to shout abuse calling us "Irish bastards". Bad mistake!

Within minutes it was mayhem, with all the Irishmen laying into the disrespectful gate crashers. Before long, there was Scotsmen's blood and bodies lying everywhere; on the floor, stage and on the stairs where they had tried to escape. The police and ambulance was called and took the bodies, depending on the physical state, to either the hospital or police station to face charges.

Trevor slept through the whole thing and Dad was delighted that the night had gone very well and even had a great finale to the night with a good old punch up! Incidentally, Dad sold most of the bottles of whiskey presented to him on the night, back to the club the following day as he was not a big whiskey drinker and, on the proceeds, had free Guinness for some time afterwards!

Dads retirement - just some of the Irish faces that could stop any clock or even gate crashers on the night!

Dixie and the suit protest

A lovely friend of my Dad's called Dixie, who frequented the club and loved the Irish ballads, would bring his cassette recorder to the club a couple of times a week and play the tracks in the lounge to us. He loved his pints and the company of his fellow Irishmen, and the night would always end up in a good old sing-song. Sadly, as time went on, Dixie developed cancer and had part of his jaw removed. However, this did not hinder him too much as when he started to recover, he returned to the club with his cassettes again. For about a year and a half he seemed to have beaten the cancer and was enjoying life again. However, the cancer returned more aggressively than before, and he quickly deteriorated.

My brother Sean and I went to visit him at home a couple of times and, despite the cancer, he was still playing his music and having a laugh and a joke with us. On our last visit, we were informed by his wife and son that he only had weeks to live. Sean and I suggested that in view of this, we could both lift him into my car and take him to the Catholic Club for a couple of pints, where he could see his old friends, probably for the last time. His son readily agreed but his wife did not.

However, Dixie, who was in the next room, overheard the whole conversation and started to get dressed in his suit. His wife started to remonstrate with him, but Dixie was having none of it and was obviously excited at the prospect of seeing the club again. Despite all of Dixie's protests, his wife would not give in and so we had to respect her wishes and sadly leave without him. Dixie passed away a couple of weeks later and at his funeral I spoke to his son who informed me that after we had left that night, his Dad had made his protest clearly to his wife, by keeping the suit on and sleeping in it! What a lovely man and what a character - RIP Dixie.

Dad and the phone box

My Dad would telephone me religiously every Wednesday from the Catholic Club and on most occasions, would talk fairly mundanely and briefly about the family and how they were doing since his visit the previous week. However, on this particular occasion, he had some extra news about the family in Ireland and so the conversation was much longer than normal. In those days, he used the pay phone in the Catholic club, which was coin operated and had the old button A to push and would then connect you to whoever you wished to talk to. If you spoke too long, the 'pips' would sound and let you know that you needed to put more coins in to continue with the call.

As I said, this particular call lasted much longer than expected and so the pips sounded. Before the call was disconnected at the end of pips, Dad asked me if I had any change for the phone on me (bearing in mind he is in Leicester, and I am at home on the other side of the city). I stupidly started to look for change in my pocket to give him! With this, the call ended abruptly.

Theresa (who was sitting at the side of the phone at the time and witnessed the whole incident), pointed out the Irish in me stating "did you know what you just did, you silly old Irish sod? I was totally unaware of my previous actions and when she informed me, we both fell about crying with laughter. I have to say that you can take the Paddy out of Ireland, but you can't take the Irish out of the Paddy!!

Dad and the lawn watch

For a very intelligent man, my father could lack common sense and awareness on occasions. On this particular occasion, he was stopping at my house over the weekend, and I was laying a completely new lawn with turf. It was summer and very hot and so the new lawn would require watering from the start. I enlisted my Dad's help and he replied, "no problem". I did not have an outside tap at the time and the fitting in the kitchen was not suitable to take the hose pipe. However, I had a flat roof extension and decided to run the hose over the roof and put the hose fitting on the tap in the upstairs bathroom.

All started well, when I asked Dad to keep an eye on the hose fitting and when ready, open the tap and let the water come through. He gave me a thumbs up whilst puffing on his pipe and the water began to flow. Initially, the water came through fine and with some force. However, after only a few minutes it started to slow down and after another few seconds was almost a trickle. I asked if everything was ok and again, he gave the thumbs up without actually replying.

The water had by now practically stopped and I was concerned, so I ran up to the bathroom. Now, my Dad, would you believe, was still puffing away on the pipe and totally oblivious to the water coming out of the side of the tap fitting at a rate of knots and spraying the whole of the bloody bathroom area. I was lost for words as I switched the tap off. When I asked why he hadn't kept an eye on things he replied firmly and positively "I did". What else could I say as it beggared belief, but then that was my Dad!!!

Dad's fish and chips and the mugger

A couple of years before my Dad passed away, a neighbour knocked on my door and informed us that my Dad was on the front page of the local paper. She went on to say that according to the paper, he had been mugged at knife point by a very large African male and had a large amount of money taken from his person. I couldn't believe it as Dad had not rung me to let me know what had happened, and the incident had taken place two days prior to my neighbour informing me.

I immediately got into my car and went over to see him. Typical of my Dad, he appeared completely unfazed by the incident and explained that he had been drinking in the Catholic Club and upon leaving the club, had decided to get some fish and chips from the local chippie. Dad always carried a large amount of cash on him as he got older and more affluent, but never had a wallet. He told me that he assumed the perpetrator must have been watching him as he took out the wad of notes to pay for his supper.

He was then apparently followed up the street by the mugger, before he felt an arm coming around his neck with a long knife in hand. The male in question then asked Dad, in a firm voice, to "hand over the money". At this point, Dad said calmly in his Dublin accent "would you mind holding the fish and chips whilst I get the money out of my pocket!?" I think the mugger must have been flabbergasted, but nevertheless told him in no uncertain terms to drop the fish and chips and use his own hand to give him the money.

The mugger then ran off, without any physical intervention from any members of the public that were present. Dad said that although he had lost a lot of money, he was not going to report it as the mugger would never be caught anyway! However, some people who had witnessed the incident called the police and Dad had to give them a statement. Dad never spoke or made anything of the incident, as he took it in his stride, but he was right in that the mugger was never caught.

Choc (Charlie) Kershaw

Before I continue with my story, I would also like to mention a lovely gentleman called Choc Kershaw (real name Charles) who originally managed the Mint group and several other groups in Leicester, and who came to see Studio Two in the early days. He asked to become our manager and arrange any future gigs. He refused to take any money for his time and efforts and, for at least the next three or four years, he kept our diary fairly full of bookings which enabled us to progress on to better things when we later formed the band 'Crisp'.

Very sadly, Choc died prematurely at the age of 50 in 1979. The story is even sadder by the fact that he had won a competition just before his passing, for a free trip to Canada with all expenses paid. Moreover, Theresa, myself and the boys, had also planned a trip to Canada at the same time to see my Auntie Eileen in Toronto, and we had made arrangements to meet up with Choc whilst over there. Sadly, it was not to be.

"Your Move" for Crisp

By early 1972, Crisp was fully established on the club circuit as a five-piece band and we had a good reputation in both Leicester and northern clubs, particularly Sheffield. We were never short of bookings from 1972 until we broke up in 1979.

By this time, Crisp was doing very well, as we had the best equipment, a very large Luton van to carry it around in and two roadies (Ray and Geordie) to set up for us no matter where we played in the country. We had several different line ups in the group over the year; we started off with Malcolm Phillips on drums, George May on rhythm guitar, Gary Bowes on bass, Colin McClean on lead guitar and myself lead vocals.

However, at the time of making records, we had Richard Hough (Chuddy) on drums, Gary Bowes on bass, Colin McClean on rhythm guitar, Steve James played keyboards, Paul Allitson on lead guitar and myself on lead vocals.

Chuddy proved to be a real character and was my closest friend in the band. He was a founder member of Showaddywaddy and also had a number two hit (in the German charts) prior to joining the aforementioned group, with a band called 'Choice' who did a cover version of Simon and Garfunkel's 'Cecilia'. Incidentally, Choice and another local group called The Golden Hammers, combined as one, to form the group Showaddywaddy back in the day.

We played with some known artists of the time on our travels, including the late comedians Marti Caine, Bobby Knutt (who appeared on Coronation Street for years) and Jasper Carrott and also groups like The Fortunes, Jonny Johnson and The Band Wagon and the Pasadena Roof Orchestra, amongst others.

Early in 1976 we decided to record some demos at Alan Jones' (Mint's studio, which was a converted garage at his home). We recorded four tracks including 'It's For You' and 'Jenny, Jenny (Dreams Are Ten A Penny)'. Later at a gig, someone approached me (can't remember his name) and said he worked in the recording industry and asked for tapes / demo's as he loved our harmonies and wanted to help us.

Within a week I had a call from Alan Hawkshaw (Alan started as a keyboard player in the group 'Emile Ford and The Checkmates' who had lots of hits in the early 60's like "What Do You Want To Make Those Eyes At Me For" and "Slow Boat To China", etc). He went on to have a successful career as a producer and arranger and gained a Grammy for his work with both Olivia Newton-John and Cliff Richard. He also wrote the themes for both Countdown and Grange Hill TV shows.

He initially stated that he would like to record us, with the intention of releasing 'Jenny, Jenny (Dreams Are Ten A Penny)' as a single. However, over the next few weeks we had few meetings with Alan who informed us that he had several songs in mind for us to record, including a track called 'Your Move' which was to be the theme tune for a literacy programme for BBC 2 TV, starring Arthur Lowe and Ian Lavender of Dads Army, as well as Sheila Hancock and the late Barbara Windsor.

We recorded 'Your Move' at Morgan Studio's in Willesden Green, London in late 1975. The thing I remember most, was the huge mixing desk which impressed and excited me. We also briefly met the Scottish band Pilot who had two number one hits with 'Magic' and 'January' in 1974 and they kindly let us use their equipment for the recording, as they had just finished a session themselves and wouldn't need their equipment until the next session the following day.

I also remember that around the walls of the recording room was lots of gold and silver discs belonging to Cat Stevens (now called Yusuf Islam) as he used the studio to record the majority of his material. We felt like we were in heaven! Our recording session went very well, and I loved doing several overdubs vocally including the falsetto part on the record.

Hearing Crisp on TV and Radio

The TV programme was first aired on BBC 2 late in 1975 and the record was released on the BUK label at the same time. The record was also played on Radio 1 and Radio 2 regularly to promote the programme. I can't tell you how exciting it was to hear ourselves on both of these media outlets, and I felt that we had come a long way since George and I started as a duo. The record itself, I was told later by Alan Hawkshaw, had sold approximately 13,000 copies, which in those days was very small for sales.

CRISP

Left to right: Steve James, myself, Paul Allitson, Chuddy Hough and Gary Bowes (a.k.a. GB).

A couple of months later in 1976, we were down in London to record a track called 'Love Makes You Cry' at the CBS studio. Having recorded it, we all felt that it could have been better. A couple of weeks later, we went down again to record a better arrangement by Alan. I again enjoyed doing several overdubs on the record and loved the experience.

I remember us taking a break from the session in the small canteen at CBS and being told by Alan that Gilbert O'Sullivan was recording in the studio next to us at the time. No sooner had we sat down, when the man himself came in and sat briefly on our table having a coffee with us. He was very shy, but nevertheless asked us what we were recording and generally was very kind and sweet to us.

At the end of the session, the recording engineer, Steve Taylor, asked me if I wanted to look at Studio One, as it was being prepared for a session the next day to record Bing Crosby. The studio was huge and had been set up for the 60-piece orchestra as Bing, I was told, sang everything live with the orchestra and usually in two takes.

I told Steve that I loved Crosby as a child, and he invited me to stay over in London to attend the recording and meet Bing himself. I was very tempted, but with work and commitments the next day I reluctantly declined. That was to be Bing's last album and he died three weeks later on a golf course in Spain. I have always regretted not taking him up on the offer!

'Love Makes You Cry' was released in August 1976 and according to our producer, the late Alan Hawkshaw, it made number 37 in the German charts, when it was released on the Polydor label. However, in the UK it was released on the EMI label but failed to make any dent in the UK charts whatsoever.

Over the next few years, Crisp continued to play the club circuit and we had many laughs together in the band over the next few years, before breaking up in 1979. (See later section performing mishaps)

As I have said several times already in this book, you never know what will turn up in life and so skipping forward to 2018, an amazing thing happened for me via my son Liam.

Liam doing the impossible!

You see, my son Liam apparently wanted to do something special for me on my 70th birthday and one of the things he considered was trying to get my old singles re-released or put onto the internet for me. Now by chance, Liam found out that one of his pupils at Kings College School in Wimbledon (where he was Director of Sport) had a parent who worked in the music industry and so he started to make enquiries into contacting him. The father of the pupil in question was a Dublin man called David Sharpe who, unbeknown to Liam at the time, was a director and very high up in Universal Music.

Over the next few months, Liam managed to obtain his contact details and took a chance by texting him, followed by several telephone conversations in which Liam, stating that it was his Dads 70th birthday and he wanted to do something very special for him (Liam is great at pulling at people's heart strings). He went on to say that I was in a group in the seventies and had recorded a couple of records. David appeared interested in this and with this Liam (as he does) used the opportunity to reiterate that it would mean so much to his Dad to have the records digitalised and released once again. Having broken David's logical mind and common sense through emotional blackmail, David relented and asked Liam to let him have copies of the records as he would look into having them released.

The old boy on the internet!

Liam let David have the records in question and to cut a long story short, David, who must have thought the records were good enough, arranged to have the records digitalised, with all the scratches removed and back to the original recording state (don't ask me how they do it). He did this with the view of putting the tracks on the internet via Amazon music, Spotify, YouTube, iTunes and even a Japanese media site, in fact world-wide - would you believe, this could mean world-domination at last for the 70-year-old!

Anyway, he also arranged to have publicity art done for the record, along with a short printout of the group's history, members, etc.

In August 2018, it was all completed, and the tracks were put onto the aforementioned media sites which blew me away, as it was fantastic to hear the quality of the original recordings again and it took me straight back to the seventies. In September 2018, I met up with David (a real genuine down to earth lovely Dubliner) and Liam in Wimbledon Village at the Crown pub where I managed to see him face-to-face and thank him for his kindness, over a few pints.

Only Liam could achieve something like this, and it would never have happened without him! I feel very proud to have such a son with such determination and drive as he sometimes makes the impossible, possible!

Now, even though they may not be the best records ever recorded, I feel proud that someone thought Crisp were good enough to make records in the first place. Moreover, for me to have those records digitalised and available to listen to on the many media sites for the foreseeable future, in order for my family to hear or indeed anyone else for that matter, is really fantastic for an old fart like me and I can't thank both Liam and David enough for making it happen.

Perhaps Liam might even get this book published for me eh! You never know what can happen in life as I wouldn't put anything past him!

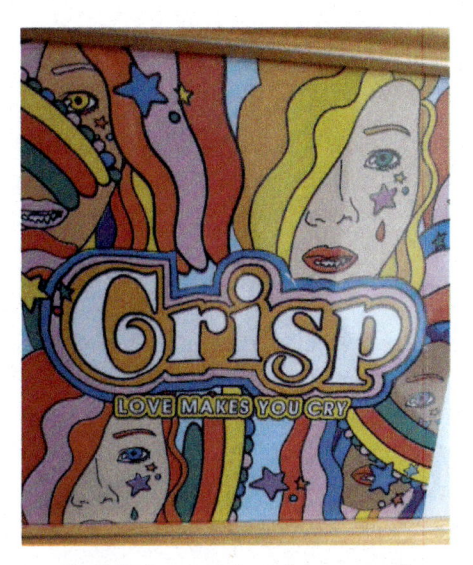

Publicity art for the record.

1977. Auntie Eileen in Leicester

In the summer of 1977, Auntie Eileen and Uncle Sean returned to the UK for a holiday. I had not seen them since they were living in Wimbledon, London around 1958 and this was prior to them returning to live in Canada again.

Theresa received a telephone call from Uncle Tony, who was in London with Eileen and Sean. They asked if they could spend some time with us and we told them to get on the next train as we couldn't wait to see them! It couldn't have worked out better, as they came up in time to attend our son Jamie's christening. They kindly gave Jamie a Victorian Crown as a christening present, which he still treasures today. We had a get together with my brothers Frank and Sean, and their respective families and it was great to see Tony, Dad and Eileen all together again.

Uncle Sean buys our record

Uncle Sean was interested to hear about my band and the fact that we had a current record out at the time, he decided to go into

Leicester city centre, to the record shop in Churchgate, and purchase a copy. He made me feel embarrassed and yet proud, as he told me that when he purchased the record, several people in front of him had also purchased a copy. He went on to say that you must be getting famous (which was totally untrue) and I didn't have the heart to tell him that he must have gone into the store on the only day that we had sold more than one copy!

The stars must have been aligned that weekend as our band was actually playing at a local club on the Saturday night. It was great to have them with me, as it brought back memories of my childhood in Ireland, and I thanked them personally from the stage and dedicated a song to them on the night.

It was a very special weekend, and we all had a great time. However, before leaving, Aunt Eileen insisted on giving Theresa 25 Canadian dollars which she said was to be used for us to visit her in Canada. Would you believe it, to Theresa's credit, she somehow saved up enough over the next couple of years, for all of us to visit them in 1980, which was very fortuitous as Auntie Eileen sadly passed away the following year.

Canada 1980

Moving forward, the trip to Canada in 1980 was like a dream, as we had never flown long distance before. Aunt Eileen picked us up at the airport and took us back to their home in Mississauga, Toronto. We had a great three weeks with them, as they took us to lots of different places, including Niagara Falls and then across to the United States to a motel in Buffalo, New York State (Theresa's dreams came true as she always wanted to stay in a motel like in the American films).

I remember we all stopped together in a family room, as Aunt Eileen was afraid that we would all be murdered in our beds as we were now in the 'States' where guns were prevalent, and cases of shootings were always in the news. Uncle Sean tried to take Eileen's mind off her thoughts that we would all be killed, by reading to us all from Gideon's bible whilst pretending to be a vicar - it was hilarious, as he was a very funny man!

We also spent a week at their caravan site in Conestoga, playing games with the kids whilst getting to know Sandra who I had not seen since she was a baby in London. I also broke my little finger whilst playing volleyball with her. The ball was spinning when it hit my finger and it left my finger pointing in the opposite direction! I was taken to the local hospital to be reset without an anaesthetic. Theresa kindly offered her hand to bite on as they reset the finger. I think she may have regretted it as I left a large indentation on the back of her hand for some time later!

Canada 1980 - You can just see my little broken finger in the splint. My lovely Auntie Eileen on the left of the picture with her 'fags' on the table (bless her, she loved a fag!), Theresa looking as lovely as ever whilst Jamie looks like he has been on the sauce!

Jamie also had his third birthday whilst in Canada and he was completely spoilt by my lovely kind Aunt Eileen. He was a very cute, adorable little English boy and my Aunt Eileen was besotted with him so much that she set up a sweet account at the site shop for him, would you believe! He would wander down every day and take his pick of whatever he fancied. We would take the kids on a hay ride every night and later, when the kids were in bed, we would have a few drinks around the campfire and reminisce over past times in Ireland.

Aunt Eileen was also stunned that I had remembered being at their house in Wimbledon all those years ago (late 1950's) and playing the LP of Slim Whitman endlessly. She still had the LP and we sat together listening to it one night, which brought back lovely memories. It was a marvellous holiday, and we had a wonderful time together. I will never forget this, especially as it was the last time that I saw my lovely aunt before she sadly died.

1978 - Finding my long-lost cousins again

Do you remember how I told you that Aunt Carmel had died aged 28 giving birth to her daughter Bernie? Well, in 1978 I decided to go back to Ireland for a couple of weeks and try to find both Bernie and her eldest sister Eileen again, as the family had more-or-less lost touch since Carmel's passing.

We stopped at Uncle Tony's (23 Rialto Street), which was fantastic as I had at last managed, after all these years, to get into the house and I remember sitting up in bed at night with Theresa whilst looking up at the ceiling and saying as if it was to my Grandma in heaven "you kept me out when I was young gran, but you couldn't keep me out forever!".

It was also Jamie's birthday whilst we were there, and I remember Uncle Tony (who adored Jamie, despite never having children himself) going out and buying him a birthday cake as well as a lovely children's suit. We had a small birthday party for him and afterwards set off to spend the day at the seaside in Skerries. I still have the photographs from the trip to Skerries with Uncle Tony and all of us sitting on a wall very contented whilst eating ice creams. We later rounded the day off with fish and chips. Happy days!

Theresa and the boys enjoying ice creams with Uncle Tony in Skerries.

Anyway, back to finding my cousins! I thought that I should start by going back to their address in Donore Avenue with Theresa and the boys. I knocked on the door for about five minutes and was about to walk away, when a neighbour, a little man even smaller than me, shouted over to me saying "Who are you looking for young fella?" in his best Dublin accent.

He was a real character standing about 4ft 10 inches tall, unshaven and a bit rough-looking, with a cloth cap perched on the side of his head. When I told him of my search for my cousins and added that it was a long time ago and therefore he probably would not remember them, he replied, "of course I fecking do" and he proceeded to tell me their family history (he knew far more than I did!).

It transpired that when Carmel died, the girls were split up with Eileen going with her Dad Ned Dempsey, who later married again and Bernie, on the other hand, was adopted by Ned Dempsey's sister and husband (Mr and Mrs Cumming). I asked the little man if he knew how I could possibly get in touch with them. Once again, he had all the information and directed me to the address of Mr and Mrs Cummings, which was just around the corner from Donore Avenue.

I thanked the little man, and we went directly to the address given and were warmly greeted by both of Bernie's adopted parents, who presented themselves as very genuine people. They were a little suspicious at first but as I told my story they realised that I was family and had nothing but good intentions. Mrs Cummings got on the phone and within minutes I was talking with my long-lost cousin Bernie (I never thought it would be so quick and easy)! We stopped and had a good chat with the Cummings before heading off to hopefully meet my long-lost cousins face-to-face at last.

Mr and Mrs Cummings, lovely people who adopted Bernie.

Bernie invited us over to her house in Balbriggan and when we arrived, her sister Eileen was already there. We spent the rest of the day swapping stories of our past and present lives, and it felt like we had never really been apart by the end of the day. From that day on, I have kept in contact with them both and over the years have had the pleasure of meeting up with them both in Ireland and England for a few jars.

In Balbriggan on the day with my long-lost cousins. Bernie on my left and Eileen on the right.

Listowel with Aunt Violet

The next day, Uncle Tony had received a call from Aunt Violet in Listowel, County Kerry. She had stopped in our house in Leicester over several Christmas's with Uncle Tony and she was now inviting us to go down to Kerry for a week. Tony felt that this was a bad idea, as he informed us that she was overtly house-proud, set in her ways and was not naturally good with children (as it turned out, he was not wrong!).

We arrived in Listowel and upon entering Aunt Violets house, we found that every bit of furniture and all of the floors through the house were covered in plastic sheeting. We felt like we were some kind of contagious visitors and to be perfectly honest it was not the best welcome we had ever had!

Violet herself was not welcoming or warm in her presentation and she pre-empted our stay by telling us that it could only be a couple of days as she had made arrangements later in the week to go away somewhere with a friend for a few days (it was obvious that she did not want us staying too long and had come up with this story. Of course, I could have been wrong). Nevertheless, I loved my aunt and told her that this was not a problem as I would never like to offend her.

Ballybunion - Liam disappears!

The next day, we took the boys to spend the day at the seaside in Ballybunion (isn't it a great name!). This day out was to be one of the most frightening days I have ever encountered. After a few hours at the beach, the tide went out and the boys wanted to paddle in the water and so I set out to walk down to the water with Liam and Jonathan to let them have a splash. At this point, Liam ran ahead of me, and I started to talk to Jonathan about the day and was he enjoying it, etc. I looked up after approximately 30 seconds to find that Liam had completely disappeared?

My heart began pounding and I began to sweat and panic. Where could he have gone? The beach was clear with few people around and so I had a clear view of the area. By pure chance, out of the corner of my eye, I spotted what appeared to be a shallow rock pool (it was actually about six foot deep) in the sand and at that moment I saw a little head and hand appear out of the water. I raced over and by the time I got there Liam had gone under again. In what seemed a lifetime, his head appeared again and I grabbed it and pulled him out.

He was naturally coughing and spluttering whilst crying, as it must have been very frightening for him (he still recalls the incident even though he was only five years old at the time). I shielded him from his mother who was busy looking after Jamie at the top of the beach and walked down to the water, asking both boys not to say anything to their mum as she would kill me! To both their credits, they said nothing and the day passed without further incident.

Incidentally, I told Theresa the story about 30 years later and to my surprise, although horrified at the gravity of what could have happened, she was very sympathetic towards me for keeping it to myself for all those years.

Liam running happily on Ballybunion beach just prior to his near drowning. The deep rock pool was just to the right of this picture.

John B Keane and the horse trader's

Whilst in Listowel, I would nip out most nights to a pub near the square, which was owned and run by the writer and playwright John B Keane. He wrote many plays and books and perhaps his most famous book was a true story that happened in Listowel called 'The Field'. It was later made into a film starring Richard Harris, John Hurt and Sean Bean. Anyway, over a few pints, he asked me where I was from and why was I visiting Listowel. When I mentioned Aunt Violet, he said he knew both her and her late husband Charlie McCarthy very well.

He was a very likeable and friendly man, and I enjoyed his company for the few hours I was with him. I have watched that great film many times since and it always transports me back to Listowel. Mr Keane's son runs the pub to this day and there is a plaque on top of the front door to commemorate his late famous father's life (it's worth a visit if you are ever in that neck of the woods)!

Whilst in Listowel, I took the boys to see the horse fair trading in the main square just in front of John B Keane's pub. Both the boys and I found it fascinating to watch with around 40/50 horses in the square and the lively banter between the traders and the public. All transactions finished with the buyers and the traders spitting on their palms and then shaking each other's hands to signify that the deal was complete.

I think that this event is probably long gone now and I am not sure if either of my boys actually remember it as they were both very young at the time. Nevertheless, I felt very privileged to have witnessed this ancient event.

Noel and the booze up in Tralee

Before leaving Listowel and returning to Uncle Tony in Dublin, I had arranged to visit an old friend of my Dad's called Noel Laven. Noel had previously lived in Leicester for some years and had decided to return to live in Ireland (Tralee his hometown) as his children had grown up and had flown the nest. Having assured Theresa that I would only have a couple of pints, I set off to visit him at approximately 7pm and the fifteen mile journey passed without event.

Having arrived in Tralee and found the house, I was quickly ushered by Noel into his lounge and instantly given a can of Guinness to toast our reunion and my safe arrival. I informed Noel that I could only have a couple of cans as I needed to drive back to Listowel later in the evening! He nodded, but I could tell that he had not really listened and was only interested in enjoying and celebrating the occasion.

Having consumed our drink, he announced that we were heading to the pub, but added to disarm me, that we would only have one drink! Before I knew it, we were knocking them back and having the best of times reminiscing and sharing the craic. We left the pub at around midnight and Noel informed me that his wife had made some sandwiches for us back at the house. By then I was totally pissed and therefore this seemed to be a great idea!

Having eaten the sandwiches and consumed more of the devil drink, I noticed that it was now 2am and I announced that it was time for me to drive back to Listowel. Both Noel and his wife attempted to persuade me to stop the night, but I insisted that I was fine to drive despite having drank what felt like a barrel of Guinness!

I am ashamed to say that I then somehow drove back the fifteen miles. To my shame I remember hitting the kerb side on several occasions and at one stage I was actually driving on the pavement for a short while. I stopped halfway to throw up and to try to gather myself together. The luck of the Irish must have been on my side, as I don't know how I ever managed to drive and find my way back without having crashed or injuring anyone, or indeed being arrested by the police. Back at Violets, Theresa was naturally waiting up for me as she was concerned. She could see that I was in a bad way with the drink and quite rightly gave me a verbal lashing before putting me to bed, bless her.

1976 - Another visit to Dublin / Diversion

Around September 1976, I decided to go back to Dublin with my Dad and two brothers. It was the first time of flying for both Frank and I, and Frank was particularly frightened of flying, and the journey over to Ireland from Birmingham was taken up with me giving him reassurance and breathing exercises to calm him down.

As we arrived in Dublin, the airport was covered in a blanket of fog. The pilot tried to land twice without success and therefore he informed us that we would be diverted to Shannon Airport (needless to say that Frank was in an awful state for the rest of the flight). However, upon arrival we were transferred to Limerick in order to catch the train to Dublin.

Dad gone missing

As we boarded the train, I noticed that Dad was missing. We looked around the station but could not see any sign of him. As the train was due to leave, we had to board it and hoped that my father would catch the next train or would already be onboard the train. As we looked through the carriages, we eventually found him, with his feet up on a crate of Guinness would you believe!

How he managed to do this in the short time spent in the station I will never know, however, the long journey was very pleasant, mainly because of Dad's endeavour and we arrived in Dublin well-oiled! For the rest of the week, we stayed at Uncle Tony's house and had many happy times drinking in McCauley's again and I also intended to catch up with some of my relatives including Joe (Boy) McLoughlin.

Joe Boy and the horses

Whilst in Dublin, I rang my cousin Joe Boy Mcloughlin, who by then had left Leicester and had married a Dublin girl called Pauline and went on to have a good rake of lovely children. He kindly offered to lend us Pauline's car whilst in Dublin and also offered to take us horse riding on the Saturday morning in the Wicklow mountains.

We set off on the day in question and made our way towards Brittas, where Joe had arranged for us (via an ex-jockey friend Pat Smith) to have the use of his horses. I had some previous experience of riding and therefore was not too daunted by the prospect. However, Frank and Sean had never ridden, and were very concerned about the whole experience.

Dad stayed in the stable yard, as we prepared by putting on the riding hats and started to amble out of the yard and up the hill towards a wooded area. We all felt like John Wayne at first as we slowly made our way out of the stable yard and up the hill towards the woods. However, as we approached the woods, the horses became livelier as their ears pricked up and they started to sense what was about to come!

At this point, my cousin Joe came up behind each of our horses with his riding crop in hand and, despite our pleas not to do it, he gave each horse a mighty crack on their respective arses, which caused Frank in particular to panic. The horse naturally bolted and went straight into the woods, and I took up my position for galloping, as I found it somewhat daunting and yet exhilarating. However, as I looked behind, my brother Frank was holding on for dear life whilst doing his best to stay in the saddle!

Things got worse for him, as the riding cap then fell forward and over his eyes and he was now riding blindly. I couldn't do anything to help him, and I was concerned for his safety, but despite this, it was a very funny sight and how he ever stayed on that horse I will never know! As for my brother Sean, he was taking to the experience of this danger with great delight (as he does love danger!).

He got into the same riding position as myself and quickly caught me up with a grin on his face whilst trying to outpace me. Anyhow, following the lengthy bolt through the woods, we somehow all made it back to the yard safely and upon returning, looked like fully experienced, on-the-range cowboys!

Dad finding Lacken again

Joe Boy decided to go back home, and we set off to explore the area, when my Dad suddenly remembered that years ago he had visited a pub in the area that was near a lake or a reservoir and went on to say that he thought it was a small hamlet called Lacken and he asked if we could possibly find it again.

We eventually found the pub at around 2pm in the afternoon and the place was full and buzzing with life. As we walked into the family run pub, we were greeted by the owner, a slim built 90 year old man, who wore a bowler hat tilted on the side of his head and was dressed very dapper, with a yellow waist coat and black trousers. He acted as if he was 20 years of age, as he performed tricks with a walking cane, by banging it on the floor tiles which sent in into the air, he would then catch it and twiddle it around his head and then in his hands, making it look like a theatre performance.

He told us that all who entered had to participate by singing or telling stories or poems. A queer fellow was playing a squeeze box with some of the keys missing. The owner's grandchildren and members of his family were all serving us, and the craic was mighty as the drinks flowed! My Dad sang 'Sweet Sixteen', I sang 'The Wild Mountain Thyme' with everyone joining in the chorus and finally my Dad and his three boys all sang 'The Rising Of The Moon' with great gusto!

I am ashamed to say, that having consumed a large quantity of Guinness as I was enjoying the whole of the afternoon and evening, I then somehow drove back to Dublin in Pauline's car, thankfully without causing further incident or harming ourselves or others (very sorry Pauline and Joe Boy)! What a day and what an experience; its one that I will never forget as it was like going back in time.

1976. A picture I took just prior to the cowboy and Lacken experiences. Left to right - Frank with the riding crop, Sean, Joe Boy McLoughlin and my Dad.

Footnote: I was recently informed by my friend Peter Goulding (an author and my book guru) who lives in Dublin, that the pub in Lacken was actually called Zellers!

Performing mishaps

We had some very funny occasions when I was in the band performing and below are just some of the incidents. On one such occasion, we started to have sound and lighting effects in the show. We did an acapella number called 'After The Gold Rush' by Stephen Stills. We would have a tape of a thunderstorm prior to singing and the lighting effects would enhance the performance hopefully!

The first time we used this was in Sheffield. We told the chairperson / compere of our plans and when and where this number would be in the programme. However, as this took place the person concerned had either forgotten or had too much to drink and, upon hearing the effects, he suddenly announced in his best northern accent to the audience as we started to sing "that the groups equipment had gone wrong" and with this he closed the curtains on us, which left us singing behind the curtains all to ourselves for the rest of the number! It was both total pandemonium and very embarrassing!

The giant turd!

We were playing locally at the West End Club in Leicester, when an incident took place which beggars' belief! However, I swear that it is completely true. We were just finishing our second spot when there seemed to be some kind of commotion in the concert room. From the stage I could see that it involved the gents' toilets, as people started to head over to that area. Suddenly, as we finished the spot, the Chairman announced to the audience that they needed to "form an orderly queue please" around the side of the concert hall, in order to take turns in viewing the object which was in the gents' toilets.

As I made enquiries with some people who had just viewed the object, it transpires that someone had apparently given birth to an unbelievable sized turd and so the word had spread, with the result that people's curiosity had got the better of them and they all wished to see this freak of nature (people never cease to amaze me!).

I never got to see the object myself, due to going back on stage. However, both the audience and all members of my group spent the rest of the night looking out for a very red-faced man who was walking with a very sensitive and funny gait!

Golden shower time!

At another club in Doncaster, an incident took place in which our drummer Chuddy was involved. Most of the venues had toilets in the dressing rooms, but on this particular occasion there was none. Chuddy was dying to relieve himself when he arrived in the evening and as there were no facilities, he decided to open a window and urinate. Unfortunately, the club secretary was passing by the window at the same time and so he suddenly received a 'golden shower'.

He was fuming when he entered the dressing room and called us all kind of names that are not repeatable, even though we tried to apologise! However, he let us finish the show and then he got his revenge on us by only paying us half the amount we were due. We actually felt that he was 'taking the piss'!

The white knuckle ride

Prior to Chuddy joining the band, our original drummer was a lovely guy called Malcolm Philips who lived in Enderby, where his mother owned a grocery shop on Main Street. One afternoon I was giving him a lift home, when I pulled in to get some petrol from Clark's garage on Narborough Road.

As I filled up with petrol, a car pulled onto the forecourt and Roger Clark, who was the world rally champion driver at the time, pulled up in his car and came over to speak to Malc (Roger Clark's father owned the petrol station, and Theresa's Dad Eric worked there part-time as a petrol attendant incidentally). Now, I didn't 'know him from Adam', however, Malc's parents were friends with Roger and his wife and used to go out regularly with them for meals and social events. Malc also knew him well and would cut his lawn for him whenever he was away on rallies.

They stood talking together for a few minutes when Malc called me over and introduced us. I don't know what they had discussed prior to this, but before I knew it Malc said that Roger was going to take us for a quick spin in his car. I left my own car at the side of the garage, and we quickly took off in the direction of Enderby.

All was fine initially, however, as Roger drove down the back narrow lanes of Enderby, Seine Lane, etc., he put his foot down whilst going through the gears swiftly, braking and accelerating through each bend with great speed and yet I have to say with great control. I was in the back seat sweating and swearing to myself for getting in the car in the first place.

We continued at great speed, as we headed towards the village of Thurlaston, and the pace appeared even quicker with each bend and turn in the road. I was shitting myself and holding on for dear life, as I don't like speed particularly.

I remember getting flung from one side of the seat to the other as we twisted and turned our way along the road. However, Malc and Roger (who was looking at me in his mirror and grinning) appeared unperturbed by it all, as they laughed and joked as we sped along the lanes towards Huncote and back round again to his father's garage.

By the time we got back, I felt sick and my legs were actually shaking as I got out of his car. I have to say that Roger himself appeared a very nice and down-to-earth man, and his driving ability was just unbelievable! I never met him again and he sadly passed away in 1998. However, I will never forget him or the experience of that car ride!

Chris Montez and the orange glow!

One of the strangest and oddest experiences I ever had was meeting the Mexican / American singer Chris Montez who had number one hits in the mid 1960's with 'Let's Dance', 'The More I See You' and 'Call Me'. It was either January or February in 1974 and Crisp were playing at a venue in Leicestershire called the Bath Hotel in Shearsby.

Mr Montez entered the room as we were playing, with Steve Fern, a local singer, composer, and session musician who I knew a little through playing at the same venues as him over the years. Apparently, Steve was a session player in his band that was touring Europe at that time.

When we came off stage, Steve called me over and introduced me to Mr Montez. My eyes seemed to dilate as I tried to look at him, as his skin was glowing a really bright orange colour and his teeth being pearly white seemed to light up the room! Not only that, but he also looked so different to everyone else, as he was dripping in gold with chains around his neck, rings on most of his fingers, bracelets on his wrists, whilst wearing a very expensive Afghan fur coat.

It was obvious that he was not from Leicester as we don't get too many people glowing orange around here, especially in mid-winter when everyone is pure white! It was clear that he had overdone his suntan under a sun lamp and I and the rest of the people in the room couldn't take our eyes off him, as the whole thing seemed surreal as we spoke to each other on the night. Nevertheless, he seemed a very nice and down-to-earth guy despite his 'glow'; I can still visualise him to this day!

"You should have gone to Specsavers"

I just want to tell you a story that not many people know about, involving a funny character that I briefly met through Steve Fern.

His name is Des Dyer, and he was the lead singer and drummer with a band called Jigsaw, who had a number one hit with a song called 'Sky High', and the record went on to sell seven million copies worldwide. However, not too many people know, that Des is also a session singer and sang on the first number one single for Robson & Jerome, namely 'Unchained Melody', which stayed at number one for seven weeks and was the best-selling single of 1995.

Des was asked by the famous hit making partnership of Stock, Aitken and Waterman to do the session and was paid a basic session fee as agreed at the time. From what I can gather, Robson and Jerome were both having singing lessons on the back of the success of the TV programme 'Soldier, Soldier'. However, their management felt that they wanted to make the recording perfect, as they wanted to launch them as a singing duo on the strength of the show but never perhaps suspecting the success of the records to go as high as they did.

After the success of their first number one, Des apparently approached their management and asked for more money as the record had sold millions and made a fortune. He was initially refused, but to cut a long story short, the record company were probably scared of him spilling the beans to the newspapers and so Des received a further substantial settlement as I recall, and I suspect he was happy with it.

Years later, the newspapers did eventually get hold of the story and Mike Stock eventually admitted that Des was brought in to assist with the Jerome part because his voice was similar, but he also added that both Robson & Jerome had sung on the single as well? I can remember reading about it in one of the Sunday papers, and as for Robson & Jerome, they went on to have more success and spent a good few years touring on the strength of the initial success.

As for Des, he is still playing after all these years, in a duo with Steve Fern called 'Fingers And Thumbs'. I bumped into him at a charity event in Newtown Linford a few years back, ironically in the toilets. I told him he "hadn't changed a bit" to which he replied, "you should have gone to Specsavers". Des is a lovely guy with a great sense of humour.

The Scotsman's credentials!

Another time, a Scotsman in a kilt was on the same bill as us. Chuddy (Richard Hough) our drummer, who could be very odd at times, did not have a proper drum seat and so he made one out of a car clutch plate would you believe, which he then covered in cloth to make it more comfortable as a seat. It was just slightly perched on the end of a metal stand and was perfect for him as he could move around independently as he played each drum, however, it was not to be used as a stable seat!

The Scotsman started his act and after several numbers, he decided to look cool by singing the next song on a stool. Both Theresa and I were watching in front of the stage and guessed what we had in mind. I remember that we said to each other at the time "I hope he doesn't try to use Chuddy's stool". Too late, as he had spotted Chuddy's stool - it was a very bad mistake!

He initially managed to move the stool into position, however, as he sat on the stool trying to look cool and professional whilst sounding like Dean Martin, he fell backwards with a loud bang on the stage floor whilst banging his head on the drums as he shot backwards, thus revealing all of his 'Scots credentials' (not a pretty sight I can tell you)!

Chuddy's drums went everywhere on the stage, and the audience were in uproar. Even the organist who was accompanying him had to stop playing, as he was laughing so much. It is one of the funniest sights I have ever witnessed and both Theresa and I were pissing ourselves laughing as he tried to compose himself again and regain some of his dignity, but that's showbiz for you folks!

Ada and the corpse!

Following playing at a local gig one Saturday night, I brought back Colin (our rhythm guitarist) to my home for a drink and a chat. He ended up doing a jigsaw puzzle later in the night with Theresa, which was quite normal on his visits. However, at around 12.30am, a knock came at the door. It turned out to be an elderly neighbour called Ada who was looking worried and somewhat distressed.

We invited her in, and she told us directly that her husband Jack was "not well", as he had not moved for a few hours and furthermore she could not wake him up! We knew prior to her visit, that her husband had been ill for a lengthy period with throat cancer and therefore fearing the worst, I left Theresa comforting her and to phone for an ambulance, whilst Colin and I went to check on his welfare.

Having entered her property, we found her husband looking decidedly dead, but nevertheless we went through the motions of checking his pulse and breathing etc. It was obvious to both of us that he had been deceased for some time, as rigor mortis had set in and with this, he was positioned in a very peculiar pose on the settee almost sitting up and looking very uncomfortable.

I went back to inform Theresa of his demise and she told me the ambulance was on its way and, upon seeing me talking to Theresa, Ada said enquiringly to us both, that she hoped he was not dead as you "can't do much about it on Sundays can you!"

With this, I returned to her house and for some stupid reason (I have often reflected on the incident and still don't know what possessed us) I thought it would be a good idea to try and put his body in a more comfortable and natural position, therefore giving him some dignity before he was seen either by the ambulance service or perhaps by Ada herself.

With this, I suggested that Colin would go behind the settee and hold his body very tightly whilst I could straighten his lower half of the body into a sitting position by pushing down hard on his knees. Sure enough, Colin went behind the body and took hold tightly, whilst I began to push down on his knees to flatten them onto a more comfortable sitting position on the settee.

Unfortunately, as I pushed down on his knees with some force, his body came up towards me and his forehead nearly collided with mine! It was a bit frightening and spooky coming face-to-face with this corpse, but nevertheless I was still determined to do the job and so I suggested we try for a second time, using even more pressure to sort him out.

The result was the same and again, I was face-to-face with the deceased! His body was like a seesaw and no matter what we did and what force we used, it was impossible to alter his shape or straighten him. After much huffing and puffing, we were both knackered and having tried for a third time without success, we admitted defeat and decided to leave him in the same position as we had found him in.

A short time afterwards, the ambulance men arrived and after a quick assessment pronounced him dead, subject to certification by a doctor. Not wishing to be disrespectful to the dead in any shape or form, but we didn't find it funny at the time but upon reflection, it was funny, and it shows that there is humour even in death!

Footnote: We invited Ada to come for Sunday dinner the next day and she initially told us she was "not really up to eating" given the circumstances. However, a couple of hours later, she did join us and she nearly ate us out of house and home bless her! Also, during the dinner, it transpired that she had worked with Theresa's Dad Eric at Dunlop's tyre factory and she remembered Eric telling her about Theresa's birth at the time (isn't it a small world?).

End of Crisp / Home life and mishaps

I had great times in Crisp and I always loved making music. **"To me music is what feelings and emotions must actually sound like!"** I still love making music to this day, particularly with my boys. The tracks I recorded over the years will always be a reminder of happy times spent together with both the band and my boys and the love that we have for each other.

However, after eight years of being with the band, we had become stale and I had enough of travelling, doing the same routine of clubs, pubs etc and so I sadly left the group in 1979. Moreover, I wanted to spend more time with my family and become more of a handyman around the house.

Needless to say, it was to take a long time for me to develop my skills and below are just some of the mishaps that became of me on my journey to any kind of proficiency as a handyman. Each mishap is completely true and even I can't believe some of the stupid things I have done during my lifetime (read on and see what you think!).

Having left Crisp, I had more time to spend with family and friends whilst creating mayhem - with my cousin, Sheila McLoughlin.

Flooding the front room

Theresa normally worked three nights a week at the hospital. On this particular weekend, she had worked four nights in order to have a few more pounds in our pockets. On returning home after the shift and having her breakfast, she instructed me to put a lamp on top of the corner unit which housed both the gas and electric meters inside it. Apart from this there were two pipes of water (hot and cold supplies) running into the same cupboard (you can already see what may happen!).

"Leave it to me" I cried with complete confidence. I inspected the job and felt where the two pipes entered the cupboard, there was just enough clearance to put the electric cable through and therefore make a neat job of hiding the cable within the cupboard where the socket was contained. As I tried to push the cable through, I realised that it needed a little more room to go through.

Now, being Irish, I decided to get my trusty drill and make the opening slightly bigger! I opened the cupboard door and stuck my head in and began to drill between the said pipes. After a few seconds, I felt a tiny bit of water on my cheek and thought little of this as I continued to drill. All of a sudden, Whoosh! The pressure took hold and pumped out at a rate of knots. I was in big trouble and did not know what to do in these early days. All I could do to hide my incompetence and embarrassment, was to shout up the stairs to Theresa in my best Frank Spencer voice. "Put your water wings on, Theresa, I think we are in trouble and may need to swim out".

Theresa came down and was definitely not happy as she shouted several unrepeatable expletives at me. By now, the whole carpet was soaking wet. She immediately sent me over the road to fetch a neighbour called Paul Newsome, who was by profession a carpenter and all-round handyman. He came over and dealt with the situation swiftly by turning off the water supply at the stop, and later welding the leak in the pipe. It took weeks for the carpet to dry out and believe it or not, the story does not end there either....read on!

The door handle

The following morning after the flooding incident, I was up early to make amends by putting a plastic handle on the door in the living room as Theresa requested. As I finished putting it on, the doorbell rang and I opened the door to find Paul Newsome with his brother-in-law, Richard, standing there.

As they both entered, Paul informed Richard that "this is the prat I told you about yesterday. He is a walking disaster!". I then tried to convince them both that yesterday was just a one-off and attempted to make my point by showing them the door handle I had just put on. I then attempted to demonstrate how robust the handle was by quickly moving it up and down repeatedly. As I did this, the bloody handle came off in my hand! Both Paul and Richard were in hysterics and could not talk as they were now crying with laughter. I offered them both a coffee to discuss the matter, but Paul replied that they were going before "anything else happened".

Metal heels and the woman under foot

One of the funniest and yet embarrassing things that has ever happened to me was via an elderly drinking friend of mine called Fred Tapping. Ironically, he was also a drinking friend of Theresa's grandmother, who I knew long before meeting Theresa (however, that's another story).

I am ashamed to say that back in the 70's and 80's, like many others, I used to drink and drive. My friend, Fred, had become terminally ill and so I decided to take a crate of beer up to his house (with his wife's permission) to have a last drink with him.

On that particular night, I was wearing some shoes that I had just purchased and had put some metal heel protectors on the bottom of each heel, to save wear and tear on the new shoes. Having finished the crate of beer and said a very emotional goodbye to Fred, I stupidly decided, under the influence of the demon drink, to walk down the passage to pay my respects to his wife and daughter and ask if I could do anything further to help them during this sad time.

As I walked down the passage, which was covered with Victorian ceramic tiles, my metal heels made a clicking noise with every step on the tiles. His wife must have heard me coming as she went to greet me on the other side of the door. I knocked on the door and, without thinking, pushed the door open.

Unfortunately, unbeknown to me, the door was a sliding door, and I took it straight off the rails! Fred's wife, a frail tiny woman, was on the other side of the door as it came off the rails and, naturally, she had put both hands up to stop it falling on herself, this resulted in her being unable to hold the weight, and the door landing on top of her! Now, in my drunken stupor, I had no idea what was actually happening and could only gaze at her daughter who was still sitting at the table speechless as she witnessed her mother being brought to the floor by my blundering stupidity!

Not realising this, I tried desperately to help by pulling the door back up several times, but I was unaware that in my drunken state that I was standing on the edge of the door and naturally my own weight made it a total impossibility for her to escape and this only added to making things worse for her poor mother, trapped below!

At this stage her daughter (who incidentally was a policewoman) took charge of the situation by ordering me off the door. I offered to put things right, but the daughter declined my offer whilst ushering me out of the house in an aggressive manner telling me that **"you have done enough and need to go home now!"**.

It was an embarrassing disaster as I left their house in shame and when I got home, I felt obliged to tell Theresa what had happened. I started by saying "I think I made a fool of myself tonight, Theresa" - what a bloody understatement this was and what a right plonker I really am!

Footnote: I still go red in the face when I think of the incident.

Wire in my head!

My neighbour Steve Foster and I were both pretty hopeless at DIY, yet despite this, we attempted to put up a wooden fence between both of our properties. It was a disaster! After several weeks, some of the posts had sunk into the ground (not enough cement or the right mixture of sand and cement) and most of the panels were falling over and generally speaking, the whole fence was 'on its arse'.

One Saturday morning, Steve called me into the garden to discuss further action to make good the fence. As he called me out from the kitchen, I was already in the process of repairing or bodging something with a long strip of galvanised wire.

As I walked over to discuss things with Steve, I forgot about the wire in my hand. We talked about the poor state of the fence generally and I wanted to make a point by showing him the top piece of wood on one post which was very loose that would need screwing again. I got hold of the top piece of wood from underneath to demonstrate how loose it was and pulled it upwards with force.

The next thing I knew was my vision was severely impaired by a piece of galvanised wire which was sticking out approximately four inches from the side of my head. You see, I had forgotten about the wire and with pulling the top off with force, the wire had entered the side of my eye socket and had gone down between the thin layer of skin at the side of my head and ended up at the back of my skull. It started throbbing and quickly became very painful.

At this point, I didn't know what had actually happened. Steve was initially speechless, and he looked in a state of shock as he surveyed the unbelievable sight of an antenna type wire sticking out of the side of my eye. He then stated in a whisper that "you have a wire sticking out of your head". I asked him to pull the wire out, but he refused. With this I pulled it out which wasn't easy.

The blood spurted out and onto Steve's shirt. At this point, my son Jonathan entered and, upon seeing the situation, rushed to tell Theresa who was a couple of doors away at our neighbour, Dot's, house. Theresa initially was dismissive of Jonathan saying "oh, your Dad's always doing something" not realising how potentially bad the accident could have been with the possibility that I could have lost my sight had the wire been just a couple of millimetres nearer my eye.

However, our neighbour Steve turned up to confirm Jonathan's story and with this, he rushed me down to the Royal Infirmary in his car. I was quickly seen by a doctor who, after seeing my X-ray, declared that no permanent damage had been done, thank God! However, he informed me that I would need to have a tetanus injection.

I was then seen by a nurse, who turned up holding a tray with the lethal syringe on it! Upon seeing this, I dropped my trousers down to my ankles and exposed my lily-white arse and prepared for the worse. As nothing happened for a couple of seconds, I turned around to see the nurse, grinning with the syringe in her hand and proceeded to inform me that "the injection, Mr Kane, is going into your arm and not your bottom!". What a prize plonker I am!

Ian and the squash incident

Ian and I decided to take up playing squash on a regular basis and so I contacted my brother Frank who had played squash for years and who had a contact at the university who could gain us access to the squash courts for free. This particular day, we were really enjoying ourselves on court, when I smashed the ball so hard that it hit the wall and completely overshot the court and ended up in the viewing gallery at the back. As I attempted to open the court door the round flat opening ring came off in my hand. We both tried to put it back on to the door without success and began shouting at the top of our voices to anyone who might be on the other courts to free us from our incarceration.

After ten minutes of shouting, we realised the others had left the building. Being Irish, I had an idea and suggested that that one of us could stand on the others shoulder and perhaps reach the top of the wall to climb over. Furthermore, being Irish, I thought it would be better for Ian to stand on my shoulders as he was much taller than me! Bearing in mind that Ian was over 6 foot tall and weighed in at approximately fifteen stone, this proved to be some task.

After much huffing and puffing, I managed to give him a leg up to my shoulder. I was wobbling like mad and tried to steady myself against the wall as the strain was immense for a little man like me. We were both pissing ourselves with laughter at our predicament. Somehow Ian eventually managed to get his fingers on the top of the wall as I went on my tip toes to gain that extra bit of height. Ian scrambled over, laughing all the way as he crashed over the top.

We thought no more of the incident (not realising what prats we had been) and continued our game before making our way back to my house to see Theresa and Elaine for an evening of booze and a curry. It was only when we mentioned the incident to the girls in passing that Theresa looked at us both and called us "thick old sods".

She then pointed out the obvious, stating that the height would be the same regardless of who was on the top or bottom and it made no sense at all for the smallest and lightest like myself to be supporting someone with Ian's weight and stature. Neither of us realised this at the time and we broke down, killing ourselves laughing when Theresa drew it to our attention. Ian is not Irish himself, however, it's no wonder that Ian is still my friend to this day as there are times when he displays the same Irish logic as myself!!!

Liam bound and gagged

My son Liam has always been lively, funny, and yet bloody annoying at times! One particular Sunday, I was watching TV with my eldest son Jonathan. Liam had been very annoying all day and so, having had enough and despite giving him several warnings to "pack it in" or I would bound and gag him, he continued to play up. So, I decided to carry out my threat by grabbing hold of him with the help of Jonathan (who was also fed up with him) and proceeded to bind his hands and legs together and place gaffer tape over his mouth. It was raining hard on the day so, to hopefully teach him a lesson, I put him out into the back garden.

Within minutes, he was drenched to the skin (he was only wearing underpants and a top when we put him out!) but despite his predicament, he was laughing all the time behind the gag (I still have the picture of him which I took for posterity with Jon and myself grinning like Cheshire cats whilst Liam is trying to curtail his laughter at his predicament - see below).

Liam began to knock on the patio door with his head as his hands were tied securely behind his back, whilst all this time Jonathan and I waved, laughed, and gave him the thumbs up, just to add to his discomfort and our enjoyment. Jonathan and I left him and went back into the lounge to continue to watch our programme.

After about five minutes, the knocking stopped, and we went to see what he was up to. Liam was nowhere to be seen, and so we looked out the front door only to see Liam hopping down the road in the direction of his Auntie Kath's (Theresa's sister) house just down the road (we lived at 12 Farmway and Kate lived at 41). Within a few minutes, we had his Grandma on the phone in a rage. Apparently, Liam had gone to Kath's house where his Grandma and Grandad were having Sunday dinner.

He had knocked on the door with his head, only to be greeted by his loving Grandma and Grandad! The rest of Kath's family were in stitches at the sight of him and were delighted as they also knew what an annoying bugger he could be! From time to time, we get that photograph out and relive the day and it still makes us laugh. However, Liam continues to be an annoying old sod regardless!!

No need for words, the picture says it all!

Falling through the car port

I decided one summer to clear out the guttering and paint the underneath soffits of the house in Farmway, by getting the ladder up to the narrow wooden maintenance walkway of the carport to carry out the said task. The car port was hand-built by my neighbour Dave Bassett and myself, with single perspex sheets as the main part of the roof. Having cleared the guttering and painted the soffit, I felt very proud of myself and decided, like a prat, to step back and admire my handywork and, would you believe… naturally, of course having stepped back onto the perspex, whoosh… I went straight through it!

Luckily enough, I put both of my arms out as I shot through and managed to stop myself falling onto the concrete drive below, with my armpits resting between two of the supporting carport beams and my little legs dangling in the air underneath the perspex. I shouted out at the top of my voice for Theresa to help me and she quickly appeared at the back door.

Having looked at my predicament, she disappeared back into the house and to my amazement came back seconds later armed with a camera and a wide grin on her face. Having taken the photo, she naturally left me hanging for some time before getting the ladder up and guiding me down safely, whilst laughing and shaking her head at my stupidity once more. I am still looking for this photograph amongst the thousands we have in our loft, and I will insert it as soon as I locate it!

I couldn't actually find the original photograph, but this is me trying to fix the hole I went through!

Jack and the post-Christmas booze up

I think it was post-Christmas 1982 when I received an early morning call from my neighbour and long-time friend, Jack Boldry. He invited me around to his house for a drink, as he had a lot of booze left over from Christmas. I told him it would have to be later, around midday, as I had a few chores to do and I wanted to chat to Theresa before she went to bed after finishing her night shift.

After Theresa had gone to bed, my best friend Ian turned up with a tray full of eggs as he did most Saturday mornings. I put the tray on top of the high-level grill in the kitchen and thought no more about them.

However, just before leaving the house, I received a telephone call from my mother-in-law, Pat who asked me if I would mind picking up Auntie Agnes and herself from the bingo hall at 3pm. "No problem, see you at three o'clock!" I replied and with this, I headed around the corner with my boys to Jack's house, just as it started to snow.

Upon entering Jack's house, I noticed another neighbour was present (Paul Newsome). "Oh no, I thought" as I knew that both Jack and Paul could take their drink, unlike myself, and so I tried to pre-empt his offer of beers / spirits stating that I would "only have a couple" as I had to make the kids something to eat and pick up my mother-in-law from the Roxy bingo later in the afternoon. "No problem", Jack replied as we all started on our first drinks of the day.

Several hours later we were all completely paralytic with drink, having consumed all the beer and then drinking our way through any spirits and wines that we could lay our hands on. There were bottles everywhere, and the house was a mess, mainly due to the kids running riot as we continued to booze, unaware in our drunken state and therefore having a total lack of supervision of our children.

Things came to a head when Jack's wife Kate turned up after finishing her morning shift at the hospital where she worked as a health care worker. She went mad at the both of us when she saw the state of her lovely home and the carnage caused by our lack of supervision. I was ordered out of the house, and myself and the kids quickly left, with my tail tucked between my legs, as I didn't want to become embroiled in the argument that had ensued between Jack and his stressed wife.

As we walked out into the street, it was now snowing heavily and being unsteady on my feet, I had the bright idea for some stupid reason of putting Jamie on my shoulders to steady me up! As I passed by the shops, I nearly slipped due to the shopkeepers clearing the paths earlier with water and by now had made it into an ice slide. Jonathan, bless him, was doing his best to warn and guide me back home, stating every few seconds "watch it Dad, be careful, don't drop Jamie" etc.

Egg tray on fire

Back in the house, I decided, in my drunken state, to make beans-on-toast for the kids and so I turned on the gas grill to make the toast, as in those days we could not afford a toaster. Within minutes, the tray of eggs I had placed earlier on top of the grill, was on fire. Jonathan again tried to warn me, shouting that the "eggs are on fire, Dad!" only to hear my drunken response that we are "having beans not eggs, Jonathan"! As the kitchen and lounge filled with smoke, the vision of Theresa appeared through the smoke and haze, as she had been woken by all the noise, smoke, and general mayhem.

Having quicky taken charge, she sorted the fire and the children out and put the house back in some kind of order. She then ordered me to bed in no uncertain terms, uttering several unrepeatable expletives towards me as I made my way upstairs in my drunken state, again with my tail between my legs.

Mother-in-law in the snow

After what seemed like a short period of sleep, I was awoken by Theresa who began slapping me around the face and then proceeded to kick me off the bed, stating "you drunken Irish bas!!!d". I started laughing and found the whole thing very funny in my drunken state, only to be told by Theresa that her mother and Aunt Agnes had been waiting in the thick snow for me to pick them up for the last two hours!

This appeared even funnier to me, as I began to imagine them standing there with icicles dripping from their noses, whilst standing in five foot snow drifts! I was killing myself laughing whilst Theresa in her frustration and anger continued to kick me on the floor.

In between all this, I could hear her mother on the other end of the phone pleading with Theresa not to hit or hurt me as it was no problem and they could easily grab a taxi to get home. Theresa's Mam, bless her, never did hold it against me, in fact she used to laugh about it herself whenever the incident came up in conversation.

The Kearney's putting me to bed (the drink again!)

Another occasion involving the demon drink took place when I received a telephone call from Uncle Alf Kearney, who was up from London to visit both of my Aunt's, Vera and Maura. Alf told me that they were all going to the St. Patricks Club in Leicester for a drink and he wondered if I could join them. Having apologised, I told him that it was highly unlikely that I would make it, due to me looking after the children whilst Theresa was working on the night shift.

Following the call, I decided to call Theresa's Mam and asked her if she would mind looking after the children for a few hours as I would love to see my relatives, particularly Uncle Alf whilst he is in Leicester. Pat and Eric willingly obliged, and I made my way into Leicester to see the family.

After just a couple of pints I announced that I would have to leave to relieve my in-laws, but in passing, I invited them all back to my house when they had finished (not thinking for a moment they would actually take me up on the offer to be honest!). Within half an hour of getting back home, the doorbell rang and in came all of the gang. Well, we started drinking and managed to drink anything that had been left over in the house from Christmas.

The craic was amazing and the hours raced by, with me drinking all kinds of shorts that normally I would never touch! I vaguely remember at around 4am feeling rather sick with the room spinning around. I was then assisted up to bed by both my Uncle Alf and Aunt Vera. They both returned back to the party downstairs without me and continued to finish whatever drink there was left. The next I remember (I think it was around 5am) was hearing Aunt Vera and Uncle Alf shouting up the stairs to me as they left the house stating "great party, Derm, see you soon".

At around 8am, I was awoken by Jonathan. "Wake up, Dad, you have got to pick Mam up from church". As I sat up in bed, I noticed I was already dressed in my clothes from the previous night and so I got out of bed and rounded the boys up before putting them in the car.

Having arrived at the church just in time, Theresa approached the car with a big smile on her face as she was thankful for the lift following a long night of nursing. However, when she kissed me, she noticed a bad aroma coming from my direction. "What on earth have you been doing?" she cried as she noticed the sick from the previous night all down the front of my shirt! I tried to explain, badly, as I was still drunk and talking bollocks. I am ashamed to say that upon returning home I told Theresa that I felt so bad and ill that I would have to go to bed as I was not capable of looking after the boys.

God love her, despite having worked the whole night, she put me to bed (looking back I don't know how she put up with me at times). Later, Jonathan told the neighbour at the bottom of the garden that whilst Mam had been working all night, my Dad had been spending all of Mam's money on booze and had been sick all down the front of his shirt! It wasn't too long after this we decided to move house as my reputation as a drunk was beginning to spread!

Over the decades we had some fantastic parties at our homes and here are a couple of pictures...

Don't know what I said, but Theresa found it funny. And one pissed up Santa and his lovely maiden!

1984 - Moving to Farmway

Having lived in Wilnicott Road for the past thirteen years, we decided it was time to move on. So, we started to look for other larger properties to accommodate the family, as we thought that my father would eventually live with us. As we had no money to speculate, I asked Theresa's Mam and Dad if we could put the house on the market and stop with them until such time that we had sold the house and could afford another, to which they both agreed, bless them! However, Gertrude insisted on the conditions that Theresa would do all the housework and she would do the cooking.

We actually sold our house within days, for the full asking price of £22,000, which was great, as we had we had originally purchased it for £2,800. Having moved in with Gertrude and Eric, we started looking around and found several that we liked, including one in Enderby that was fully detached and in brilliant condition, with a large garden that backed onto the local cricket ground and park. However, it was two hundred pounds more than our budget and so we didn't pursue it (looking back we can't believe that we turned it down for the sake of a few hundred pound, however, we didn't want to get into debt).

Having looked at several properties, none of them gave us that 'gut feeling' of being the right one. However, as we scanned the local area, we noticed a sign up at 12 Farmway, a detached, three bedroom house in the same street as Theresa's sister, Kate and her husband Colin Hayward. Kate and Colin married in 1972 and went on to have five children, Tammy (Tampers), Scott (Toppers) Grant (Granny), Dean (Deano) and Blair (Billy Blair).

Having rang the estate agents, we arranged to get the key and have a look around the house. As we entered the property, the door partly fell off its hinges and basically the place was in poor condition, whilst needing lots of work. Nevertheless, it felt right to both of us and therefore we decided to put in a bid. Strangely enough, the agency said that someone else had put in a stronger bid and that the owners were now taking it off the market.

Corrupt estate agent

We felt gutted and somewhat suspicious as why had they let us see the property in the first place and how come, within a day, the whole thing had changed? Having thought that this was the end of the matter, several weeks later, Theresa's sister Kate saw someone entering the property and stopped to enquire. The person concerned said she was a relative of the owners who now lived in Wales, and she stated that the couple concerned were desperate to sell the property as they had been on a bridging loan since leaving and the rates for the loan were crippling them financially.

She went on to say that the estate agents had told them that nobody had put in a bid since they left and therefore they advised them to reduce the price of the house. When Kate told her of our recent offer and what the estate agents had said, she was upset and alarmed. Kate asked her for the phone number of the owners in Wales so that we could contact them directly and explain the situation.

Having contacted the owners directly and explained what had happened, they were very upset as they had been on the bridging loan for the past year and a half and were virtually broke trying to keep up with the payments. Our hearts went out to them! We said that we were sincere in our offer and would pay the full asking price and to show our commitment, asked them to take the property out of the hands of the estate agent immediately, to which they agreed.

The following day, the owners received a bogus call from the Halifax Building Society, telling them that we could not get a mortgage and therefore they needed to put it back on the market (it was obviously the estate agents making the bogus call as they were conducting a crooked scam). We then received a call from the owners saying that they had trusted us and could not believe we could do this to them! With this we asked for their solicitor's phone number and promised to put a deposit down the same day as a show of our sincerity.

We put down a deposit of £3,000 with their solicitor later that day and within a short time, following all the legal transactions, the house was ours.

We spent the following six months doing up the house to make it habitable. This was all done whilst living with Gertrude and Eric and after work most nights and at weekends too. Both Theresa and I would work on the project until late each night. We were completely knackered but happy to own this lovely house and at the time of writing, we have lived happily there for the last 38 years)!

Kate pounding on the skip!

Theresa's sister Kate would also help us at the house on occasions and supply us with tea, biscuits and sandwiches as we worked and she was also a dab hand at using her weight whenever the skip was full, to jump up and down on it for hours, squashing it down to make more room for rubbish (you could see her bosom's flying in every direction possible, as she relentlessly pounded and pulverised the skip whenever she carried out this task - it's a wonder that she didn't knock herself out!).

I would even fetch some of my new neighbours around to witness the sight of this mad woman sweating and jumping happily on the skip whilst carrying out this vital job - and what a sight it was. I think they must have wondered what kind of family were actually moving in!

Colin Hayward

All this was happening at number twelve, whilst Kate's husband Colin (an Italian looking man, clean cut and very smart, standing about 5ft 7 inches tall of medium build and the most chilled and relaxed man you could ever meet) was supposed to be looking after his children but would be sitting in his favourite chair reading his paper at their home.

In fact, on one occasion when Kate was doing an evening shift at British Telecom, Theresa was alarmed to see Kate and Colin's kids still playing in the dark in the street, while Colin was still in his chair reading at 10pm at night. "No sweat", said the chilled Colin, as Theresa sent him out to bring them in before Kate came home. From then on, Theresa would keep a regular eye out for the kids in the evening and warn Colin in plenty of time so as not to upset Kate.

Anyway, back to the story, whilst reading the paper, Colin would always be eating monkey nuts and leaving the shells all around his chair and following this, he would start eating copious amounts of satsuma's. All this took place while twiddling with his hair as he ate his goodies and being totally oblivious and unaware of where his children were or indeed what they were doing! Apart from this, he was obsessed with technology, world news, the media, new roads being built and cricket!

From time-to-time, he would come up to our house to inspect the progress we were making, and you could always hear him coming as he had a habit of jangling his keys wherever he went, and he would enter the house swinging the keys whilst twiddling his hair as usual. What a character he was!

Having moved in, we enjoyed the company and support of Colin, Kate and their children over the following years, with impromptu

BBQs at each of our houses, family get-togethers, parties, days out and holidays together whenever possible (we thought it was the start of many more holidays and outings together). However, this was sadly short lived as Colin would sadly pass away only two years later (see section 1986 - Dad and Colin pass away).

Footnote: Moving forward to 1991, Kate married again to Joe O'Flynn (born 5th December 1946, died 27th September 2016). More about Joe later in the book (see sections 1997 - Quizzing with Jon and Joe).

Left to right: Paul Hayward (Colin's brother), Kate, baby Tammy, Colin and Theresa (who is pregnant with Liam in this picture).

Liam, the dentist and the Chimp

Just a quick story folks involving my son Liam, who was having dental troubles at the time, and ended up with him having to have several of his teeth removed whilst under gas by the dentist (gas was regularly used by dentists back in the 80's - thank god, not anymore!). Anyway, Liam had previously had teeth removed when he was younger whilst under gas and this had left him mentally scarred as he reported that following the treatment, he felt sick, and his head had been in a "spin" for several days afterwards. Naturally, and very understandably, he was really frightened at the prospect of having to go through it all again, but nevertheless, the treatment was necessary and therefore he was booked in to have the job done.

Come the day and poor old Liam was shitting himself as I took him for the treatment, and I did my best to take his mind off what was inevitably to come, by discussing football or whatever I thought might distract him from thoughts of the 'devil dentist' whilst on our journey to the surgery. Having arrived for the appointment slightly earlier than arranged, we found that we were the only ones in the waiting room and having booked in with the grumpy nurse, who appeared to be looking down her nose at us, and who I am sure could quite easily tell that Liam was obviously very nervous, but did nothing to allay his fear and anxieties like a good nurse should. She then informed us, in a very off-hand way, that we might have to wait as it had been a busy morning and the dentist needed to catch up and prepare to get the room ready for us ('miserable old bitch', I thought, as it costs nothing to be pleasant!). With this she departed into the treatment room, leaving both of us alone in the room.

Poor old Liam looked really frightened and was nearly in tears by now and so I thought "feck this" and impulsively in a blink of an eye I had the bright (but perhaps stupid) idea, to pick up his spirits and distract him by jumping up on the chair next to a very large oak table in the middle of the room and from there, jumping onto the table itself where I began to do my very best impression of a mad chimp.

Well folks, I was on the table for several minutes, hunched up like a chimp whilst scratching underneath both armpits, doing twists and turns and also throwing my head back while grunting and panting making chimp type noises with both of my lips puckered up like a real chimp, engrossed in whatever chimp-like behaviours I desired. I was completely gone and into my part as a chimp and loving every minute of it, as by now Liam was in stiches, laughing his head off at his mad father and as for myself, I have to admit that I was completely in my element.

Luckily enough, no other patients or visitors came into the room whilst all this was going on as I am not sure what they would have made of my antics (although I was not embarrassed at all, in fact I loved it). However, the fun was fairly short-lived, as the grumpy-arsed nurse came back into the waiting room and, no word of a lie, she did not crack a single smile or say anything at all as she witnessed me leaping around on the table in my mad chimp state.

By now Liam had stopped laughing and once I was aware of her presence, I also stopped and looked around at her only to find her staring at me with an intense anger that would stop any clock or even frighten the devil himself! However, she never spoke a word, other than asking Liam to follow her in and then proceeded to wave her index finger at me as if I was a naughty boy, indicating that I should get down and wait in the chair for Liam like a good boy - what else could I do folks!

I have to say that some 'feckin' people have no sense of humour at all (would you agree?). As for Liam, the treatment all went well on the day and I recently spoke to him a few days ago on the phone about the incident to see if he could remember it and his reply was as follows. "I don't remember anything other than you jumping up on the table like a madman and me cracking up". Well folks, that's good enough for me as my mission had been completed!

Malcolm Greenwood's van and the Irish builders

About a year and a half after moving into Farmway, we decided to get an extension built to enlarge the tiny kitchen and eventually get a bedroom built on top of the kitchen to accommodate my Dad, when we could afford it. Dad suggested several people at the Catholic Club who could help; one being George Cafferty to do the brick work and the other being Dennis Connolly to do the plastering.

Having spoken to George, I agreed to pay him a daily work rate and we both spat on our palms and shook hands to seal the deal. However, Dennis would not commit to a price but kept on assuring me in his broad Armagh accent that he would save me pounds and I should I take him on.

Having agreed the job with Dennis, he then asked me if I had a van (which I thought was strange at the time) and I answered "no" but then informed him that I had a friend who would lend me one if needed. Dennis then told me to pick him and a friend up from the Catholic Club the following Sunday morning at 9am, to which I agreed. I naturally assumed, innocently, that we would be going to a builders' merchants to pick up whatever was required to do the job.

I borrowed my friend Malc's van and drove down to the club, as arranged. Dennis and his mate got in and I was instructed to drive up towards the Uppingham Road area of the city and into a council housing project that was being undertaken. By now I suspected that whatever Dennis and his mate were going to do, it would not be legal! However, I said nothing and tried to look as inconspicuous as possible as they asked me to follow them down an entry to the back door of one of the houses.

Shoulders to the door

Without a word, both of them put their shoulders to the door which gave way quite quickly and revealed a stock of building materials being stored in the house. I was now an accomplice in the crime as we entered the house and Dennis and his mate grabbed sacks-upon-sacks of plaster, finishing plaster, plasterboard and whatever else they required for the job.

Having loaded the van, we set off with the stolen goods. I remember being very worried about being stopped by the police and thinking 'no wonder he said he was going to save me pounds'! After dropping the goods at my house, I took Dennis and his friend home and finally returned the van to Malc.

When I told Malc what had happened, he initially started laughing about the situation and then with realisation he said "bloody hell, you could do time for that" only to have me reply "yes, but you would probably go down with me, as it was your van that the goods were in!"

Over the following weeks, I became the project manager and did the labouring for George when he started the building and what a fantastic job he made of it. He would be paid cash in hand weekly by myself and strangely, he would go missing for a few days afterwards (he might have been on the booze possibly?). Nevertheless, he was a great builder, an honest grafter and a real gentleman to boot.

As for Dennis and his mate, they did a cracking job of the plastering and were absolutely right when they said they would save me pounds! George, Dennis and his mate have all sadly passed away but I often think of them and laugh about that time we spent together and I feel grateful to have met such great characters during my lifetime.

More about Malc later in the book (see; Malc saves the day section).

Footnote: Dennis Connolly was a lovely man and I remember his kindness when my mother was diagnosed with motor neurone disease. Dennis would come to our house regularly and put my Mam in her wheelchair and then take her to the Catholic Club, where he would carry her upstairs to spend the night in the company of her fellow countrymen and women (his kindness will never be forgotten by me).

1985 – Dad, Strasbourg and Sandra Lacey's wedding

In 1985, Dad and I were invited over to see Sandra getting married to her future husband, Andre Keller, in Strasbourg. It was the first time my Dad had travelled anywhere other than England & Ireland! It proved to be a very happy trip in which I got to know Andre and his lovely French family (The Kellers) who lived in a village outside Strasbourg called Duppingheim.

I also saw Uncle Sean Lacey and his new German wife, Edie. I remember going into Strasbourg town centre with Dad, Edie and Sean and having a good old drink. On the way back to our apartment, a woman approached me in a very friendly manner and started to enquire where I was from and why I was there, etc. She then asked me back to her flat and I remember thinking (under the influence of alcohol) "what lovely people live in this city."

I then called to the others and told them that we were all invited back to her flat! I could see that the woman was not too pleased with this, as she tried to discourage the others from following. Uncle Sean then grabbed hold of my arm and informed me that the friendly lady was in fact a prostitute! Anyway, we all had a good laugh at the situation before heading to the nearest bar to continue our drinking spree.

Whilst in Strasbourg, Guinness was in short supply at most bars and so Dad took to drinking red wine. He did this with great ease and despite drinking Guinness for most of his life, took to the wine as if to the manor born. Neither my Dad nor I could speak French and I only knew a few words and so I decided to do all the ordering for booze and food, speaking in broken English with a French accent (just like Peter Sellers in the Pink Panther movies). Now then, this seemed to work somehow, and my Dad was most impressed and told people upon returning to England that his son was almost fluent in French! It was great to spend some time with Dad on my own and I felt very close to him during that week.

The wedding itself was a very joyous occasion, with all of us walking around the village in a procession whilst all the villagers clapped and danced and cheered as we passed by. Later, after the ceremony, we went to a castle to have a twelve-course meal, lasting five hours, followed by music, dancing and lots of booze. What lovely memories, I shall always treasure them!

Left to right: Dad, Maureen (Uncle Sean's sister), myself, Andre and Sandra, Edie and Uncle Sean, The Mayor of Duppingheim.

1986 - Colin Hayward and Dad both pass away

Looking back, Theresa and I both felt that it was fate for us to get that house in Farmway, as sadly, in 1986, Kate's husband Colin passed away, leaving her with five children. As we were living in the same street, we were able to support her and the children through this horrendous period whenever they required help of any kind.

Over the forthcoming years, we thought of their children, Tammy, Scott, Grant, Dean and Blair, as our own. It was an awful shock to the whole of the family, as Colin, who was only 45 years old at the time, appeared fit and well and in the prime of his life. Despite this, he was booked in to have a routine heart procedure and I remember taking him in on the day prior to his operation.

It was early on a sunny June morning as I took him onto the ward. Thinking all this was routine I quickly said goodbye and told him I would see him tomorrow, stupidly thinking that nothing could go wrong! However, as I walked off towards the entrance, Colin called after me and said, "are you not going to wish me luck?".

It struck me at that moment that this was not like Colin to be concerned or sentimental. Having wished him good luck, he grabbed me and gave me a hug. This was definitely not like him! I left the ward somewhat perplexed at what had just taken place and made my way to the car.

As I started the car, I looked up towards the ward, and there was Colin, looking out of the window and waving at me (this was sadly to be my last enduring memory of Colin). I had a very strange, unnerving feeling that I could not explain as I waved back. I drove off to work initially feeling uneasy but quickly put it out of my mind, convincing myself not to be silly as all would be well.

When the surgeons carried out the operation the following day, they found that his heart was badly diseased and despite all their efforts he sadly passed away on the table. The whole family was devastated, particularly Kate who never really got over it and I remember having to pick up Colin's daughter Tammy from school and tell her that her Dad had passed away. It was one of the hardest things that I ever had to do.

Father Nolan takes a tumble!

I can recall Colin's funeral with great clarity and despite the sad occasion, there was still some humour to be had on the day, which Colin himself would have appreciated. After the church service, we all got into the hired funeral cars and waited for the priest, Father Nolan, to join the cortege to proceed to the crematorium. Father Nolan, an old school priest, was quite elderly with very bad hips and therefore he struggled with his mobility generally. He had particular problems getting in and out of cars and found the best and most comfortable way to do it was to stand with his back to the car, get his backside onto the seat and then pull his legs into the car.

Unfortunately, the large Rolls Royce hired for the family on the day of the funeral, had the seats set well back on each side from the car door. Oblivious of this fact, Father Nolan did his usual trick by opening the door, turning his back, and attempting to sit down on the seat, which of course was not actually there!

The whole of the cortege was watching this with bated breath as we witnessed Father Nolan disappearing into the void with his religious crook / staff flying in the air and eventually hitting the ground, all this whilst he was showing the soles of his shoes as he hit the inside of the car floor with a bang!

Theresa and I, despite the sad occasion, were crying with laughter, as he sat back up from the car floor in a dishevelled state with his Biretta hat falling over his forehead and his glasses twisted over his eyes like a scene from the Morecambe And Wise Show!

By now the funeral directors had realised what had happened and two of them went to his assistance by attempting to pull him back up. However, due to his weight and lack of mobility, they were initially unsuccessful as they pulled him back and forth, back and forth like a seesaw but each time due to his weight and mobility he would disappear back into the car with a large bump!

Eventually, they did manage to get him back on his feet whilst restoring some of his dignity....bless him. It was very funny to watch, despite the sad circumstances and Colin would definitely have loved it! The rest of the day was a blur to me, apart from remembering that my Dad (who was very ill himself) telling me directly and factually as Colin was cremated, that he would be the next to pass on.

Father Nolan (long before the tumble) with Jamie on his communion day.

Dad / whiskey / 'no utopia' and last goodbyes

My Dad was correct, as he passed away in September of the same year. Prior to this, he was diagnosed with cancer and lived with us for approximately three or four months. My Dad was never scared of anything or anyone to my knowledge and so it came as some surprise that on the night before his passing he showed some fear of his forthcoming demise. Theresa was on a night shift and at around 3am I heard him calling me, whilst banging on the wall for my attention in the next room.

When I entered his room, he asked me to sit with him for a while which was very unusual for him. I held his hand as he told me he would pass away tomorrow and was a little frightened of the prospect. I tried to give as much assurance as possible in the circumstances. I tried to distract him from dwelling on his fear, by talking about his life in general and then asking if he had any observations, advice, or wisdom that he could pass on to me as my father.

He thought for just a moment, before replying that there is **"no utopia"** in this world. This meant little to me at the time but subsequently as I passed through life, I have found his words so profound. I also remember that before I returned to bed, he told me that I had been a great "comfort to him" as his son and his words have sustained and comforted me over the years.

The following night, he instructed me to get a bottle of whiskey and phone my brother Sean so that we could say goodbye together with a little dram! Having got the whiskey, we managed to get through it quite quickly, whilst reflecting on good times and giving comfort to Dad. However, with time my Dad got weaker and weaker and so I supported his head whilst pouring the whiskey into his mouth. However, the whiskey started to run down from the corner of his mouth and naturally I thought that he had enough and so I took the glass away from him.

As I did this, despite being only minutes away from departing this world, he told me in no uncertain terms that "I'm not fecking dead yet so put the glass back in my mouth!". What spirit my Dad had, even on his deathbed. I loved him for that; what a character he was!

Within minutes, he left us for good. I loved him very much and only wished that we had this kind of relationship earlier in his life; however, "**such is life**" to quote Ned Kelly!

Dads funeral / wake

I could say so much more about events leading up to my Dad's passing and subsequent funeral (however I will leave this "To those who know", to quote my son Jamie) and as I don't want to be negative or unkind to anybody and so I will keep it fairly brief with just some of my observations on the day. On the day of his funeral, the church (New Walk Catholic Church) was packed, mainly with the Irish community, which to me was a sign of love and respect that he had accrued during his time here in Leicester.

It was a proper Irish funeral with all the 'paddies' coming in line at the end of the service to shake the hands of each and every member of the family whilst saying "so sorry for your loss!" This hand-shaking and respectful comment was to continue throughout the day and evening at my Dad's wake! Following the service, my Dad was laid to rest with my mother in the Saffron Lane cemetery.

My Dad always wanted to have a proper send off with an Irish wake and so my brothers and I put a large amount of cash each behind the bar at The Catholic Club to celebrate his life, with lots of the demon drink (Guinness mainly) and the 'water of life'. As the day progressed, with Irish music playing in the background, my boys mixed with the Irish crowd as my brothers Frank, Sean and I celebrated our Dad's life whilst slowly drowning our heartfelt sorrows in drink (we were all very close and supportive of one another on the day).

Liam on the demon drink

However, unbeknown to me at the time, some of the Irish crowd who knew the boys, started to ply Liam & Jon with drink and Liam, although only thirteen years old, was only too happy to accept with the result that by evening time he was well and truly "pissed" on Guinness and Irish whiskey!

With Liam being inebriated, we grabbed a taxi back to my brother Sean's house to sort Liam out and hopefully continue with the wake with some of our close Irish friends who had also joined us. Theresa put Liam to bed after he had vomited and made him comfortable and safe for the remainder of the night, whilst Jon and Jamie stayed downstairs listening to stories and Irish songs.

Sean put on Irish traditional music which was played very loudly as we all sang along at the tops of our voices, with some weeping in between from my brothers and myself. It was all so very raw and emotional with a mixture of heartache, pride and love which brought back memories of my upbringing and childhood in Ireland as I sang along.

We sang and cried into the early hours of the morning before catching a taxi home with the promise that we would keep together as brothers as we needed each other now that Dad had passed on. Sadly, this was not to be, but that's yet another story!

It was a great wake, just as my Dad would have wanted and a fitting end to his life. Despite my early relationship with my Dad, I have some wonderful memories of him, and I still miss him to this day.

The priest's predictable greeting

Prior to marrying Theresa, I had promised to help her bring up any children that we may have during our marriage in the Catholic faith, at least until they reached the age of eighteen, when they would be able to make up their own minds regarding religion and to this, I kept my word, as the boys attended mass every week until they each reached that age.

On this particular Sunday evening, I took both Liam and Jamie to church and upon arrival it was fairly packed so Liam went to the back of the church whilst Jamie and I sat together on the second row from the back (thank goodness as it happens, as we could make a swift exit).

Without being disrespectful or indeed unkind as I would not wish to offend or hurt anyone, the priest at that time (who shall remain nameless) was perhaps the most boring, un-motivating and un-Christian person of the cloth you could ever meet.

His services (in my opinion) were regimented, disingenuous and without any kind of passion or belief and therefore he appeared to be going through the motions with each service. He would say exactly the same words of greetings every single week (never changing a single word) so much so that every parishioner could repeat it in their sleep!

Anyhow, you know how sometimes things can really strike you as funny or you have an image in your mind that you can't shake, and you can't stop laughing about? Well, on this particular day it happened!

As the service started, the priest welcomed visitors with his normal speech and spoke completely verbatim as he did every single previous week, I began to say the same words as the priest, under my breath, with Jamie joining in as I went along. This built to a crescendo with his usual phrase "visitors bring something very…..**special**"!

As he uttered the words **very ……special,** Jamie and I both said the same word aloud whilst trying to control our laughter, as we knew exactly what he was about to say (we really couldn't help it as we were too far gone by this stage!)

By now we were both completely helpless whilst trying to contain our laughter and the more we tried to contain it, the worse it became as we both kept hearing the priest's words in our heads…. "**very ……special.**"

Breaking wind and the fat lady

Like I said, the more I tried to contain it, the worse it became, as by now in my effort to suppress my laughter, I let out several loud large farts which, thankfully, not too many people heard, as by now the congregation were singing a hymn.

However, as I looked behind to see who may have actually heard me, I was confronted eye to eye by a large lady who was singing the hymn and looking indignant whilst giving me the 'evil eye." Again, this struck me as funny as being brought up in the Catholic faith, you were taught never to laugh or misbehave in church and yet here I was blasting away with my shoulders heaving up and down as I continued to try to suppress my non-containable laughter.

I was now feeling the pressure of the fat lady eyes on me from behind and I tried to grasp at anything to get me out of this hole I had dug for myself. I then turned my attention to Jamie who was still killing himself with laughter and so I tried to shift the blame on him.

I tried, laughingly, to berate him whilst slapping his arm and trying to sound and act like a responsible parent saying "don't be so rude - pull yourself together - stop showing me up - you're in church you know - behave yourself!". However, this didn't work as when I was trying to contain and suppress my laughter as I scolded him, I let out several more loud farts with the result that we were both rendered helpless!

It was pathetic! As we were both too far gone with that mental image and the sound of the priest in our heads, I felt we had to abandon ship and get out of the church before the whole of the congregation would realise what was happening and take revenge on us.

It was so embarrassing as we left our pew, still trying to supress our laughter with looks that could kill from all those parishioners behind who had witnessed our behaviour. Having got into my car, we drove to the centre of the village, and we continued to laugh for another half an hour as we waited for the service to finish (to make it look like we had attended the whole service) before we headed back home.

However, would you believe as we walked in the door, despite feeling like we were acting normal, as our laughter had subsided by then, Theresa asked directly and searchingly "what's happened now?". How does she know these things, I ask?

Footnote: I hope my description of the event does not put us in a bad light as we didn't mean to be disrespectful to the priest, parishioners, or anyone else concerned, however sometimes no matter what the circumstances are, you can't help but see the funny side of life....it was bloody hilarious nevertheless! However, once again it could be a case of you had to be there to see and hear it or maybe to quote my son Jamie **"to those who know!"**.

Boys leaving home & walking / outings with Ian & Elaine

In the early 1990s, things began to change with the boys leaving home. Jonathan was the first to go in 1990 as he went to Coventry University to study Technical Communication. Liam went next in 1994 to Loughborough University to study PE, Sport Science and Management Studies. Both Jon and Liam got their degrees within their subjects and Jonathan went on to work successfully within the IT Security industry, whilst Liam became a teacher at City of London Boys School before moving to Kings College School, Wimbledon as Director of Sport.

Jamie followed his brothers in 1996 to study Drama and to pursue his ambition to become a musician and recording artist. He achieved his dreams having several CD albums released in which he wrote his own songs and played most of the instruments on the recordings (what a talent!).

This left the house very quiet, and our lives seemed to have changed overnight and so Theresa and I decided to start courting again by having date nights and spend more time walking and meeting friends and generally having more of a social life. We bought all the gear for walking and what a sight we looked in our matching anoraks!!

We walked a couple of times a week, subject to work and family commitments, and initially walked in Leicestershire followed by the Peak District, Wales and then later in the Lake District, which we loved. We would visit regularly to climb most of the tallest and most beautiful mountains including Snowdonia, Scaffell Pike, Helvellyn and Blen Catha. In between these walks, we would meet up with Ian and Elaine for meals at each other's homes and daytrips out together.

Eventually, Ian and Elaine started walking with us and having holidays together, as we spent many happy times in each other's company both in England and abroad. We travelled many times on holiday to Italy (my favourite country) with them, visiting Lake Garda, Verona, Lake Como, Rome and Venice, to name a few.

Incidentally, Ian also befriended my old friend Rocco Ambrico in later years and visited him and his wife Elana in his mountain village home of Tricarico in the Bacilcata region of Southern Italy. (More about Rocco and Ian later in the book - see 'Meeting Rocco again').

However, back to the story, to this day we all remain the best of friends and both Theresa and I feel so lucky to have shared so many happy times together with our special friends.

Coombe Abbey medieval night with our best friends, Ian & Elaine.

1990 - Birrs Sportswear closes

With hindsight, the 28 years I spent in tailoring were not (generally speaking) the happiest years of my life. My home life was fantastic, but work was mundane, a hard slog and I never really liked the job. I would commence work at 8 each morning and usually finish at 6pm. I would then spend another hour delivering outdoor work, in the company van, to home workers who were either machinists or hand stitchers. This meant that I would normally get home around 19.30 each night - a long old day!

Birr's Sportwear premises comprised of two floors and when we had a delivery of bales of cloth (usually 8-10 bales at a time) weighing on average 500lbs, I would have to carry each one on my shoulders up two very narrow flights of stairs to the second floor and then walk the full length of the floor to the cutting room table where all the bales were stored. Believe me, this was a no mean tough task for a small man like myself!

I learnt my trade on the shop floor with first-hand experience of machining, pressing, overlocking and any other jobs required to make garments. However, my main job was cutting and drafting / designing. It was bespoke tailoring mostly done by hand. However, we did some readymade stuff which I used a large cutting machine for.

On one hand, tailoring provided a living (albeit a relatively poor one), providing enough of a salary to pay the mortgage but certainly nothing left over for luxuries. Theresa had to work three nights a week as a nursing assistant to supplement my wages and provide the extras for the family (Theresa was fantastic at managing the little money that we had and to this day, I don't know how she did it).

Extra work to make ends meet

Apart from working in tailoring full time, I also worked extra days at the weekends for a builder called Chris, doing footings for which I was paid £25 for each footing I dug by hand. The work was very hard especially in the winter when the ground would be rock hard. However, the work was made bearable, as my mate Ian Parkinson and next-door neighbour Jack Boldry, also worked with me doing the footings. The banter was second to none throughout the day with us throwing clay at each other, singing songs, and generally making the best of the situation, but nevertheless, we were all grateful for the extra money.

Moreover, during the 28 years spent in tailoring, I had some very hard lessons in life. Firstly, before owning the firm, my boss Harrold Birr was a mean old sod who kept my wages very low throughout the years, despite working my balls off for him. Secondly, when both myself and partner Mick Woodfield bought the business off him, he drove a very hard sale despite knowing that trade itself was changing with mass foreign imports taking over the market and the fact that we could not compete with their prices which undercut us as a business. To be fair, I don't think I was ever cut out to be a businessman, as I think that I am much too soft by nature!

Having bought the firm, I discovered some years later, that both our secretary and Mick had been taking money regularly from the business, as most of the transactions were cash in hand from customers. However, looking back, it never did either of them any good as they both died prematurely a couple of years later. As for myself, I never took advantage of anybody in business and slept each night with a clear conscience. Moreover, with hindsight as I have said before, I was never a business-minded person and was, by nature, a very trusting person which is not always a good thing.

When we eventually liquidated the firm in 1990, I paid all of the 36 workers their dues and left the business owing no-one. I also learned to never trust banks! Despite having a good turnover of approximately half a million a year and the firm conducting their business through Natwest for about 45 years, the bank did not support us in any way shape or form. However, they did suggest that I put my house up as security for a further loan in order to keep the business going.

This was the final straw for me and, having talked it over with Theresa, we did not want to risk our home and the potential of destabilising our family. I felt quite down for the following few weeks, with overwhelming thoughts of being a failure in life. Having no formal qualifications and being poorly educated and with no confidence in myself, I felt that I was not really employable and could see no future for myself.

Malcolm "I'm sick on it" Greenwood saves the day

At this point we had no money in the bank and only had £11 a week to survive on, as it took several weeks for any dole money to come through. However, my faith in people took over again, as my next-door neighbour Malcolm (Malc) Greenwood, had recently moved out to a new house which was more or less a derelict property. Malc, upon hearing my recent problems, suggested that I work for him for a couple of weeks doing labouring at his property, by knocking down walls and outbuildings as well as moving tons of earth and building materials.

Malc (bless him), paid me a £100 a week, cash in hand, for my efforts and looking back he could have done it himself as he was a builder by trade! Malc saved the day for me as not only did the money help, but I found that this gesture lifted my low spirits. Malc, a very funny man and an out-and-out Leicester man, had his own Leicester vocabulary and I could mention many more, however, here is just a couple of examples. Work became "wuk" and I am sick of it became "I'm sick **on** it". It was almost like a foreign language which Malc spoke fluently!

However, he has a great heart, and I am sure he only did it out of pure kindness and because of his friendship with me and the relationship we had built up over the years. Incidentally I was privileged to have been his best man at his wedding to his wife Gail prior to all this and we continue to be the best of friends to this day!

Malc "I'm sick on it" Greenwood and his wife, Gail with Theresa and me on their wedding day.

Theresa was initially very understanding and sympathetic to our situation and she somehow managed to get us through this very difficult time. However, following the work for Malc, I had not really looked for work in earnest, and was taking more to the demon drink around our local pub on a fairly regular basis to wallow in my self-pity. Theresa then took action to wake me up to reality by tearing into me (quite rightly) and reminding me of my responsibility to my family. With this, I had the 'kick up the arse' that I needed, and I started to look for work, but did not want to go back to the job of tailoring or hosiery.

My brother-in-law, Kelvin Ford, suggested working as a health care support worker in psychiatric services (where he himself worked) but I initially dismissed this idea. However, about a week later there was an advert in the Leicester Mercury for health care support workers in forensic nursing. To be honest, I didn't know what forensic nursing really meant! However, I decided to apply for the post anyway and give it a go.

A couple of weeks later I went for the interview and despite knowing nothing of nursing mentally ill offenders, I somehow managed to get the job and this proved to be the happiest part of my whole working life, which lasted just over 21 years, before my eventual retirement.

Incidentally, two of the panel who first interviewed me were Bridie Collins and the other being Carey Maisey, who incidentally turned out to be lifelong friends and both of them were a great support to me during my career, particularly Bridie Collins whom I adored as a great friend, fantastic nurse, and a wonderful human being.

Skipping forward, Bridie sadly passed away on 12th April 2019 (the very same date as our wedding anniversary, would you believe) after being diagnosed with leukaemia, bless her. She was only sixty years of age and the world, in my opinion, is a much poorer place for her passing!

Forensic nursing tales

Before commencing on the following chapters regarding my work in forensic nursing and later with the community forensic team, I would like to inform the reader that all of the patients and some of the staff's names have been changed to protect their identities and ensure confidentiality.

In 1991, I started my first shift on the wards, where I was to remain for the next thirteen years of my career before I moved to work with offenders again in the community for the following eight years.

My work involved nursing and caring for mentally-ill or mentally disordered offenders, mainly held under sections of the mental health act - whilst dealing with every kind of offenders imaginable, including arsonists, bank robbers, rapists, paedophiles, psychopaths and murderers.

Moreover, during my career, I nursed single, double, triple, and even quadruple murderers and although daunting at times, the work was fascinating and interesting and, as I say, the most enjoyable part of my working life.

My work setting had a forty-foot fence all around the grounds with CCTV cameras monitoring the environment day and night from the main control by the control officers.

As a health care worker, I was employed by the NHS, but governed by the Home Office, as most of the patients were Home Office restricted patients and therefore dangerous, whilst requiring a secure environment. Moreover, working on the wards, you are not allowed any keys until you complete your basic security training, which usually takes several weeks to complete.

Starting on my first morning involved going through the security air lock at the front of the building and handing over any car keys or anything else that could potentially be used as a weapon or to breach security to the control room staff (this was the daily routine).

You would then be issued with a 'pit' alarm which is attached to your belt, and should you encounter any emergency or potential danger to yourself or others, you would pull the 'pit' which in turn would set an alarm off throughout the ward, informing a response team of your exact location, who would then attend immediately to the incident. Anyway, on my first day, I was picked up by a qualified member of staff who accompanied me down through the many locked doors and into the recreation and ward areas.

"Do you like Jesus?"

As I passed through the recreation area, I suddenly found an arm coming around my neck in a tight grip. The voice from behind asked me "Do you like Jesus?" to which despite his grip, I managed to utter / splutter "I do". The member of staff asked 'John' (I shall call him John for the sake of confidentiality) in a calm and jovial manner to put me down as you "don't know where he has been."

With this, the arm loosened its grip, I was released, and I turned around to find John with a beaming smile on his face. Not all patients within secure settings are violent, as John, who was diagnosed with schizophrenia and delusional beliefs regarding Jesus and the Bible, was one of those who you couldn't help but like and we had a great therapeutic relationship during his time incarcerated.

Basically, I took to the job like a duck to water from the start. I felt that many of the patients I encountered over the years in forensics reminded me of the characters I had met in life, both good and bad! Also, during my upbringing, violence was never too far away, especially in the Irish community and so I did not find the environment too daunting to work in.

I was initially based on a rehabilitation ward. The work, as the name suggests, is helping the patients after years of incarceration to adjust to the outside world and give them the necessary skills to hopefully find work and a place in the community and also give them help and advice on ways to stop them reoffending when they are eventually discharged back into the big wide world.

This involved becoming the patient's advocate / keyworker, taking them on trips into town, back home to visit parents and family, and generally assessing their ability to function in these settings and reporting my findings back to their consultant.

Billy Boy

It was on this ward that I started working with an old friend, Bill Carpenter, who I had known for approximately 25 years through my brother-in-law, Barry Ford.

Bill is a real character, standing about 5ft 6 inches tall, rotund in stature, a bit of a thespian, weighing approximately 17 stone with a comic personality second to none. Bill was also the Social and Recreation Officer, which involved arranging entertainment and activities for the patients throughout the year including bingo, quizzes, live bands, shows and guest speakers, etc.

He quickly suggested that I become his assistant and right-hand man and within a couple of weeks, I took up the part-time role with the blessing of management. Bill advised me from the start to "always carry a clip board" as people would think I was always working and planning activities!

This was sound advice and would serve me well for the thirteen years I spent in the role. For the next few years, Bill and I, armed with our clip boards, managed to look busy arranging activities which sometimes involved leaving the wards to see bands, arrange for shows to come into the hospital, disco's, lighting and fireworks, hog roasts and BBQs in the summer, etc.

In fact, some of our time off the wards was spent in cafes occasionally after having completed our arrangements and so long as you carried your clip board when you returned to the wards, no one ever questioned how much time you had been gone....it was great!

Hostage negotiations

During my time on the ward, I learnt the basics of forensic nursing whilst attending many lectures and teaching sessions, including Home Office approved control and restraint methods and also a hostage negotiation course. Billy and I both passed the hostage negotiation course together (with flying colours) and used our skills on a least two occasions when patients had barricaded themselves in their bedrooms. However, we managed to talk them out of the incidents safely without harm to themselves or others.

Despite the ward being rehabilitation, it was not generally violent, as the patients were settled on medication and treatment regimes and potentially were due either to step down to a lower forensic setting or move back into the community, under supervision. However, sadly there were some tragedies whilst I was on the ward (which I won't go into detail on) with two fatalities (one being a hanging and the other an overdose).

Green and learning the ropes

Another incident of note which made me think and reflect (as I was green and still learning the ropes) was the case of a patient who was incarcerated for paedophilia. Over a period of time, the patient agreed to be chemically castrated in order to prevent future sexual offences against children.

However, following his treatment, I was talking to him at length about his previous offences and mentioned that he must be pleased to have had the castration, as this would prevent him from further offending when he is eventually released back into the community.

I was really surprised when he replied, without a moment's hesitation, that "I probably will re-offend as for me it's not just the sexual thing, but it's as much about having power over another human being!"

I was shocked but I tried not to show it, as he went on to explain and ask me a question. "You know how you see your wife as pretty and attractive, with nice curves and assets and therefore it is only natural that you would want to have a relationship with her? Well, it's exactly the same for me but I fancy children!" He went on to say that he didn't want to feel this way about children but he couldn't help his emotions and feelings. He finished off the conversation asking me the question "how would you feel if someone said to you that you couldn't have a relationship with females ever again?"

I am not defending the patient in any way, shape, or form, as I find the protection of any child to be the most important role of any society and having children and grandchildren myself, I honestly found the whole subject very difficult to deal with.

However, as a nurse, I had a duty of care and part of my role was to help offenders from re-offending. Now then, I had never really thought or even considered the perpetrators perspective or how difficult it might be for them to fight their most basic and natural urges. However, his question really took me by surprise and stumped me and I found it difficult to answer initially. Nevertheless, after composing myself I told him that irrespective of his feelings, society has a duty to protect the most vulnerable (starting with children) as they hadn't got the capacity to make choices or give consent and therefore it was totally against the law to even consider such an act.

I remember thinking at the time that my reply was probably inadequate, as the patient gave no indication that he had heard me or was even considering my views. However, I was only starting out in my new career and still had a lot to learn, but the incident made me realise what a difficult field of work I had entered!

Footnote: The hostage negotiation course was devised and run by our then head of our Psychology Department, Paul Britton, who went on to become a police serial killer profiler. Paul also wrote a book which sold millions, about the very first case of DNA solving murder in the world (the murders of Dawn Ashworth and Linda Mann by Colin Pitchfork) in which he assisted the police with his profiling. The book is called 'The Jigsaw Man' and is well worth a read if you have the chance!

Paul also did a follow up book about our forensic setting called 'Picking Up The Pieces'. Once again, this is a very good read.

Holidays and forensic capers at the Carpenters Arms

One of the bonuses of working on the rehabilitation ward was the outings with the patients into the community – taking them home to their families for the day, going to concerts, shopping and visits to parks and entertainment venues (I really loved it as you got to know the patients outside a locked environment and therefore, they saw you as a human being and not just as a custodian).

One particular year, some of the patients (subject to consultant and Home Office approval) had the opportunity to go on holiday for a week to Cornwall. Billy and I, as well as our manager and several other staff, were asked to go as escorting supervision staff and naturally we were delighted, as this meant double pay as you were away from home for the week and would you believe, we would receive a weeks' time owing in lieu of the trip!

We spent the week in Polzeath, not far from the beach, in a building owned by a local hospital, complete with bunk beds and all amenities for rehabilitation, including activities of daily living such as cleaning and cooking, etc. However, the building was right next to a pub called The Carpenters Arms would you believe!

Needless to say, this was very convenient, in fact a little bit 'too convenient', as it meant just a couple of steps from one environment to another. Over the week, Billy Boy and I made many trips to the pub. We had a great time together in that pub and the craic was ninety (but that's another story).

Over the week, we took trips to all the local sights and across the water to spend the day in Padstow with fish and chips on the front at the end of the day - the patients loved it! However, Billy Boy really wanted to take the patients on a fishing trip (mackerel fishing) and despite the weather being good inland, whenever he tried to book the trip during the week, he was told by the skipper that the sea further out from land was too rough to take anyone, much to Billy Boy's disappointment.

The fishing trip

On the day prior to leaving Polzeath, Billy Boy tried once more to book a fishing trip and this time the skipper reluctantly agreed, albeit with some reservations. The skipper turned out to be right to have reservations, as when we left the harbour it was very calm, just like a mill pond, but the further we went out at sea it became a little rougher. However, once we had dropped anchor it became much calmer and Billy Boy quickly put his line over the side and within minutes, he brought up fish after fish on his line with dilated pupils 'as if he had gold on the end of his line,' whilst pulling them on board by the bucket full

Back on land, Billy spoke incessantly about his fishing ability and the amount of mackerel he had caught when in fact everyone on the boat including patients had caught loads. Well reader, that's Billy Boy for you!

It was a fantastic holiday for all concerned and the patients spoke of never having a real holiday in their life and never having experienced anything in their life like a fishing trip. As for myself, I really enjoyed the sight of the patients experiencing these events. Moreover, as I said earlier, I actually got paid double for doing this and also a week in lieu to have off duty at the convenience of the ward. This certainly beat my wages and my conditions whilst I was working for Birrs Sportswear. Anyway, upon returning to Leicester, I brought back a load of mackerel home to Theresa and she was absolutely delighted as she loves fish. Isn't life great... there is always a silver lining!

Billy Boy and myself in Cornwall, just prior to the fishing trip.

Acute Admission "Beirut"

Having worked on the rehabilitation ward for a couple of years and cut my teeth regarding the basics of psychiatry and nursing, I was asked to go and work on the Acute Admission Ward, which was very understaffed at the time and known as 'Beirut' due to the amounts of assaults on staff from acutely ill and psychotic patients.

The majority of the patients on the ward suffered from mental illness with psychotic symptoms and were usually admitted via the courts, following being sentenced or for assessment with the view of a consultant submitting a report to direct the judge as to whether they should be admitted to a locked environment for treatment or should no illness be assessed, then the route should be via a prison sentence.

Most staff refused or tried to get out of working on the ward, but I fancied the challenge and change of working practice. Now, I could write a separate book about my unbelievable experiences in forensic nursing and in particular the Acute Admission Ward, however listed below are just a few of them.

Political correctness gone mad

Well reader, nursing is full of bureaucracy at the best of times and most of the time I think that there is a reason for it - in order to protect, safeguard and provide guidance and structure to the system. However, in 1991 the Government of the day (the Conservatives), introduced The Patient's Charter, which was again revised in 1995.

Now, I am all for patients and human rights, but I have to say that sometimes common sense does not prevail as in this case. Bearing in mind that our patients are not incarcerated for stealing sweeties and are potentially very capable of harming others through violence, the Patients Charter was taken literally and applied within the hospital. This meant, for instance, that from having supervised shaves monitored by staff, they could now have them unsupervised as directed by the charter!

As I said earlier, the ward was under-staffed, as the normal compliment of staff was 26 and, at the time of this incident, was down to 15 members of staff to cover the whole of the 24-hour shift. On the day of the incident, as I walked onto the ward for my afternoon shift, I was greeted by the shift co-ordinator.

At this stage of my career, I was still an unqualified B grade member of staff. However, I was informed by the co-ordinator that there was no ward-based qualified members of staff available for the shift and therefore as I knew the ward and its patients better than any other staff on the shift, I would be considered to be in charge, as they could only provide a qualified member of staff from the other wards for one hour at a time!

Of course, this was illegal as I was not qualified and so I asked the co-ordinator to write down in the co-ordinators book my official protest and objections to this decision and note that I would not take the responsibility for the shift. This was duly noted! But the co-ordinators plan went ahead, nevertheless.

Violence

Within twenty minutes of the shift starting, a male patient asked to have a shave and so, as protocol dictates, I looked in his notes and care-plan to see if there was any reason not to let him have his requested shave. Having done so and discussed the matter with the rest of the staff on shift, including the on-loan qualified member of staff, it was agreed by all concerned.

However, I had a niggling feeling in my stomach about this patient and so I asked another member of staff on 'sharps' duty to follow him down to his room and keep an eye on him through the observation spy hole in the patient's door to ensure safety on the ward. Just then, a female patient (it was mixed gender wards in those days) started to crack off at another patient and so I removed her from the environment and took her into a side room to calm her down. I was only in there a couple of minutes later when I heard this almighty screaming by a female patient followed by banging and shaking on the door of the room I was in.

As I opened the door, I could see the colleague on 'sharps' wrestling and trying to subdue the patient who had requested the shave. At this point I hadn't a clue what was happening, but I grabbed hold of the patient and we both managed to bring him to the floor. As we brought him down, my colleague screamed out in pain as the patient managed to cut the top of two of his fingers off with the razor he had requested.

Having restrained the patient, he was taken by the response team to a seclusion room on another ward and I then had to deal with the other female patient who was still screaming at the top of her voice.

What a sight it was, as she had been cut with the blade by the male perpetrator who had managed to cut some of her ear off and then had proceeded to cut her throat, but luckily enough the female had dropped her head and with this he cut straight though her cheek so much so that you could see her tongue and inside of her mouth as the cut flap opened wide - it wasn't pleasant as there was blood everywhere!

It naturally took me a long time to console and calm her down, given the circumstances. However, she refused hospital treatment point-blank and would only accept myself steri-stripping ('butterfly') her cheek back together and putting a dressing on her ear - the task took me one and a half hours to complete.

Later in a debrief, it transpired that the member of staff on sharps had not followed the patient to his room as I asked and within minutes the patient had removed the blade and carried out his attack.

The following day she did agree to treatment at the hospital and I received a lovely note via the escorting staff from the plastic surgeon at the hospital, informing me that I had done a lovely neat job of putting her cheek back together again.

Footnote: Following this incident, a discussion took place between management and the Home Office, with the result that management went back (sensible, in my opinion) to having patients' shaves supervised by staff.

As for the victim of the attack, she received compensation for her injuries. Regarding the perpetrator, he was transferred to a more secure setting the next day and sadly a couple of months later it was reported that he had hung himself.

The gangster in the negligee

During my time on this ward, I met some real characters and apart from the violence there was also some very funny incidents involving patients as in the following case. This particular patient (we shall call him 'Derek') was quite notorious in his hometown, for his confrontations with the police whenever he became mentally ill - psychotic. The police would usually send out the riot squad to contain him whenever they felt he was a danger to himself or the public at large and so his hatred for law enforcement grew over the years.

On this occasion, he was admitted to a ward following an incident in his hometown by the police, who brought him onto the ward on a stretcher with his hands being handcuffed and his knees and feet being bound with strong plastic tie grips, all this whilst he shouted and swore constantly with unrepeatable expletives as they admitted him!

Derek had no problem with nursing staff whatsoever (only police) and as soon as the law had left, he became his normal, quite reserved yet polite, self. I got on with Derek from the word go and built up a good trusting and therapeutic relationship with him. However, I was not prepared for the sight that greeted me several weeks later when I was on a night shift.

During the night, patients were allowed to smoke in the lounge area under observation from staff so long as after finishing their fags they would return to their respective bedrooms.

The ward lighting was kept dim at night to naturally encourage sleep and on this particular night, I was sitting in the nursing station when I saw a dimly lit strange figure appear at the bottom of the ward (I couldn't make it out at first) and make his way up the ward to the nursing station.

I really couldn't believe my eyes as he got nearer as Derek was wearing a pink lady's baby doll negligee complete with frilly knickers! I really was taken aback as he politely knocked on the door and asked in his deep gangster / film star voice, to "give me a light!" - I don't know how I kept from laughing as I shakily lit his fag whilst containing my suppressed laughter.

I couldn't get over the unbelievable parallels between the tough gangster and this vision of the same person in the baby doll negligee. But as I have always said, you never know who or what will turn up in life as this incident proved! However, read on regarding further exploits of Derek.

The large built male, Billy boy and the midget

Several months later, Derek managed to escape from his escort whilst on escorted, approved leave and he made his way back to his hometown. Over the next week, he managed to avoid the police and authorities whilst laying low. However, he was eventually spotted in the town centre and the riot squad were again mobilised to return him to our ward, as he was still under a valid section of the Mental Health Act. Having taken Derek to the town centre police station, we received a call asking if he could be collected from the station as soon as possible, as they currently didn't have the resources to return him to the ward.

With this, Billy boy, myself and a very large built male on the ward took a minibus to collect Derek from the station. When we arrived, the desk sergeant looked very surprised and asked directly "where are the rest of you?" Having informed him that it was just us three, he scratched his head and said "it's on your heads then" as we walked towards the cell containing Derek.

Having looked through the cell spy hole we found Derek to be fast asleep on the bench. We quickly made a plan, with me being selected to go in first with his medication as I knew him better than the other escorts and Derek also trusted me.

This was all done in seconds as I shook Derek gently yet firmly and said "wake up Derek, its Dermot. Can you take these meds for me and then we can get you back to the ward?" In his half-awake state, he said "oh hello, Dermot" and agreed with a slight smile as he came to and swallowed the meds. Within seconds and with extra verbal encouragement from Billy Boy, I had him out of the cell and onto the minibus as we chatted away about getting him something to eat when we arrived back at the ward.

As we left, the desk sergeant told Billy Boy that he couldn't believe what he had just seen, as he explained that the police had to get the riot squad to arrest and contain Derek on every single occasion and yet the 'midget' had actually gone in on his own, got him to take his meds and then got him onto the bus in the blink of an eye!

I believe life is all about building strong relationships, earning trust and treating others as you would like to be treated yourself - as illustrated in the above case!

Eating glass

As I wrote previously, the ward comprised of mixed gender and from time-to-time relationships did develop between patients as they shared time together from each ward in the main recreation area.

On this particular night, I had just walked onto the ward to start my night shift and before I even took my coat off, I just happened to look across from my nursing station and saw a member of staff being punched to the ground by a patient on another ward. I naturally pulled my pit and ran towards the incident and was joined by the response team as we entered the ward.

The patient was quickly subdued by the team and taken to another ward where he was placed in seclusion. Having returned to my own ward, the alarm went off again as another incident on the same ward took place. As we responded we entered the room of a female who had cut her wrists superficially and the staff managed to attend to her wounds whilst giving her support and calming her down. About an hour later the alarms went off again on the same ward and same room. As we entered her room the female was coughing up blood as she had managed to get hold of a light bulb and was eating the glass. Staff immediately telephoned for an ambulance whilst other staff administered as much medical assistance as possible under the circumstances.

The door breakthrough

However, as the team attempted to help the female, unbeknown to us her boyfriend, who was on an adjoining ward separated by two doors with see through panels, had been watching the incident in his girlfriend's room through the glass panel and he was now kicking and shouting as he knocked the doors through, as he thought staff were trying to harm the love of his life.

It was surreal and unbelievable as he kicked the locks off each door with some force and made his way into his girlfriend's bedroom, punching every member of staff who was standing in his way as he attempted to get to her - it was mayhem to say the least! However, he was restrained by staff and taken to seclusion to calm down and have staff explain the situation to him once he was calmer.

The female was taken by ambulance to the nearest hospital under escort for treatment and eventually made a full recovery after a few days in hospital without too much permanent damage to her throat, thank God!

However, the night wasn't finished, as later in the early hours of the morning, another incident took place requiring a restraint of two patients who had been fighting. It was nearing the end of the shift that all the paperwork was completed, and the ward was settled, but at least the shift had passed swiftly without my feet even touching the floor.

"Killing for company"

It was while I was based on this ward that I attended a lecture given by the criminology and serial killer author Brian Masters, who wrote the million selling book "Killing For Company". It's a brilliant read and was later made into a TV film called 'Des' starring David Tennant.

What a fascinating and engaging man Mr. Masters was, as he delivered his lecture on the serial killer Denis Neilson, who had murdered at least sixteen men. Mr. Masters went through Neilson's life in detail and went to great lengths to point out some of the issues and incidents in his life that had a large bearing on his offending. For example, his grandfather had brought him up in Scotland and was the role model in his life up until his sudden death. Neilson never really got over the loss of his grandfather as he had provided love, warmth, company and stability in his life and being very much a loner, he longed for these comforts for the remainder of his life.

His background and longing for love and companionship, according to Mr. Masters, was directly re-enacted with some of his victims as, following murdering them, he would keep them in his bed and sleep with them or sit them in a chair and greet them on a daily basis as he came home from work - hence the title of the book 'Killing For Company." I recall Masters finished the lecture by telling us that following his interview with Neilson, as he left the cell, Neilson asked him to make him sound "interesting" in his book! Ironically, Paul Britton also had the same request from some of the serial killers he had interviewed during his time as a profiler. As if serial killers were not bizarrely and morbidly interesting anyway!

I find the whole subject of serial killers morbidly fascinating even to this day, as I have always been fascinated by people generally and love to know what makes them tick.

Talking of serial killers, whilst I was on this ward, I was part of an escort party taking a patient back to Ashworth High Security Unit and as we took the patient onto the ward, I saw the infamous serial killer Ian Brady (partner to Moira Hindley in the Moors children murders - both of whom have since passed away). It was only a brief sighting of this old and withered man, but it still sent a shiver down my spine nevertheless!

Impetuous staff

Before I move on with my story, I would just briefly like to tell you about the only time I ever had a slight injury during my career in forensics. A fight took place between two patients on my ward and the alarm went off and I was on my own when it happened.

As protocol dictates, you should never intervene in an incident until the whole of the response team is present in order to restrain or deal with an incident. As it happened, a very large, young, inexperienced male member of staff from another ward, who I would describe (without being unkind) as impetuous, full of testosterone and alpha male in character, was first on the scene and before I could say anything to him, he jumped straight in between the two patients.

I naturally had to help him as he was on his own and I had very little choice. As I went to assist him, one of the patients involved in the fight spotted me coming and timed his elbow perfectly to pull back and strike me in my right eye. However, I have to say that I count myself very lucky in over 21 years of service to have only suffered this very slight injury.

Footnote: Regarding mental illness and personality disorders, I loved my time on the acute ward, as I have genuine sympathy for patients with mental illness as, generally speaking, they have **little or no insight** to their condition and behaviours and therefore are less responsible for their actions (mentally ill patients do respond to medication and can live relatively normal lives providing they keep taking the prescribed meds).

However, conversely speaking, patients with personality disorders generally **have insight** to their actions and behaviours and therefore, in my opinion, are far more dangerous and unpredictable (personality disorders are less likely to respond to medication although this is becoming more prescribed by clinicians over the past few years).

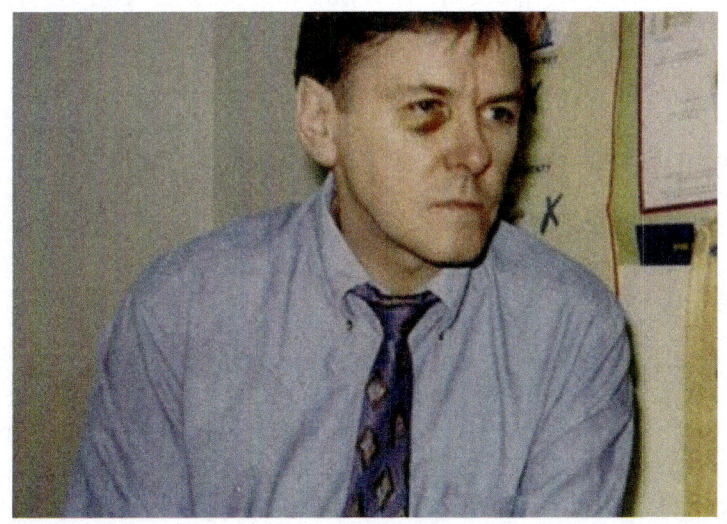

My one and only slight injury in 21 years of forensic nursing.

The personality disorder ward

Following my time on the acute ward, I requested to go to the personality ward, as I knew very little regarding personality disorders and wanted to develop my skills and knowledge in that particular area. However, I won't prolong my writing about the time I spent on this ward, but nevertheless, I have to say that I learnt so much about patients with these disorders and really learnt a lot about myself and my own personality (it really made me think and examine my own personality traits!).

Basically, I believe we all have personality disorders, it's just about the degrees and depths of the disorder and how it affects our lives and our interactions in society. Generally speaking, personality disorders lack empathy, compassion, sympathy, etc.

However, the majority of our patients were at the top end of the scale with psychopathic disorders and offending crimes to match - exhibiting grandiose ideation, self-importance and narcissistic traits, amongst others.

Treatment for the patients usually involves talking therapies to get a better understanding of their own thoughts, feelings, and behaviours with the long-term goal of identifying strategies to resolve problems and help them change their attitudes and behaviours. I found working with these patients on a daily basis to be exciting and yet mentally draining at times, as you challenged their thoughts and behaviours.

Anyway, having been on the ward for a couple of years, I was approached by the professor who devised the ward and the treatment of patients within, who informed me that he wanted to "second me!" I naturally thought he meant to send me to another ward or another hospital, however, he informed me that he wanted me to take my training to become a qualified mental health nurse, would you believe!

I was really taken aback by his request and immediately replied that I wouldn't be capable or intelligent enough to take the three-year course, to which he responded confidently "yes you would" and he went on to say that I needed to discuss it with my wife and give him my decision within the week.

Having talked it over with Theresa at great length and drawn up a list of advantages and disadvantages to take my training, the list was far bigger in favour of taking the plunge and so it was to be! However, I still had many self-doubts about taking the course, particularly regarding my irrational thoughts and fears from my past, of my Dad's warning that I was "thick" and also that I was now in my early fifties!

The oldest student in the world

I started my course at De Montfort University in February 2001 at 53 years of age! It was initially very embarrassing, as I was obviously the oldest in that cohort. However, this was short lived as my fellow students quickly accepted me for who and what I was. Moreover, I became a father figure for some of them if they needed any support, advice or help and due to my previous experience of nursing on wards, I had a head start and could provide input into discussions and teaching sessions regarding nursing practices in those settings.

Now I could write another book about my experiences during these three years of training but that is for another time. Nevertheless, the three years went so quickly and it was a fantastic experience, especially for someone like me who never ever thought or dreamt for one single moment that I would ever go to such an institution - but there again you never know what will turn up in life!

However, there was to be one more hurdle to jump before I completed my course to become a qualified mental health nurse!

Childhood memories return to haunt me

In my last year at university, I had to sit my final exams and it was during this period that I experienced a near breakdown with some psychotic symptoms. You see, in the run up to the exam, I began to experience major anxiety, whilst having flashbacks of my father punching me in the head all those years ago whilst telling me I was "thick."

As time went by, and the exam got nearer, I became more preoccupied with the past and thoughts of self-doubt and failure. As a mental health auxiliary nurse, I was aware that this was happening and it was affecting my life and family (Theresa must have thought I was going mad, bless her!). The thoughts were so invasive at times that I became angry with myself, my wife, my family and the world in general and I believe I drifted into a psychotic state at times, with destructive thoughts and behaviours during this period.

It came to a head, when my son Jonathan, Theresa and I were going to watch an international football match at the newly-built Leicester City stadium (Walkers Stadium) between England and Serbia & Montenegro on June 3rd (Jonathan's birthday) 2003. On the way to the match, I began to feel frightened, anxious and paranoid as I walked and mingled with the crowd and found the whole thing overwhelming. Again, my logical and nursing brain told me it was major anxiety causing this irrational thinking and behaviours, but once again I was powerless to stop the process.

During the match (which was incidentally John Terry's debut) I froze and couldn't concentrate on the game whilst feeling so overwhelmed by it all. I felt so frightened that I turned to Jonathan and asked if he could take me home. I think he was shocked and perplexed at my request and really didn't know what to say or do (poor old Jon!).

However, at this moment of complete loss of control, it was like a rational switch had flicked in my head (I don't know how or why) but I started to use CBT (Cognitive Behavioural Therapy) on myself by taking control of my irrational thoughts and putting things into perspective, whilst using deep controlled breathing to bring my racing heart back to a normal rate. This was a turning point for me, mainly for exercising some control over myself. However, this was only the start as I said and as the exam got nearer, I was constantly battling against my irrational thoughts and symptoms and the fear of my Dad's warning that I was "thick!"

On the day of the exam, I had lost it again as I entered the room and was filled with dread to the point that I was frozen with fear. As the exam started, I remember that I had to get hold of my pen with both hands and use both of them to push and actually write on the paper. I recall the psychotic feeling of my Dad standing right beside me in the exam whilst his voice was telling me over and over again that I was "thick" (I swear the experience was so real and I now understand how psychological trauma, either past or present, can affect mentally ill patients).

I don't honestly know how I got through it, but I did, and to my surprise I later found out that I passed. Looking back, I came close to having a psychotic breakdown but with my experience as a nurse and my own inner strength (combined with the support of my loving family), I came through it all.

The experience made me stronger as I realised I am not thick nor am I the brightest either, by the way! However, I have moved on and put my Dad's words and actions to rest at last. Moreover, the experience improved my understanding of mental illness as I had experienced it myself first-hand and therefore, I think I became a better nurse and a more understanding person generally!

Community forensic mental health team

In February 2004, I went back as a qualified registered mental health nurse to the wards and the transition was relatively easy and comfortable, so much so that I got promoted to a higher grade within six months. However, towards the end of that year, I received a telephone call from my old friend, Bridie Collins, who by now was working with the community forensic team. Basically, Bridie informed me that a post was coming up with the team and she felt that I should apply for it. To cut a long story short, I did apply and to my surprise I got the job.

This proved to be the most interesting, exciting and the happiest part of my working life. However, it was combined with the dangers of working independently most of the time with mentally ill offenders in the community.

Once again, I could write another book about my time with the team and the many stories and incidents I attended over the years, however this is just a quick summary of a few of them.

Lone working basic working practice

Before I continue with my story, I would just like to quickly explain the basic working practice for working independently in the community. In essence, it is normal to work solo on most occasions. However, risk assessment is on-going with all of the patients and should risks increase with a patient, you could visit the patient with one, two or even three colleagues to ensure safety for all. In some cases, you could enlist the assistance of the police if deemed necessary.

Every day working included each of the nurses taking turns to become the co-ordinator for the day. This role entailed the co-ordinator making a log of all patient's visits with the time of arrival and departures from each patients visit. The nurse would phone the co-ordinator at the end of the visit and inform them that they were safe. Should the nurse not phone at the agreed time, the co-ordinator would attempt to contact the nurse and if unable to make contact, the co-ordinator would either go directly to the patient's home address, with colleagues in support, or request the police to attend should they have safety concerns.

The walking group

Having settled into the role, one of the first things I did was to set up a walking group with my colleague and friend, Bridie Collins, who at that time was our team leader. It was one of the best things I ever did in nursing! Every two weeks we would take the patients out in a twelve seater minibus with me as the driver and Bridie as the tour guide. The basic aim of the group was to improve the level of patient's fitness and encourage socialisation. The trips would include visits to museums, cinemas, parks, stately homes, country walks and shows. The patients loved it as many had never really seen the countryside or had the opportunity to visit places, due to impoverished backgrounds, being in care, lengthy incarcerations or even just living in cities for the majority of their lives.

I won't bore the reader with all of the trips and fun we had with the group over the years, however, I will tell you about one of the trips which proved to be both funny and yet so thought-provoking for the patients. I had the idea of taking the group up a mountain as over the years the majority of the walks had mainly taken place on flat terrains, due to all of the patients being smokers and some of them with fairly acute lung problems mainly due to their excessive smoking and overall lack of fitness.

Having discussed the idea with Bridie we sought the permission of their forensic consultant which, after lengthy consideration, he reluctantly approved. We built the patients fitness up over the following months to the point that they would only have a fag hourly at stops, as we praised and encouraged them to believe they could actually climb a mountain.

"The mountain and a fag every few yards"

Come the day and we set off early-morning to climb Kinder Scout, which is 2,087 feet high and the only mountain in Derbyshire. After a lengthy drive, we arrived at the carpark in Hayfield and from there we had about an hour's walk to the foot of the mountain. The group was initially in high spirits and full of expectation as we set off. However, as the terrain became steeper and more uneven, members of the group became less confident and took to smoking fags to calm their nerves. It took us nearly two hours before we reached the bottom of the mountain!

At this point it was a sheer climb to the summit and some of the patients began to have self-doubts and spoke of returning to the minibus. However, both Bridie and I gave encouragement and support to the group, which seemed to work, as all the group agreed to give it a go! With every step taken there was much puffing and panting, with a stop for a fag every few yards, whilst some of them complained that it was impossible for them to reach the top. Nevertheless, they all kept going with our encouragement and support until they all eventually reached the summit.

The smiles on each of their faces having reached the summit is hard to describe, other than saying they all had a beaming grin on their faces and were buzzing with excitement and happiness as they had managed to actually climb a mountain - it's something I will never forget as I was so proud of them all! We sat and ate some sandwiches as they took in the magnificent view, before having another fag and then making our way back down. The return journey was even slower, due to fatigue and most of their legs had by now turned to jelly, as they pushed and encouraged each other onwards.

Back on the bus, it was great to hear them all talking of their achievement with some of them realising that if they could climb a mountain, they could do anything they chose to do. I can't tell the reader just how much it meant to them as, metaphorically speaking, they had all been climbing mountains for most of their lives via their mental health problems and unstable upbringings.

Tragedy and the coroners court

I had some very sad cases during my time in community forensics, including two of my patients committing suicide by hanging themselves. Neither of the patients had given any indication of their intentions and their lives appeared to be fairly fulfilled with no mental health crisis at the time. One of those suicides was particularly sad in that he was found by his own mother!

You see, on the day in question, his mother had visited his home as she did every Saturday morning to help him clean his flat and also to take him shopping. On that particular morning, she had entered his flat with her own key as normal, only to find the flat was empty. She assumed that he had popped out to get some fags or visited a friend nearby to catch up or arrange a meeting and so she naturally sat down and waited for his return.

After approximately half an hour she needed the loo quickly and so she entered her son's toilet and pulled the door behind her which incidentally she noted at the time was heavier than it felt normally. As she turned around to sit on the toilet seat, the poor woman came face-to-face with her son who was hanging from a metal clothes peg on the back of the door.

Sadly, he had been deceased for some time, having taken his own life during the early hours of the morning. I can't imagine how she felt or the shock she must have encountered, I only know that she was traumatised very badly and would consequently ring me up from time-to-time to talk it over, in an attempt to come to terms with the incident. For some reason, she refused counselling.

Attending the coroners court on both occasions was quite daunting in that I had to compile a report and submit my nursing notes for inspection. You are also called to give evidence regarding your observations and feelings regarding the patient's mental state and behaviours prior to his suicide. The coroner on both occasions was quite satisfied that all the procedures, protocols and notes had been followed to the letter by myself and the team. Despite this, I felt very down at the time as you always reflect and wish you could have done more to prevent such terrible tragedies.

My last case-triple murder

Approximately a year or so before my retirement, I was given my last case which proved to be quite a task and not without its problems and risks. The client in question had emigrated to the UK and had resided in England for the past thirty years. In his country of origin, he had four other siblings, all being females. His father owned several plazas and was considerably wealthy and my client, being the eldest and a male, was given assurance by his father that upon his death, he would inherit all the properties and his estate. However, his father died and for some unknown reason, left his entire estate to be shared between his four daughters instead! Initially, my client went through the courts to contest his fathers will, however after a period of two years, he was getting nowhere with his claim, other than it costing him a fortune.

With this in mind, my client returned to his country of origin and whilst there, somehow managed to get hold of a revolver to 'put matters right' between his siblings and himself. Having visited each of his sister's homes, he shot all four of them point-blank, killing three of them outright and putting the other in a wheelchair for the rest of her life. He then managed to avoid being apprehended by the police for three days whilst on the run, before managing to return to England. Upon his return, he went to his GP and informed him of his misdemeanours and was subsequently taken to a secure setting for assessment.

To cut a long story short, after a lengthy assessment within the secure setting, which naturally considered his extreme dangerousness and risk to the public, our team agreed to take the case on when he was released back into the community, and he was eventually released approximately a year later into our team's care with myself as his named nurse. Prior to and after his release, I had to attend weekly MAPPA meetings (multi agency public protection arrangements) whose main concern was for the safety of the British public. These meetings involved police, the Home Office and Interpol for foreign intelligence, probation, DWP, children's welfare and any other agency that was involved in the case, who would give up-to-date intelligence and feedback from any dealings or concerns they had regarding the family and the patient himself.

Now then reader, as his offence took place in a foreign country with whom Britain had no extradition treaty, this person would never face real justice for the three murders and the life-changing injuries to another. Moreover, because of his crime, there was naturally outrage from his family in different places throughout the world, as they learned about his crime, and they began to make threats of killing and raping his wife and daughters as part of honour killing to avenge his heinous crimes. The family were naturally scared for their own safety and due to imminent threats from their family abroad, a decision was made by the MAPPA organisation to move both the patient and his family (all paid for by the state) under the cover of darkness to a new home in another part of the county.

Being a nurse, I naturally had to treat all my patients with respect and dignity and try to help them in any way possible, despite any feelings I had personally regarding their crimes. Before and after any visits to the patient's home, I would have to contact the police and inform them of the time of visit, duration and place of visit and following the visit, provide feedback to the police particularly if I had any concerns for his mental health or safety of his family.

To be honest, I was scared myself at times, particularly when I went through a period when police intelligence (via Interpol) informed me that a family member was going to assassinate the patient, as they had obtained a gun and a location that the patient was now living in. Thank God it came to nothing, but I admit that I was scared that should it have gone ahead, the gunman, knowing my luck, would probably miss his target and get me instead! Moreover, I thought I am not really paid enough to be placed in this kind of danger.

Anyway, I managed to survive and on 28th February 2013, both Theresa and I retired on the same day. My colleagues put on a great bash for me with Irish flags and bunting all around the meeting room with Irish music playing and all the female staff wearing aprons with large, busted bosoms featured on the front of the aprons, as they all knew my obsession with female breasts. The food was fantastic, and a great time was had by all (see retirement section for pictures).

As I finish this chapter on my fascinating, enjoyable and sometimes scary career in forensics, I would like to include in my book, this poem I wrote called the **Purpose Of Life**, which I initially wrote for my patients, but as I wrote it, I realised that it reflected my own life simply and to the point. It's particularly poignant in that some of my patients (who had terrible sad and tragic lives and would consider ending it all) used to ask me what is the point of it all and what's the meaning of life?

Now, I am not religious at all and it's very difficult to give them hope with inspirational words as I had not walked in their shoes and had never suffered as they had with extreme abuse and other unmentionable problems during their lives. Nevertheless, I thought about my own life and despite whatever difficulties I had faced over the years I always had endurance, purpose, and goals in my life regardless.

And so, with this in mind, I would tell them that in my opinion, the purpose of life is a life of purpose (no matter how small the purpose - even to get out of bed each morning, just to brush your teeth and have breakfast, for example, as each purpose is like a building block leading to a fuller life), as without purpose in your life, it is just an existence.

What is……The purpose of Life?

The purpose of life, is a life of purpose,

For if we don't have purpose, we don't have life

If we don't have life, we only exist

So don't just exist, be determined to live

But in order to live, we have to have purpose.

And so,

The purpose of life, is a life of purpose.

Bill Carpenter / the lost glasses and the hole in my cornea

Just a quick story of another mishap which involved me digging in Bill Carpenter's garden. You see, Bill suffered a heart attack in 2014 and so he asked me to take care of his vegetable garden as he wasn't able, and in return, I would get half of the produce grown, which was fair enough. Anyway, I made a great job of it, as the soil, after much labouring, became very fine and ready for planting. However, during the many times I had attended to the patch, I somehow lost the glasses I was wearing in his very large garden and thought no more about it until the following year when I was digging up the produce of my labour, which happened to be corn on the cob!

Having put in my garden fork and levered up the large cob, I noticed there was something hanging on the end of the fork. Upon close inspection would you believe, was my missing glasses from the previous year! Now what would the odds be, on my fork not breaking or even missing the glasses, I don't know, but after a quick clean under the tap I put them on saying to myself "these are as good as new!"

Later that year, when Bill was moving to another house, he invited me to dig up some bushes from his property which I had admired for some time. To cut a long story short, as I put the said bushes in my car one of the branch stems caught on the door frame and as I tried to pull it into the car from the inside. As I pulled hard, the branch suddenly shot forward with some force and hit my right eye, resulting in my eye streaming, and a lack of vision, combined with unbelievable pain. Down at the infirmary, after having drops and eye scans, they informed me that the accident had resulted in a hole in the centre of my cornea. It took two years for that bloody hole to grow over and lots of considerable pain during that period. It could only happen to me. What a plonker I really am!

1995 - The IRA interrogation

In 1995, Jon and I made a trip back to Dublin and we stayed at my cousin Bernie's home in Shallon, near Finglas. We had a great week in Dublin but one thing that really sticks out in my memory is our visit to Moore Street in central Dublin. I wanted to buy some traditional Irish CD albums and so we had gone to the Dolphin Records store in Moore Street, as I had previously found what I wanted in that particular store. Having had a good look around and purchased what we desired, we came out of the store and made our way up the street towards the top end of Moore Street. As we walked up, I noticed an old pub on the right-hand side of the road, with the Irish flag flying outside.

Having been up that street many times, both as a child and adult, I had never actually taken note of it and therefore I suggested to Jon that we should pop in for a pint of Guinness and a look around. We entered the dark and dingy pub, with bars on the windows, which gave it the appearance of being a pub / prison straight from the Victorian age.

I was immediately struck with the sight of Irish flags everywhere and collection boxes for the IRA, along with posters informing anyone interested in forthcoming marches and protests in support of a united Ireland. As we stood in the doorway surveying the sight with some trepidation, Jon stated that perhaps it was a bad idea to enter as he didn't like the look of the place as he felt "very uncomfortable", being only a 'Plastic Paddy'. However, I said it will be fine as I stepped forward towards the bar, leaving Jon at a table near the entrance.

Feeling slightly uncomfortable myself, I decided to put on my best Irish accent to order the pints and therefore not cause any offence or alarm to any of those present that I might possibly be working for the British Government! Having ordered the drinks, I was quickly approached by a man standing at the end of the bar who, without introduction, asked me my name, where I was from, what had brought me to Dublin and why had I come to that particular bar.

He also wanted to know my father and mother's name and where they had lived in Dublin. I gave him a whistle-stop tour of my life and details he required and mentioned that both sides of my family, Kanes and Kearneys, had supported the 'cause' during the rebellion (by the way reader, this was when Ireland was fighting for freedom and **not** when the IRA carried out indiscriminate bombing of the public in England).

Following our brief conversation, he said nothing but appeared satisfied as he walked back to the end of the bar without acknowledging or giving any indication what had just taken place between us.

The woman with the pipe

As I walked back to the table with the drinks, I could see that Jon was very nervous and twitchy. I told him what had happened and that all was well and added that we could leave after we had consumed our drinks if he still felt unsafe. Whilst drinking what turned out to be the best pint of Guinness I have ever tasted, I noticed out of the corner of my eye, an old lady sitting on her own to the left of us, smoking a long white clay pipe! I had not seen this sight since I was a child in Dublin, when occasionally you would see the odd woman smoking a pipe.

The woman in question was probably in her late seventies or early eighties and she wore a shawl around her shoulders whilst sitting, smoking to her hearts content. When I drew Jonathan's attention to her, he nearly fell off his chair. It was amazing to see this as it looked like something you would have witnessed in a bygone age and we both felt privileged to have seen it with our very own eyes.

By now we were enjoying the pints and sights and so when I asked Jon if he would like to move on he said, "no let's stay for another" and so we did! Jon and I often talk about that remarkable day, and I feel quite sad that both Dolphin Records and the old pub have since gone, along with old memories of Dublin.

Footnote - Having researched the pub on the internet, I am fairly certain the pub was called Tom Mahers at 46 Moore Street.

Jon & the bus driver

Just to digress from my story for a minute, later in 1995, Jonathan himself made a business trip back to Dublin and stayed again for the few days with my cousin Bernie and her husband Ray on the north side of Dublin in Shallon.

Jon decided to get the bus into Dublin for a few hours and Ray dropped him off at the bus stop in Finglas, with the promise to pick him up when he returned at the same stop. Jon, having spent time in Dublin, went to get the bus back for the return journey. Unfortunately, he got on the wrong bus!

As the bus made its way on the north side, Jon became aware that he didn't recognise any of the previous route he had taken and so he made his way up the bus to speak to the driver. On his way up the bus, he asked two old ladies if this was the bus for Finglas? They explained that it was indeed going to Finglas but going to a different part of Finglas to where Jon had started out from and would be a LONG time before it would go back via Finglas.

Uproar with the drunk and the old ladies

Jon then made his way up towards the driver, followed closely by the two old ladies, who by now had got the bit between their teeth into something SO exciting! Whilst Jon spoke to the bus driver about where he could get off and get back to Finglas, as the bus was trundling along, a drunk, sitting nearby, also became interested (as they do in Ireland) and began to interject and voice his concerns for Jon and his predicament. Having ascertained Bernie's address from Jonathan he was told by the driver that it was the wrong bus and he was miles away from the location.

By this time, the bus was in uproar and the driver being under pressure from the old ladies and the drunk to get Jon back on track, relented, saying "feck it" and with this, made a three point turn there-and-then and headed away from his prescribed destination towards Finglas. Unbelievably, he drove off the main route by making a short cut through the estate, navigating his way through parked cars and tight corners, and eventually dropping Jon in the centre of Finglas where Ray was due to pick him up and NOT where the bus was supposed to be going!

Ray watched open mouthed as the bus came out of the estate from an entirely different direction as normal. Jon couldn't believe what had actually happened and finally thanked and shook hands with all concerned, for their kindness as he left the bus.

The drunk also decided to get off with Jon as he said he fancied a pint (he probably thought that Jon might buy him one for his efforts). However, Dublin is a unique place with characters by the bucketful and like so many other Irish stories, it could only really happen in Ireland!

1997 - The quiz with Jonathan and Joe O'Flynn

Having lived in Farmway since 1986, we had joined the local social club belonging to the firm Jones and Shipman's, a local machine-making engineering company that was situated just around the corner from us in Watergate Lane.

In its heyday between 1960 – 1980, Jones and Shipman's had employed 2,500 workers and would export its machines all around the world, as they were front runners in machine engineering. However, by the 1990s, the number of employees was down to 200 and the firm was close to closing down. Nevertheless, the social club (known as Shippie's) was thriving and full of life with shows, social events, parties and quizzes all being put on.

'Ringers'

On this particular occasion, Jon, Joe and myself were having a drink in 'Shippies', when an announcement was made about a forthcoming Grand Quiz, to raise money for charity in memory of a deceased member of the club named David Woods, with the trophy bearing the deceased members name on it being presented to the eventual winners. As we knew most of the regular people in the club and as there was always banter and laughs between teams in previous quizzes, we decided to enter as a team calling ourselves the O'Kane's, which gave Joe the heads up for O' combined with Kane. The competition was held weekly, and I think there was three or four knock-out rounds to be contested before the actual final.

Anyway, on the day of the first round, we sat as a team behind a proper desk opposite our opposing team, complete with a card in front of us with the team's name on it and to our surprise with proper buzzers just like you see on the telly!

We stormed through the first round easily and our opponents took it all in good humour and without resentment as you would expect, and it was exactly the same on the second round. However, as the weeks went by, some of the team's appeared to be taking the whole thing very seriously and we noticed that despite us only having the three of us in our team, others were by now entering up to six people. Not only that, but new faces also began to appear in the teams who were obviously 'quiz ringers' and this got all of our team's backs up!

On the day of the semi-final, some of our opponents were definitely ringers, as I recognised some members of the team from quizzes held at the local Winstanley (Winno) pub. We were determined to beat them, as two of them in particular, were always winning at the Winno quizzes and besides being up their own arses, they acted smugly and without any sense of humility every time they were on the winning team. It proved to be a tough old battle at the semi and very close, even up to the very last question, that was directed at Jon. "Who won the very first Football World Cup?"

Had to do it!

Jon, who was seated next to me, hesitated but I remembered the answer as "Uruguay in 1930!"

Now then, I have to be honest and say that I then took the decision (with a little shame) to give Jon the answer quietly out of the side of my mouth without hopefully being seen by anybody, as rightly or wrongly, I didn't want the opponents to win as they had ringers in their team!

Jon gave the answer, and we were through to the final. You should have seen the faces on the losers as they stormed away from their table glaring at us and in a right huff before leaving the club! I felt some guilt for giving Jon the answer, but nevertheless, I was glad on the other hand to see the back of them.

The winning cup full of booze!

The final came with most of the Ford family in attendance to cheer us on. The final wasn't close as we managed to win it without any real problem and the opposing team shook our hands and congratulated us on the victory.

Joe, being very competitive, was in seventh heaven and in very high spirits, as he headed to the bar to have the cup filled up to the brim with Carling lager. He held it aloft and kissed it as if he had just won the world cup itself and the three of us took turns to drink from it. We finished the cup and continued on our drinking spree, delighted to have won and with some sense of justice at having made the final by beating the ringers.

Footnote: As I work my way through this and other stories in my book, I keep coming across coincidences, karma, fate or call it what you like and this was evident again in the case of The David Woods Memorial Trophy story as, would you believe, Theresa had nursed David Wood in the Leicester Royal Infirmary just prior to him passing away with Leukaemia!

Our prestigious cup.

Footnote: The following year, Jones and Shipman's sadly collapsed and the site was sold to a housing company, who built a small estate on it. As for the club, the members wanted to buy it but were unsuccessful in their bid. 'Shippie's' club has long since gone but it still holds lots of great memories for me, not least winning that cup.

Joe O'Flynn and the Hitler story!

Shortly after our magnificent win of the prestigious cup, Jonathan, Joe and I were having a few beers at the Jones and Shipman club when, for some reason, the subject of Hitler came up (can't remember how or why!). Anyhow, I informed Joe that I thought I had read somewhere that Hitler had actually visited England long before his rise to power, to visit his half-brother and sister-in-law in Liverpool?

With this statement, Joe started killing himself laughing and said "piss off, what do you take me for?" I then tried to persuade him that I thought the story was probably true, as history showed us that Bridget Elizabeth Hitler (nee Downing - an Irish Dublin girl from Tallaght, would you believe) had married Hitler's half-brother Alois Hitler in London in 1910 (it's true, look it up yourself).

By now Joe was pissing himself laughing and called me "deluded" whilst stating that he was having none of it. Several of the people on the tables near to us had overheard our conversation and we had piqued their interest and now they started to join the speculation on the subject with some saying it could be true whilst the majority felt that it was not. Basically, the overall consensus from them was that it was a load of old rubbish, with Joe pumping them up whilst adding the comment "prove it then!"

Immediately taking up his challenge, I said "OK" and announced with determination that I would produce the evidence over the next few weeks for them.

Proof that Hitler was in Liverpool!

A few days later I received a call from Jonathan, who told me that he had looked it up on the internet and confirmed that the story of members of the Hitler family living in the UK was true... but not that Hitler actually visited Liverpool! With this, Jon had the brilliant idea of using his knowledge with computers, to pretend he had; to scan pictures and false evidence written by himself into a book to confirm the story of Hitler in Liverpool. Jon (who was living in London at the time) said that he would be back in Leicester a few weeks later with the said evidence, to reveal his findings to Joe and the Jones and Shipman crowd.

Over the next two weeks, I made several visits to the club and with each visit I whipped Joe and the crowd interests up by stating that "I have the evidence and I told you so" and went on to tell them that Jon had absolute proof of my story, in the form of a history book and he would be presenting it to them all when he is next in Leicester.

It was probably about three weeks later when Jon arrived at the club with a history book and papers in hand, and as I had announced his coming over the past few weeks, a large crowd had assembled to see the evidence for themselves on the day. The crowd were so into this story by now that one of the guys, named Ken Nixon (Nicco) who was a mate of Joe's, had even pencilled a moustache just like Hitler, under his nose - it was Hitler frenzy on the day!

Hook, line and sinker!

Jon put the book on the table and went straight to the faked page containing the false text, written convincingly by himself, which stated that Hitler had indeed visited his half-brother in Liverpool in 1934, prior to his supreme rise to power in Germany and enjoyed a few days in the city with his relatives seeing the sights, visiting museums and theatre's and even visiting Liverpool Football Club.

According to the book, it gave him the opportunity to catch up with his half-brother and get to know his Irish sister-in-law, as he had not attended their wedding. Most of the crowd looked a bit shocked with the tangible evidence presented in front of them and the group, including Joe, started to believe that it was perhaps actually true.

Jon then went on to open some of the other pages, with a real theatrical performance, saying "just look at these if you want more proof." There is even photographic evidence of his visit to Liverpool. As the crowd looked closer in disbelief at the pictures of Hitler taken outside famous places in Liverpool such as the Liver Bird Building, Lime Street station, etc they all looked a bit stunned, and the crowd went very quiet.

Jon then changed the mood somewhat, by starting to show them even more proof on the next page with pictures of Hitler with his arms around lots of different famous Liverpool celebrities including Ken Dodd, Bill Shankly, Cilla Black and even The Beatles. At this stage, it slowly began to dawn on them that they had well and truly been completely shafted and taken for a ride by Jon!

They all started to burst out in spontaneous laughter and despite being 'turned over' by Jon, he was congratulated by the crowd on his brilliant scam. Lots of drinks were consumed by us all after this and Joe would often refer to the story in the years to come, of the brilliance of Jonathan's book evidence and what a brilliant day it was!

1998 - meeting the four Jackson girls again

By the late 1990s, both Jonathan and Liam were living and working in London and, as it happens, so was my cousin Sandra Keller (nee Lacey) and her husband Andre. Andre was working at the French Embassy at the time and, via the Embassy, he was given a beautiful, enormous flat in Courtfield Gardens in South Kensington to reside in (very posh indeed - you could have driven a small car around the flat it was that big).

They had two lovely children by then - Brian and Sean - and so whenever Theresa and I were in London with our sons, we would visit them to catch up and see the children and sometimes stop overnight. We had many happy occasions together in that flat over the years they were in London, with Sandra cooking us lovely French food, washed down with equally good French wine!

On one particular occasion, Sandra and I were reminiscing about family and past times, when the subject of our cousins, the Jacksons, arose and we both said, "wouldn't it be great to see them again?" and so the seeds were sown. Now, the only one I had kept in touch with was Moira, but I had not seen the other three sisters since leaving Ireland in the late 1950s and so both Sandra and I agreed to get in touch with Moira and attempt to have a reunion with the Jacksons, before Sandra and Andre had to return to France.

Having contacted Moira, a reunion was arranged for us all to meet up, several weeks later, on a Saturday night at an old pub in Holloway called the Queen Victoria (incidentally, the pub was actually a country cottage retreat for Queen Victoria and Albert between 1830-1860 and is now, or certainly was, a listed building).

Anyway, to get back to my story. On the night in question, some of the girls turned up with their, by now, grown up children. Moira with her girls Lesley and Jacky, Eileen brought Sandra, Yvonne, Jane and Julie. Vera came on her own (I think) and, last but not least, came June and her husband, Charlie Wilson.

Despite not having seen each other since the late 1950s in Dublin, the family ties were still very strong and within a few minutes we picked up where we had left off. Over the next few hours, we had a good old drink as we laughed, chatted, and caught up on each other's lives, whilst a duo called The McNamaras played Irish music, who were very good indeed (I still have their CD which I purchased on the night). It was a great night and a wonderful reunion with all of us experiencing the feelings of warmth, love, and a great sense of family!

Theresa, the pellet and back to June and Charlie's

The night went all too quickly and before we knew it, we were all saying our goodbyes outside the pub, when a shot from a pellet gun was fired from a nearby estate, which hit Theresa in her back would you believe! Luckily, it did not penetrate, as she was wearing a thick winter coat at the time but thank God she was not hurt. With this, we quickly left the area for our safety, and we went with June and Charlie to stay overnight at their house.

Back at their home, June kept trying to feed and ply us with more drink (like most Irish woman do) with all kinds of foods including thick Irish sandwiches with lovely fresh ham, cheese, etc. Having done this, she then offered to cook us egg and bacon, bless her!

It was my first meeting with Charlie Wilson and what a lovely guy he was! An ex-boxer and the fittest man you ever saw, standing about 5ft 7 inches tall, slim-built but strong as an ox and a friendly smile that would knock you out. As for June, she was a lovely kind and generous lady, standing about 5ft 1 inches tall, who looked like the perfect mum or grandma with her glasses and perfectly quaffed hair, combined with her gentle smile.

As both Theresa and Charlie headed for bed, I spent an hour or so just sitting and talking to June about our childhoods in Dublin (it was lovely just reminiscing with her) and during the conversation my Grandfather Kane was mentioned. I told June that I would have loved to have known him but sadly he had died long before I was born. I then went on to say that I had never even seen a picture of him. With this, June immediately sprung up and went to fetch a photograph album down.

There was my Grandad Kane's picture! I found it quite emotional seeing his image for the first time, and June gave her assurance that she would get me a copy done and post it to me. She kept her word and I received the copy a week later.

It was to be many more years before we would all see each other again, due to work commitments and life in general. However, read on, as we did meet up again (see later chapter - The Kane Girls in Leicester).

The trapped willy story

Reader, please don't read on if you are offended by any kind of painful genitalia stories!

One of the most embarrassing things that has ever happened to me, occurred when we had arranged to go out for a drink with my old mate, Dave Williams and his lovely wife Marion (Maz). It was midweek on the night in question, as we headed off towards Peckleton village to drink in the Brown Horse pub. Having had a few sherbets, I needed to have a pee and so made my way outside, across the yard and into the gents toilets.

Once relieved, I quickly pulled my zip up without looking or minding where my 'crown jewels' were situated, and in my haste, I somehow managed to get my foreskin caught completely in the middle of the zip. It was unbelievably painful to say the least! I made my way to a cubicle to have both some privacy and attempt to sort things out. I tried pulling the zip back down only to find it so much more painful that it brought tears to my eyes and (I think I might have said the odd swear word!). I then attempted to pull the zip up which made the situation even worse and caused some bleeding in the vital area.

By now, I had been in the toilet for ten minutes or so and the rest of my party actually started to wonder where I was! Dave came out to the toilet and sheepishly called out my name. Having told him of my situation, he started laughing, as friends do! By now I didn't know whether to laugh or cry myself and so I asked Dave to bring the car up near the toilet and get a coat to cover over me so that I could make my escape, hopefully without too much embarrassment.

I undid my belt and let my jeans down below the belt line in order not to have any pull on the zip and its grip on my vitals! By now it was pissing it down with rain but luckily enough, nobody was about, as I made my way to the car hunched over in pain and looking like 'Quasimodo, the Hunchback of Notre-Dame'.

The trip back home was painful with each turn and bump in the road. Having arrived home, Theresa suggested taking scissors or a sharp razor blade and cutting around my vitals! "no bloody way!" I said, as I started sweating and was completely alarmed at the prospect. I took myself off to our bedroom with a razor blade, whilst all of them were killing themselves laughing downstairs.

Being a tailor, it was no real problem to cut the stitching each side of the zip, to allow the escape of my manhood from the grip of the sharp-toothed fiend! Boy, it felt like bliss, and so I joined them all again downstairs in the lounge and we reflected on the incident, whilst killing ourselves laughing. Incidentally, the next day as I left work, I noticed a piece of paper under the windscreen wipers of my car. It was from Dave, and it read, to my amusement "zip-a-dee-do-dah, zip-a-dee-day!" We still meet up with Dave and Maz regularly and we often reflect and laugh about my misfortune that night.

My 50th birthday and the reunion with the Dublin Kanes

To celebrate my 50th birthday in 1998, I decided that I wanted to return to Ireland with my three boys and my brother Sean, in order to look up family and friends, see the country and generally celebrate this milestone in my life. Prior to going back to Ireland, I had obtained some addresses from my cousin Sandra, of the Kanes, as I particularly wanted to see Aunt Frances (nee Armstrong, born 3rd July 1922 and died 20th June 2011) whilst in Dublin.

Aunt Frances had married my Dad's younger brother, Uncle Gerry (born 8th January 1920, died 13th March 1978). They had eleven children together - Willie, Geraldine, Helen, Linda (the queer one), Gerry, Pat, Trevor, Steph, Olivia, Jackie and Marcella – phew, I think that's all of them!

Uncle Gerry and Aunt Frances's wedding on 1st August 1943. My Dad is on the left looking like a very smart 'Charlie Chaplin', whilst standing next to the very handsome newlywed couple. The couple on the right are Aunt Frances' sister and brother, Doris and William Armstrong.

Anyway, back to my story! We had made arrangements to meet the Kanes at a pub called The Bayside in Raheny on the night we arrived. I decided to take my car over to Ireland, as I wanted to get about and visit as many of my old haunts as possible. The overnight ferry journey from Holyhead to Dublin was mainly uneventful and having arrived in Dublin, I had arranged to see my cousin Joe Boy at his home. Having kindly given us breakfast, he asked if we would like a short sleep to recover from the journey. As we were all sleep mad, we quickly accepted his offer and slept soundly for the next four hours.

Following the kip, we thanked Joe Boy and Pauline for their hospitality and headed into Dublin to find our cheap accommodation in D'Olier Street at a hostel named Ashfield House (we called it 'The Cells' as it resembled a prison).

That night, we took a taxi ride over to the Bayside Pub. The boys and I were a little apprehensive about meeting the Kanes, as we were unsure of the reception we would receive. The first five minutes were a little bit tense, as both parties sized each other up.

However, we need not have worried, as after a few gulps of Guinness we talked as if we had known each other all of our lives.

We had a right old session with everyone singing the ballads and rebel songs. Aunt Frances even sang a tune on her own, bless her. We caught up with family news in Ireland and made links with everyone as to who they were married to and how many children they had. At the end of the night, everyone was well oiled, and the feelings of family and belonging was very evident and special, as everyone kissed and hugged each other warmly!

I really took to my cousin Trevor, and I felt that from our very first meeting, we were going to have a special relationship. This proved to be true, as our friendship and closeness has grown over the past 25 years. As we were heading off for Galway and Connemara the next day, we arranged to meet up with the family upon returning to Dublin the following Saturday, in Temple Bar, before catching the ferry back to England.

Having mentioned that we were going to Connemara the next day, Trevor Kane said that he would "see us on the road" as he would be going to Galway himself the next day. We took this with a pinch of salt and thought no more of it. We all woke with a very large hangover the next morning and following a late breakfast, headed off for Connemara.

The journey was largely uneventful until we got near to Galway. Someone said that they needed the toilet and so I spotted a small shop on the other side of the road and decided to pull over. Having just pulled into the car park another car pulled up beside us, with the owner sounding his horn and waving to us. We couldn't believe our eyes….it was Trevor Kane!

We were delighted to see him again so soon and began to hug and embrace him. He informed us that he had been keeping his eyes out for us all day and, upon leaving Galway to return to Dublin, he had spotted us heading in the opposite direction and pulling into the shop. We were all amazed as the odds on this happening were unbelievably high. I am convinced this could only happen in Ireland as it is a magical place!

The awful smell

Having completed a tour of the west coast in which we visited Galway, Westport in Connemara and ended up visiting our lovely friends Derry and Mick Flynn in Donegal. They used to live in Leicester and both of their sons, John and Andy, had gone to the same school as my boys and been close friends. However, they now lived in Fanad, a tiny village north of Letterkenny in Donegal. We stopped with them for a couple of nights, and it was lovely to catch up with old friends.

Sean, the boys and I, with the beautiful Donegal scenery behind us

However, on the second night, we asked if we could go for a pint to the nearest pub. Derry and Mick advised that we should wait until at least 10pm before going out to the pub, as nobody would be in until then, as most of the community were farmers and it was normal for them to go out between 10-11pm when they had finished their work on the farm. We thought this was a bit over the top and suggested that we could go at 8.30pm if that was ok with them. Reluctantly, they agreed and having arrived at the pub, sure enough, we found the place to be empty apart from us.

Over the next couple of hours, we drank many lovely pints of Guinness with Derry showing the way, by keeping up with us on pints. Derry herself is a lovely, kind, yet formidable woman, standing only 4 foot 8 inches tall, nevertheless she was determined to drink us under the table as she stated that she would show us how "the Irish drink!" Between 11 and 12pm the place began to fill up and by 1am the place was buzzing and I think we left the premises at around 2am.

When we arrived back at their house most of the party naturally made a dash for the toilet, including Liam and Derry. I started speaking to Mick for a while outside before moving back into the house. As I walked in, I was met with the most unbelievable pungent smell you could ever imagine. I went mad at Liam again, as he was always farting and creating all kinds of unnatural smells. I went straight to his bedroom (which was just opposite the toilet) to check if it was him.

As he was not present, I began to shout madly at Jonathan and Jamie that our "bloody Liam was showing our family up" and making me feel ashamed! Just then the toilet door opened, and I expected to see Liam, however, it turned out to be Derry who was very unsteady on her feet and had the largest contented, yet pissed smile on her face that you have ever seen as she passed us by! Liam then came in from the lounge, innocently trying to find out what all the noise was about and found us all in a heap, crying with laughter and when told the story, he started laughing himself. It was yet another great night on our tour and the craic was indeed ninety!

Liam & the Derry air exposure

Before I get back to the story and our return to Dublin, I would just like to tell a funny story about Liam and Derry. Liam was about 15 years of age and would visit Derry's home regularly when they lived in Leicester, to see his mate John (aka Corky). When visiting, he would generally knock and enter as did Derry's boys whenever they came to our house.

On this occasion, Liam knocked and entered as usual, and as he went into the lounge to see the boys, he was confronted with the sight of Derry completely naked bending over the video player, apparently to eject a videotape! According to Liam, it was a sight to behold! Derry (bless her) then turned to Liam without batting an eye lid or blushing and stated that "you have seen the worst and everything from now on is a bonus!"

To this day, Liam's mates still love the banter and joke about the incident as Derry, knowing that Liam was coming around, had been waiting and watching for the opportunity to show off her vital assets! We still laugh about it as a family and Liam has never really got over the trauma of it.

The 'Leaving' and Liam takes another pounding

The following morning, we headed back to Dublin in order to meet and say goodbye to the Kanes before catching the boat back to England. We met up with the Kanes at lunch time in a pub called Oliver St. Johns Gogarty's in Temple Bar. The place was heaving, even though it was early and as we walked in, we saw all of the Kane family waiting for us.

We spent the next four hours or so drinking and having a great time with our new-found, brilliant cousins. I had to go steady on the drink, as I had to drive everyone back to the port to catch the ferry, nevertheless, I still sunk a good few pints. I took to all my cousins instantly from our first meeting at the Bayside Pub, however, Trevor, in particular struck me as someone special and we seemed to have the same sense of humour and outlook and values in life, and I felt like he was more of a brother than a cousin.

Anyway, the few hours passed way too fast and before we knew it, it was time to leave. I am not exaggerating but as we stood up to say our goodbyes, everyone was in floods of tears, as the feelings of family and love was very prevalent in the room. We all hugged and kissed and promised to keep in touch and I invited them all to come and see me in Leicester whenever they could manage it.

As we walked down the road to the car and turned to wave goodbye, we could see them all outside, waving whilst wiping their eyes at the same time. It was such a powerful feeling of love for our family that we were also wiping our own tears at the thought of leaving them. Back in the car we reflected on the occasion, and all agreed the meeting with the family had been a very special occasion and one that we were unlikely to ever forget.

As we drove to the Dublin ferry port, initially in silence, Liam began, as usual, to annoy everyone, particularly his brothers, who were sitting each side of him in the back seat and by the time we reached the port, I too had had enough! As we pulled up to join the queue of cars waiting to catch the boat, Liam started to annoy me by putting his finger in my ear.

That was the straw that broke the camel's back! With this, I quickly undid my seatbelt, got out of the car, opened the back door and began to give Liam a good clattering. Everyone else in the car also thought it was a great idea and they also began to pulverise Liam. Sean even leant into the back from the front seat to add to the punching! Despite the rain of fists coming down on Liam, he continued to laugh at his predicament whilst all the people in the cars behind us looked completely astonished and bewildered at what they were witnessing from the gang of hooligans in front of them. Nevertheless, we all felt much better for having got it out of our systems by giving Liam a good pulverising!

The Kane girls in Leicester and the Jacksons turn up!

A few weeks after our wonderful trip to Ireland, several of the Kane girls including, Olivia, Jackie, Stephanie and Geraldine decided to come to Leicester and stop with us for a few days. Theresa and I were delighted at the prospect of seeing them and having spoken to Olivia by phone, she informed me that Vera and June Jackson might possibly get up to Leicester at the same time, as they were aware of the girls visit and would also like to meet me again, as they had not seen me since I was a child in Dublin (it transpired that the Jacksons had always kept in touch with my Uncle Gerry and Aunt Frances during their trips back to Ireland, usually to visit their mother Tessie's grave).

Having spent a few days drinking and having a great time with girls, we received a call from Vera Jackson saying that they were on their way up to visit us in Leicester. A large car pulled up at the house during the afternoon and I watched with anticipation to see what my long-lost cousins would look like after all these years.

However, I was amazed and astonished at the sight of the driver getting out first, with a very large smile on his face. He was a giant of a man, standing approximately 6 ft 6 inches tall and weighing twenty stone or more! It turned out that this was Brian Higgs (Vera's Jacksons husband). He was quickly followed by Vera, June and her lovely husband, Charlie.

Once again, there was a lovely feeling of family and love for each other as we all kissed and hugged. Theresa naturally fed everyone (what a woman) and following this, we headed to the Winstanley pub for a good drink. We had a great night catching up on all the family and reminiscing about old times in Dublin and London. They all stopped for the night and there were bodies everywhere, but it didn't matter as we were all well-oiled and how Brian managed to fit into our relatively small bed, I will never know!

Before leaving the next morning, Vera informed us that it was going to be Brian's birthday later in the year and invited us and the Dublin crew to attend. We were naturally delighted to get the invite so that the Kanes, Jacksons and Caseys could be together again in force.

Kane boys in Leicester

It was not long after this that the Dublin Kane boys turned up in Leicester to stop for a few days. They were all interested in history and so I took them on daily tours of the city, including the Jewry Wall roman site, the 15th century town hall and museum, and both the New Walk and Newark museums. This was done in between popping into most of the city pubs for liquid refreshments and usually finishing off at the famous Winstanley pub in the evening. Jamie joined us for a few jars most evenings and it was great to have all the Kane boys together.

At this stage of my life, my brother Frank had not spoken to me for years, nevertheless, I wanted him to have the opportunity to meet the boys as he had not seen them since his childhood and so I arranged for them to meet Frank and his family at Molly Malone's pub in town, whilst I waited at another pub across the road as they got together.

After a lengthy chat with Frank, in which they caught up on each other's lives, Trevor mentioned the lack of communication between Frank and myself and how sad it was to see us apart. Trevor (with the best intentions) went on to encourage Frank to take the plunge and get back in touch with me.

However, despite Trevor's best efforts to encourage Frank to start the ball rolling between us again, and maybe us all spending time together whilst the Dublin Kanes where in Leicester, Frank sadly declined the suggestion and wouldn't budge. It was to be many more years later that we did eventually get together again (however, that's yet another story!).

The few days that they were here went all too quickly and before we knew it, it was time for them to leave. Regardless, the craic had been fantastic, and we had a great time as usual and thank goodness there was to be many more times that we would be together again over the next few years.

Dressing up in the New Walk Museum, Leicester. Left to right: Trevor, Pat, myself and the big gentle giant, David Bridgette.

Brian Higgs 60th birthday; Meeting of the Jacksons, Caseys and Kanes again!

Brian's 60th birthday party was held in a hall somewhere near Luton (can't remember the actual venue). All of the Dublin Kanes said they would attend and so we had arranged to stay with them at the same hotel in Luton town centre. All three of my sons came down for the do with us and brought their respective girlfriends too.

During the afternoon before the party, we all went on the lash with the Dublin Kanes and stayed on it from lunch time until closing time at the end of the party. The craic between us all was fantastic with everyone laughing and joking whilst catching up and talking about our reunion on the trip to Dublin and the subsequent visit of the Kane girls to Leicester and life in general. By this time, I had got to know each individual Kane more and had realised that cousin Pat was one of the funniest men you could ever meet. My lovely cousin Pat stands about 5ft 6 inches tall and is of slim-build with a moustache and has the cheekiest grin you have ever seen.

Throughout the day, Pat was telling us jokes and recalling funny incidents he had been involved in over the years, especially when he was in the navy with his brother Willie, and they were based together in Cobh, County Cork at the Haulbowline Naval Base. Pat was very well known on the base, not least for being the only man who ordered the Beano comic to be delivered each week and he was always seen with it tucked into his back pocket as he carried out his duties. His brother Trevor told us that Pat clung to the Beano like mad and added that "woe betide anyone who tried to take it from him or even tried to borrow it".

Pat Kane - guard duty and the vicar

One such story Pat told us, was when his brother Willie was on night guard duty and Pat had returned from a night out in Cobh, after having a good drink with some of his shipmates. Apparently, as they approached the base, Willie called out "who goes there?" as protocol demands in the forces. Upon hearing this Pat replied, "it's your own feckin brother Pat, for God's sake!"

Once again Willie asked who goes there, only for Pat to approach him pointing to his face stating "don't you recognise your own brother?" Willie apparently told him that he would be on a charge if he didn't provide both his rank and number. Pat was by then in a rage and told Willie in no uncertain terms his rank and number whilst adding like a child that he was "going to tell his mammy about this!" That's Pat for you!

Incidentally whilst Pat was telling us these stories, a vicar came into the pub to have a pint and read his paper and he sat down next to us. The vicar ordered a plate of chips and began to read the paper. At this point, Pat seemed to lose interest in us and became engrossed in the vicar, his paper and most of all his plate of chips. As the vicar tucked into his chips whilst reading his paper, Pat began reading the headlines on the front page. The vicar noticed this and peered over the top of his paper as if to ask what he was doing.

Pat engaged him immediately and the two of them soon began discussing world events as well as inquiring where each other came from and how they ended up in each other's company. During the discussion, Pat began to take chips off his plate very nonchalantly, whilst carrying on with the conversation. You could see by the vicar's face that he was shocked but was too embarrassed to say anything.

As the vicar went to take a chip off his own plate, Pat tapped his hand as if to say "naughty boy". By this time the vicar understood Pat's humour and was laughing at Pat and his cheekiness and by the time we all left the pub the two of them had become the best of pals.

After having a bite to eat ourselves and having consumed a lot of alcohol during the afternoon, we were looking forward to seeing the Caseys / Jacksons as we boarded the mini-bus to go to the party in high spirits.

The party itself was fantastic, with all the family in top form whilst drinking and catching up on each other's lives. There was a real sense of belonging to family in the hall, as we all danced and laughed with each other. It was also an opportunity to get to know some of my cousins again after so many years. One in particular was my lovely cousin Eileen, who I took to straight away as she was so kind, loving and gentle. She was about 5 ft 3 inches tall, with slim build and blond curly hair and she always seemed to have a permanent smile on her face which would light up any room. Apart from this, I loved her children Sandra, Terry, Julie, Yvonne and last but not least, my favourite, Jane.

Over the following years we would regularly keep in contact with Eileen and her kids and, in 2014, Theresa and I would go to visit Jane and her lovely husband Nick, down under in New Zealand were they now lived (I will go back to this later - see Singapore New Zealand 2014). At the end of Brian's party bash, he made a lovely speech about his 60 years of life, his family and extended family and how lovely it was for us all to get together again. Despite his huge frame he was a real softy inside and he began to cry as he continued with his speech.

All of us were in bits following his speech and as I said previously, there was a real sense of love, family and belonging in the room. We all hugged and kissed at the end of the night and promised to keep in touch and it concluded a fabulous night and reunion of family as we headed towards the bus to take us back to our accommodation.

Pat Kane the flight attendant

However, that was not the end of the night exactly, as once onto the bus, cousin Pat pretended to be a flight attendant preparing for a flight by counting each of the passengers as he went down the bus touching each person's head as if to indicate the count. He then went to each of the overhead compartments and opened and shut each of them as if to convey they were safe and secure for the flight to take off! Pat finished off his act, by pointing out the escape exits on the bus in case of an emergency, indicating each exit with his hands just like a real flight attendant would do on a plane before it took off - we were all pissing ourselves laughing. It was bloody hilarious!

As the flight, sorry, bus took off, we all began singing at the top of our voices, some popular Irish songs for the remainder of the journey back to our accommodation, with Pat taking control of proceedings by standing in the middle aisle of the bus conducting his audience whilst singing along himself - it was both joyous and infectious!

What a great night it was and what a fabulous family I have!

Meeting of the clans at Brian's 60th. That's Brian towering above myself in the white shirt on the left of the picture.

Our 30th anniversary in Dublin

In 2001, Theresa and I decided to go to Dublin to celebrate our 30th anniversary with many of the direct family coming over from the UK to celebrate too. Unbeknownst to Theresa, I had decided to retake our wedding vows again in Dublin and also arranged for the three boys to come to Dublin early to surprise her at the ceremony, which was to be conducted by a very dear friend and priest, Father Pat Costello, at the Blessed Sacrament Church in Bachelor's Walk, just off O'Connell Street.

We knew Father Pat from his time when he was a priest at the Blessed Sacrament Church in Leicester and we have always kept in touch.

On the Thursday, I took her to the church to meet Father Pat and informed Theresa that we would be retaking our vows. Father Pat told us that the ceremony was to be held in one of the side rooms of the church. As Father Pat led us through, Theresa saw, to her amazement, the boys standing in a row waiting for us, and the look on her face was priceless!

Father Pat, Theresa and I – look at the shock on Theresa's face, seeing the boys!

Father Pat attempted to carry out the ceremony but by then, Theresa was reduced to a blubbing wreck, and she could not utter a single word due to her continuous crying, as we all hugged and kissed each other (**she never did say I do and reflecting on this, I can't help but wonder why!**). However, it was a very emotional ceremony with Father Pat giving us the blessing and it was all made very special by having both Father Pat and our lovely boys there.

My cousin Trevor Kane and his wife, Gerradine were also due to attend but never turned up, and I later found out they had been sitting in the church all the time, as the ceremony was carried out in a private room adjacent to the church, unbeknown to them!

On the Saturday night, the Kanes and Kearneys had organsised a party for us at Shelbourne football club to celebrate our 30th Anniversary.

Theresa's brother, Barry came over for the bash along, with Kate and Joe, Tammy and Ben and Kelvin, who also flew over for the celebration and the boys and their girlfriends, who were already here. It was a great night with everyone celebrating in the Irish way and all sides of our families getting to know each other over a few beers with Irish music playing all night. The feelings of love and having all sides of the families with us, made it fantastic night and it was yet another memorable night to add to our ever-growing collection.

Footnote: Moving forward to April 4th 2009, Jonathan married Lilian (Nee Thomson) in his village of Old Basing and he wanted Father Pat to conduct the ceremony. Once again, Father Pat stepped up to the mark by flying over from Ireland and carrying out a joint ceremony with the local vicar - what a great human being and priest he is! The wedding itself was fantastic, but that's a story for another time!

2002 - Ian Parkinson tries to join the Kane family

Jamie married Claire Brown in 2002 and the majority of the Dublin Kanes came over for the wedding and what a great and joyous occasion it was. Now, I could write a separate book about each of my sons' weddings as they were all amazing but that's for another time!

However, I have to put in this book, the story about Ian wanting to become an honorary member of the Kane Family and I hope my following description of the event does it justice, as it was so bloody hilarious! However, it could be a case of you had to be there to get it!

The following day after Jamie's wedding, we had arranged for the Dublin Kane clan to eat at the Winstanley (Winno) pub. In those days, the Winno didn't do food, but the landlady kindly obliged us by putting on a two course Sunday lunch, as a thank you to the Kanes for making the effort to attend the wedding. Anyway, the whole crowd of us carried on drinking, as we had done the previous day at the wedding, and the laughter and the craic was indeed mighty throughout the day and evening.

After finishing our food, we all continued to mingle, and Ian approached Linda Kane's husband, the big man himself Dave Bridgette (the big soft teddy bear). Ian apparently asked him how he got on with his in-laws, as they always seemed to be very close and have a great time in each other's company, to which Dave replied that he loved them all and went on to verbally compliment the Kane family as a whole but added cautiously "that I am still only their brother-in-law".

With this, the cogs were turning in Ian's head and he plucked up the courage to ask Dave if he thought that there was any chance that he could become a member of the Kane family and went on to ask Dave if he would "put the word in for him?"

Dave started killing himself laughing and replied in his deep Dublin accent as he walked away from Ian, "ah you must be joking, don't feckin' ask me, I can't get in myself, and I have been trying for years!"

Ian and the Trial by Jury

By now some of the family who overheard this conversation, started to become involved in Ian's request to join the family and before long the word had spread like wildfire amongst the Kane clan, with some of them backing his simple request whilst others were shouting for his blood! At this stage, Trevor and Pat had become involved and suggested a family trial of Ian, in the hope of getting a decisional balance as to whether he was in or out of the family!

A table and chair were placed in the middle of the room and Ian was summoned to appear in front of the Kane jury, with Trevor and Pat as judges. Poor Ian, he was now bombarded with questions from the judges and jury and also from each quarter of the room by other family members including myself.

Questions included: what can you bring to the family that we haven't already got? What if the family needed money - could you help? With money being mentioned, my ears pricked up and I got my two-penny's worth in stating that although he was my best friend, Ian could be "mean with money at times!"

I was only joking when I said it, as Ian is a very generous man with his money (most of the time anyway!), however, it caused a riot and pandemonium broke out with Jacky and Linda stating that they "didn't want him in the family and if he is in, then we are out", whilst Gerradine, Pat, Big Dave and Trevor were in all favour! Most of the others basically just sat on the fence as they were unsure as to whether they wanted him or not! Bless him! Ian was bewildered by the whole of the family reaction and could not defend himself one way or another as he was speechless with the onslaught.

The whole of the room was going mad at this stage with some of them in groups pissing themselves laughing at Ian's predicament and others in couples discussing the situation as if Ian's life depended on the outcome!

Ian's final test and continued debate

At this stage, it was suggested that Ian could try the Beer Mat Flipping Test as a last resort. I told Ian that having been in pubs all our lives the Kanes were experts at this and so it was expected that he would be able to flip at least five beer mats on the trot to pass the test and become an honorary Kane. To give Ian credit, I think he flipped two out of the five as everyone waited with bated breath. A large cheer went up as the last one was flipped and signalled his failure! Some were very happy with this and others in the family felt sorry for him, but as usual, Ian took it all in good fun with a big smile on his face.

The uproar and debate continued throughout the day with people discussing it in toilets (both male and female), around their tables and whilst having fags outside the premises. Some were laughing about it, and some were speaking about it seriously! It was very, very funny! Even some locals who could hear it all from the lounge area became involved as they knew me and kept enquiring if Ian had got in or not. It all resulted in Ian not being granted his wish to join as there was no consensus of opinion in his favour from the family.

Ian took it all in his stride (even though he still says that I stabbed him in the back on the day) as he knew them all by now and loved their Irish sense of humour and attitude to life. He still talks about the incident to this day, whenever we reflect on the Kanes visits over the years.

However, I don't want the reader to think that it was all serious as it wasn't. It was just wonderful Irish humour and good-hearted banter and craic from my lovely family and friends. The Kane family all love Ian, even though he didn't make it into the family. It was a great laugh and yet another great memory!

By the time we left at closing time, the whole pub knew all about it as they could hear our laughter, debates and overall uproar throughout the day. The pub itself had come alive with the Kane clan in it and at the end of the night, the landlady thanked us all for a very entertaining day and said that the Dublin crew were welcome back anytime.

This was not too surprising to hear, as the pub started to run out of beer as the day progressed and it's no bloody wonder really as the Kanes had been drinking in the Winno every day since they had arrived the previous Thursday and the landlady's takings over those few days must have been astronomical!

2003 - My Ford brothers and Brian and Nigel Clough

Over the years I have enjoyed the company of my brother-in-laws, 'the Weakling Brothers', Barry, Kelvin (old bean), Trevor and Joe O'Flynn and periodically, we would go abroad together as a collective group, calling the trips "the Jolly Boy's outings." This particular time, we were heading for Amsterdam in Holland and Joe also brought along Tammy's partner, Ben. Having arrived at East Midlands airport early in the morning, the boys wanted to head for the bar after checking in for our flight and so I took a stroll around the complex as it was a bit too early for me.

To my surprise, I spotted both Brian Clough and his son, Nigel, collecting for Children In Need at each end of the concourse. I couldn't believe it! Mr Clough was a hero of mine for what he had achieved at Nottingham Forrest Football Club on a shoestring and so I felt a bit overawed at meeting him. Nevertheless, I took courage and approached him, placing a few bob in his collection tin without saying a word to him. He replied in his strong Northern accent "thank you, young man" and smiled at me, as I turned and walked away.

I was mad at myself for not actually speaking to him and asking him about his life in football. Moreover, I would have loved to have had my picture taken with him, but I had no mobile phone in those days, and I was not carrying a camera at the time. However, such is life, and it was nevertheless an honour to have met him, albeit briefly.

Rugby world cup with weed and cake

Having arrived in Amsterdam, we went on the town for a few drinks and a meal before eventually going back fairly early to our hotel for a night cap, as we wanted to get up early in the morning to watch England play Australia in the Rugby World Cup. The next morning, we were straight on the beer as we watched the exciting game with Jonny Wilkinson scoring in the final seconds with his historical last-minute drop-kick over the posts to win 20-17.

England were also the first European country to win the Rugby World Cup and so we had watched history being made. What a result! We were all going mad with excitement and the rest of the day was open for celebrations.

Dermot the art critic!

We caught a cab into the city as, before hitting the booze, the boys wanted to visit the Ann Frank Museum and the Van Gogh Museum. However, the queue for Ann Franks was too long and so we headed to the Van Gogh Museum. It was not the best to be honest and I did my best to pretend to have some understanding of art by doing my best impression of the television artistic historian, nun Sister Wendy!

Kelvin's observations

That night we went to the red-light district to see for ourselves if all that we heard about the place was true. Sure enough, there were women in every window scantily dressed whilst doing strange poses, it was unbelievable! Kelvin then made a statement which had us all killing ourselves with laughter as he observed that most of the girls in the windows were actually men!

When asked how he came to this conclusion he replied that he had observed each person closely and had noted that most of them had very large 'Adams apples' which was proof that they were in fact nearly all men!

Kelvin had obviously not been looking at the same assets that we had been looking at and for some time afterwards, we continued to piss ourselves laughing at his statement and bizarre observations.

High on the must-see sights for the boys was a visit to one of Amsterdam's coffee shops, to sample the semi-legal weed and so the following afternoon we headed towards the nearest one.

On the way, my brother-in-law Kelvin suddenly went missing (as he does everywhere he goes). Joe was the first to notice that Kelvin was talking to a total stranger and walking away with him. He alerted us and we quickly caught up with them only to find that the stranger was trying to sell Kelvin a range of every kind of drug known to man! Having dismissed the man, we asked Kelvin why he was talking and walking away with the man, to which he replied, I couldn't understand what he was saying and so I followed him to find out what he wanted!

Following this, we found a coffee shop and entered to sample the delights. I am anti-drug myself and as an ex-forensic mental health nurse I had seen the damage first-hand that these drugs can have on people's lives. I had never ever taken a drug in my life but felt compelled to try it to see the effects and the appeal to regular users. I reluctantly tried a very small bit of hash cake, whilst the others all smoked the biggest spliffs they could possibly purchase.

Initially, there was little effect, however, within a short time we were all laughing and giggling. Trevor and Kelvin both had their fill of cake and joints, and the gear must have been strong as within half an hour Baz and Ben were sitting opposite each other on a table, staring constantly into each other eyes in a catatonic, and yet, loving state! This constant staring continued for a couple of hours before Baz showed some form of life by crying out "help me" several times.

Kelvin was on fire during the whole trip and couldn't get enough of the substance and my overall enduring memory of the trip is one of Kelvin in the coffee shop, smoking the biggest joint on one side of his mouth, whilst smiling, laughing and trying to shove a very large piece of hash-cake in the other side of his mouth!

Eventually the drugs wore off and we headed back to the hotel, where we stayed on the beer all night and what craic we had as Kelvin held court, telling jokes with us all killing ourselves laughing under the lasting effects of weed and drink.

The next morning before we flew back, I remember that as we had our breakfast, we saw Trevor lurking in the garden bushes of the hotel looking decidedly ill whilst vomiting - all this whilst we all tucked into our hearty breakfasts while giving him a cheery smile and wave from our window as we did so (it's a man's thing you know!).

What a great time we all had and it was one of the funniest trips I have ever been on with all of us laughing, from the very first day we left the UK until the day we returned.

Left to right: Joe O'Flynn with "The Weakling Brothers", Barry, Kelvin (old bean) and Trevor. Picture taken at Liam and Donna's wedding!

Prague and my boys turn up

A couple of years later, there was yet another 'Jolly boys outing' arranged this time to go to Prague with the usual crew namely the 'Weakling Brothers' and Joe O' Flynn. It was late February when we flew out and I remember clearly that it was bloody freezing as we arrived in the city but nevertheless our spirits were high. Over the five days in the city, we visited Prague Castle which, according to the Guinness book of records, is the largest continuous castle complex in the world, with an area of over 70,000m^2. The castle itself was built in the 9th century and it commands a fantastic view of the city from its high vantage point and it's a really great place to visit if you get the chance.

Another interesting site to visit is St. Cyril's Church in the city. The church is famous for the WW2 operation called 'Daybreak' in which several Czech parachutists returned to their city to assassinate the SS General Reinhard Heydrick. They successfully ambushed him and shot him point blank on 27th May 1942, however he survived but did eventually die on 4th June from his wounds.

Following the assassination, the parachutists fled to the church and after fourteen days, someone blew the whistle on them, resulting in 700 hundred SS troops surrounding the church and shooting most of them. Eventually those who had survived in the basement of the church were killed when the SS troops flooded the basement and they all drowned.

However, the highlight for me was seeing my two boys Jonathan and Liam who, unbeknown to me, had flown in on the previous day to ourselves. As the Weaking Brothers and I entered the hotel to check in on the day of arrival, I took little or no notice of two people reading papers with their faces hidden behind the papers in the hotel lobby.

It was only when Baz (who knew about the boys coming over to surprise me) said, "look over there Derm" and as I turned to look, I saw them both put down the papers and head towards me with beaming smiles on their faces. It was a complete surprise to me. I was really flabbergasted as they had apparently flown out especially to spend some time with their Dad on his birthday. Now then, how lucky am I to have such wonderful and thoughtful sons who had flown out all that way for just two days. I really am blessed!

Anyway, the boys stopped for the following two days in which we laughed, drank many a pint and enjoyed the company of each other and their uncles whilst naturally taking the piss out of each other as we went along. Yet another great memory!

2005 - America with Trevor and Geradine Kane

On many a visit to my cousin Trevor and his wife Geradine (Gerr) in Dublin, Trevor mentioned several times about his love of Elvis Presley and stated that he always wanted to visit America and see Elvis's home, Graceland. Having mulled this over in my mind, I suggested that all four of us should save up and have a trip together to fulfil Trevor's dream. And so, it was agreed that 2005 would be the year to take the plunge.

We embarked on our three-week adventure on 29th September 2005 and after a non-eventful flight, we landed at Newark airport in New Jersey, where we caught up with Trev and Geradine to await the connecting flight to Birmingham, Alabama. After another three-hour flight, we were all knackered and therefore we all slept soundly for the whole of the flight before we finally arrived in Birmingham at 11pm.

We hired, and consequently, picked up a very large people carrier at the airport and what a beauty it was. Automatic, with all mod cons and every electrical gadget you could imagine at your disposal on the steering wheel, to make your journey more comfortable. It was, as I say, "the dogs bollocks!" I nominated myself to do the driving and Trevor agreed to navigate. The helpful girl at the hire service gave Trevor directions to the hotel where we were to spend our first night (and what a mistake this turned out to be).

Trevor's navigation skills!

Having spent time with Trevor in Ireland over the years, he always arranged everything and appeared to know exactly what he was doing and so I naturally assumed that he could easily carry out the task of navigating. By this time, it was night as we set off, with Trevor looking serious whilst studying the map, as if he was planning the route. Having spotted the first highway sign I asked Trevor should I turn East or West to which he slowly replied "errrmmm, East, I think".

We continued along the road for another half hour with Trevor turning the map sideways, upside down and in every direction possible, whilst not filling me with confidence in his ability to navigate. After another half an hour of turning on and off the highway as instructed by Trevor, it was clear that we were lost. Having been given directions from Trevor, when I asked him why we were heading East when the destination on the map was in the West, he stated that "it's the same thing isn't it?" I couldn't believe that he didn't know his 'North from South' or his head from his arse!" Just to confirm this, Gerr shouted loudly from the back seat "let Theresa navigate as he always gets us lost!"

Trevor was quickly demoted from navigator with an embarrassed look and yet a slight grin on his face, whilst Theresa took over the directions. Within a very short time we arrived at our destination - The Wingate Inn - hip hip hoorah! Now we can get some shut eye, we all thought. Wrong! After waiting another half an hour, the laid-back receptionist finally allocated our rooms. Great we thought, even though the room we had was a smoking room, but hey, it was a room and we could finally get some sleep.

A short time after Theresa and I were snug in bed, the phone rang, and Theresa answered. "Hello, it's Trevor here - we haven't got a room!" Apparently, when Trev and Gerr had got to their room, there were two people already in their bed and were non-too pleased to be woken. The receptionist then gave them the last room left in the hotel. But would you believe it, there was a couple in that room too! By now Trevor and Gerr were very tired and well pissed off and although they didn't want to, they were then taken by a cab to another hotel, and we knew not where!

In the morning we tried to locate my long-lost cousins without any success or help from the receptionist. It took an hour for her to track them down and finally they were located as they arrived by cab. We thought it was 11.30am by this time but then we realised it was a different time zone and so we put our watches back another hour. At least we all had some sleep and with this, we took off excitedly to see Elvis's birthplace in Tupelo, Mississippi, USA!

The drive was without incident, and we took in the countryside before our arrival in Tupelo, Elvis's birthplace. It was a fantastic sight to see the wooden shack they called home that was built by Elvis's father, Vernon. However, I was very surprised to find it was in the middle of a housing estate and this made it look quite surreal - I guess the estate must have been built long after the shack was built, when it stood alone in the countryside. The shack itself was very simple and sparse with little in the way of mod cons, which reflected the poor background that Elvis is said to have come from.

The woman in his house was great and gave us loads of information about his early life, as she knew him personally, via her Dad owning the local petrol station which Elvis used regularly. Trevor was in seventh heaven as he hung on to her every word as she told us what a gentleman and modest man he was back in those days.

We took loads of pictures before we left to look for a hotel for the night. Trevor and I went into a shop to get directions for a decent hotel which we wrote down. But somehow, owing to both of our poor navigating skills, it wasn't to be as we ended up in an entirely different hotel, which wasn't the best but at least it had a bar!

We had something to eat and then in the evening went to a bar that was supposed to have some live music, however it didn't and was just records being played. I remember that there were several strange looking girls doing strange dancing and, to be honest, we got the uneasy feeling that we were watching a scene from the film Deliverance, in which the cast were dancing to 'duelling banjos' if you know what I mean?

Trevor landing in heaven

The next morning, after breakfast, we set off for Memphis and decided to head straight for Elvis's home, Graceland. It was amazing and looked just as you saw it in films and in old footage with Elvis in his prime. Trevor couldn't believe he was actually there. When we arrived, we didn't know what to look at first, but eventually we made our way to the entrance of the house to do the tour.

The house itself was much smaller than I imagined and was quite brash and gaudy in décor. I loved Elvis but was not a fanatic like Trevor. However, I was blown away by each room that we entered, with hundreds of gold, silver and platinum discs on each of the walls and photographs of Elvis receiving awards from heads of state, royalty and also with stars and famous personalities that he had met during his relatively short life.

Later, we saw his private aircraft, with gold taps in his own bathroom, and following this, his huge collection of limousine's and motorbikes, before ending up at his grave. I knew he was a big star but the whole tour made me realise what a giant and groundbreaker he was for rock'n'roll and the music world in general!

Outside Elvis's Graceland with Trevor.

After the breath-taking tour, we booked into the Heartbreak Hotel on Lonely Street would you believe, with Trevor on a high, living his dreams and looking completely overawed by the whole Elvis experience. It was in this hotel that Trevor met an Irish Elvis impersonator named Mick Murphy (not really an Irish name is it?) and the two of them got on like a house on fire as they drank the night away.

Moving forward several years later, Trevor met up with him again back in Ireland at a golf captains day in Julianstown, as Mick was performing that night, and would you believe it, they recognised each other and sat up all night drinking again - isn't it a small world!

That night we went to downtown Memphis and what a sight it was, with great live music in each bar and the motorbikes and Hells Angels racing up and down Beale St. The atmosphere was fantastic as we supped away our beers whilst taking in the wonderful sights and sounds.

The next day we caught the shuttle bus to go to Sun Studios. We took lots of photos of the place, with Trevor and me standing on the actual spot where Elvis stood recording, pretending to sing into the actual mike that he used. It was a great tour around the studios and at the end of it, Trevor and I made separate recordings. Trevor's recording, to be fair, was really good and I don't really want to talk about mine!

Whilst we were packing to move on, Trevor went swiftly back to Graceland yet again, as he was buzzing with excitement and wanted to take some last-minute photographs! We then set off for Nashville and on the way, stopped off at Shiloh. This was a site of a battle in the American civil war and following this, we picked up the Natchez Trace which is an old Indian trail that leads straight to Nashville. We arrived in Nashville about 8pm and Gerr and Theresa made an executive decision to stay in the Holiday Inn, as it was too late to go looking around. I nearly fainted when I saw the price (just joking!).

Missing in action

After freshening up, we went down for something to eat. There was a lady called Dina Carrol singing live in the hotel and what a great voice she had. We spoke at length to her and bought one of her CDs. Later in the evening, the girls were feeling very tired and so they both headed off to bed, with Trevor and I stating that we wouldn't be long ourselves.

However, as we finished our drinks, we were really enjoying ourselves and therefore we didn't want the night to end. Without thinking, we both looked at each other and I said "shall we grab a cab and head downtown to a bar with music" to which Trevor agreed without even a blink.

We got in a cab and asked the driver to take us to the nearest bar with music and so he did. Having spent a couple of hours drinking, we decided to head back to our hotel, as it was now 2am. Once outside, we got into a cab and the driver said, "where to?" Both of us went blank, as neither of us could remember what our hotel was called or indeed could recall the address or location and so we started giggling like two silly teenagers at our stupidity and present predicament, whilst under the influence of the demon drink!

We both attempted to provide some kind of information, whilst clutching at straws, stating that the building was very tall and large with swing doors, lots of rooms, white in colour with lots of people in it etc, which was no bloody use whatsoever to the poor old driver!

Bless him, he had a great sense of humour and started laughing at these two drunken Irishmen in his cab, and to his credit he decided to take us around the local area to see if we could recognise anywhere or shake up our memories. However, as we drove around, I started to remember that it was close to an American football stadium, as I saw the floodlights from the ground prior to us leaving the hotel. The driver knew instantly where it was and took us straight to the hotel and what was even more surprising, he refused to take any money from us, telling us both that it was one of the funniest fares he had ever picked up and we had made his night.

Trevor - like a lamb to the slaughter!

As we pulled up outside the hotel laughing our heads off, we saw Gerr waiting in front of the foyer, with her arms tightly folded, tight-lipped whilst looking decidedly angry and ready to blow. I slid down behind the driver's seat hoping not to be seen, whilst Trevor's demeanour completely changed from being on a high whilst laughing his head off, to a whimpering, frightened wreck! Furthermore, his body language changed as, without saying a word, he got out of the cab with his head down and he became like a meek lamb, with his shoulders dropping and a look on his face that was like that of a naughty boy, having to face up to the consequences to his stern headmaster!

I was still in hiding in the back of the cab as I witnessed the scene and I couldn't help laughing out loud, even though I felt for him, as Gerr ushered him inside and up to their bedroom to face the music with a verbal lashing. However, my laughing was short lived, as when I got to my room, I hadn't got my 'feckin key' and I started to sweat and worry as I knocked on the door many times before Theresa, who kept me waiting, opened the door with a look on her face that would stop any clock…. need I say more!

Next morning (2nd October), Trev was still in the doghouse with Gerr and I was still suffering from a very bad hangover! We couldn't get a room for that night in the same hotel and so we checked out and left the car in the car park and took a cab to downtown Nashville, a great city with nearly every bar having live music. We had a few jars before we took a horse and carriage ride around the city. I've never known a horse fart so much as we took a slow ride around the fabulous city centre. Later, having picked up our car, we booked into a hotel near to Grand Old Opry Village, which we found without any trouble. It appeared that we were getting better at directions! In the evening we went to a great steakhouse, and I remember that, apart from the steak being great, the whole of the floor was covered with empty peanut shells and it crunched as we walked across it.

After seeing the Grand Ole Opry in the music village and doing some shopping, we headed for Pigeon Forge and Dollywood near the base of the Blue Smokey Mountains. On the way, I picked up a hitchhiker (as only I could and I must admit he did look a bit rough). Theresa, Gerr and Trevor all went quiet in the car, as I am sure that they felt that being American he would possibly kill us all. After dropping our guest off, they all gave me a hard time about picking up strangers and the importance of car safety.

Eventually, we arrived in Pigeon Forge and booked into a hotel. The place was buzzing as it was decorated up for the annual harvest festival. We then took a stroll around the town and came across a great country / bluegrass type band playing in a bandstand with fiddles and banjos and traditional instruments.

Whilst they were performing, an elderly couple came onto the stage and started to dance, as you see in films, with the man in hillbilly dungaree's, placing his thumbs behind his shoulders straps whilst doing the 'do-si-do' and dancing with his partner. It was fantastic! They were obviously locals and not just there for tourists to see, as they were shortly joined by other locals who turned up and joined in at will. I could have watched them all night and I was fascinated by the music and the dancing and also the sight of other locals turning up to play in the band, as they reminded me of the pubs back in Ireland and the sessions when anyone could join in.

Later, we decided to look for something to eat and found, to our surprise, that most places didn't sell alcohol and were closed at an early hour. However, we eventually found something to eat and then went to bed early as we were all looking forward to Dollywood the next day. Gerr and I were loving the early nights as we both loved our kip, however Theresa and Trevor thought they had joined AA through lack of alcohol!

Dollywood here we come!

Next morning, we set off to go to Dollywood. We were waiting at the trolley stop for a lengthy period, when we decided to walk to the next stop as it was a boiling hot day, and we were frying just waiting. A young couple joined, as they obviously must have thought we knew what we were doing, (they obviously didn't know us!). We ended up walking all the way in the hot sun to Dollywood and we were all knackered when we arrived. Dollywood was not what I had expected, as it was much less commercial than I had been told and the stalls were mainly selling locally made products, such as handmade instruments, furniture, clothing, locally grown food, which is why Dolly Parton had opened it up in the first place, to support the local community. Fair play to her, I say. Dollywood was great!

We watched several acts including Dolly's uncle's band. Apparently, he co-wrote 'I Will Always Love You' with her. The local food was very tasty. We also went on a train ride with the driver pulling the American style train whistle, with the haunting deep sound which I really loved. Later, we went on a water log-ride, in which Ger got completely soaked to the skin, bless her. Trevor and I bought a couple of cowboy straw hats which we thought would make us blend in with the locals! After an amazing day out, we returned to Pigeon Forge and went to the only restaurant that served beer and wine - it was a great end to the day. Heavenly!

Dermot and the floating Dollar Bills

The next day (4th October), we headed off to explore the Smokey Blue Mountains. We went up to the very highest point - Clingmans Dome - and what great views we had. It was spectacular! Following this, we then headed for the Indian Reservation Cherokee. It was the Cherokee New Year and so a big festival was going on with lots of shops and stalls. So, not missing an opportunity, Gerr and Theresa naturally went shopping in the village where there was a lovely Christmas shop, which Theresa can never resist by the way! With the girls out of the way, Trev and I decided to go for a swim and already having shorts on, went straight to the outside pool at the hotel.

After a relaxing swim, Trevor and I stayed in the pool and started talking about the trip so far and all its highs and lows. It was then that I spotted something floating at the other end of the pool. It looked to me, without having my glasses on, to be a chocolate wrapper in the distance and wondering how it got into the pool, I decided to investigate. As I swam nearer it took on a different form and looked like a wallet - surely not!

Bugger me, it was my wallet! You see, I had forgotten it was in my back pocket of my shorts and, by now, although it was floating, the whole of its contents were completely soaking wet. I started to panic and swear at the thought of Theresa coming back and finding out (as she always does) what had transpired and so Trev and I quickly headed to my bedroom to get the hairdryer to dry the dollar bills before the notes either tore or even disintegrated with the water damage.

There were hundreds of bills scattered all around the room, some being dried with the hairdryer and others placed on the windowsill to dry, whilst others were being patted with towels. Despite this, we couldn't help but laugh at my predicament as you can do very little else. However, all was well, as we managed to dry most of the bills before the girls returned from the shopping trip - but as usual, as Theresa entered the room, she somehow smelt a rat and asked Trevor directly "What has he done now?" How does she know these things?

That evening, we all headed out for a meal and a few drinks. However, Trevor and Theresa were both very shocked when they were informed by the staff that the reservation was alcohol free! Having finished our meals, we went back to our rooms for an early night feeling completely dejected by the lack of alcohol.

The following day, we went back onto the Cherokee reservation where they showed their old crafts and traditions. We then headed for the artificial town of Helen via Tallulah Gorge. The Tallulah Falls were amazing, as the gorge is like everything in America – VERY BIG! It was like a miniature Grand Canyon! Having spent time walking around the gorge, we started out to visit Helen, a completely artificial Bavarian town complete with false snow, would you believe - only in America! Despite being artificial it was quaint and nice to see anyhow.

We awoke to rain on the 6th October, our first day of rain since leaving England. It was raining cats and dogs and so the girls couldn't go around the shops, so we headed for Chattanooga. We paid a visit to the aquarium in Chattanooga, the biggest in the world - once again, only in America. Later we stayed in a hotel that turned out to be the worst of the holiday and apart from Trevor having a thing about a lovely big black southern cook called Ernestine, who couldn't boil eggs, there was little else of interest to report! However, I have to say that having stopped in Chattanooga, we never did see the train or indeed the station!

Trevor's white-knuckle ride and meeting John Kearney

On Friday 7th October, we headed for the city of Atlanta with Trevor at the wheel for the first time and having made a balls-up with his directions earlier in the trip, he sure made up in his driving through Atlanta. Unbeknownst to him, we entered the city for the first time to twelve, yes, twelve lanes of traffic going each way. To Trevor's credit, he appeared to keep calm, even though I thought he was shitting himself as his knuckles went white with his pressure on the steering wheel and sweat appearing on his forehead. However, I have to say, fair play to Trev for getting us there in one piece!

We had booked into Atlanta for three nights, as I wanted to meet up with a cousin of mine on the Kearney side called John, who I had not seen since he was a boy back in Dublin. On Saturday, we met John, who turned out to be a very slim, good looking 6ft 5" tall truck driver, who looked even taller in his Stetson hat, but was a very gentle, kind, and generous man who spoke with a dual Irish/American accent. I took to him straight away and we spoke at length about all aspects of our lives and family both past and present.

He kindly took us all up to Stone Mountain - a plateau mountain rather like Table Mountain in South Africa. The views were spectacular of the surrounding area and the city of Atlanta itself. In the evening, he took us to a great Irish pub where the craic and Guinness was very much to our liking.

Hurricane Katrina - change of plan

The following day, Trevor and Gerr went shopping and this gave us the opportunity to meet John and his lovely children and spend the day with them. We had a great time getting to know them all over a meal and a tour of their lovely city and I felt somewhat sad leaving them, as owing to the distance, we would probably not see them again. It all went too quickly and before we knew it, the time to move on from Atlanta had come. However, during our time in America, Hurricane Katrina had hit the southern states and having planned originally to go to New Orleans, which was a place I always wanted to visit, we were now directed by the travel company to go to New York for our own safety.

On 10th October, we dropped off the hire car at the airport and got ourselves and luggage booked in very quickly, as we were looking forward to our three-day stop in New York. Going through security, Gerr got picked out for further security checks as did I (it happens to me most times when I fly for some reason). However, it was a good job Trev didn't get stopped, as he had bought a penknife in Dollywood and somehow managed to get through security with it - what they would have done if they had found the knife instead, God only knows! After a decent flight, we landed in the 'Big Apple'.

We caught a cab to take us to our hotel, but what a miserable feckin driver we had. He must have won a competition for the most miserable taxi driver in New York! Furthermore, when we arrived at our hotel, we were all very disappointed as this could have won a prize for the smallest rooms in New York (even for two little people like Theresa and I) as you couldn't swing a cat in it. I think we could sum this hotel up as being posh and modern in style but still crap! However, we got freshened up and then went out in the pouring rain to Times Square, which was very bright, busy and wet!

Later, we found an Irish bar and settled in for a few drinks and whilst having a pint, the owner came over to welcome us and asked where we were from. It turned out that he came from the same village as Gerr in Cavan and knew her family and friends - Gerr was delighted as was he. He then wished us well and left our company, however, a short time afterwards his barman came over and informed us that he had left instructions to get us a round of drinks. What a nice gesture – happy days!

The following day, would you believe, it was raining again, we were even issued with rain capes by the hotel but it did eventually stop raining thank goodness. We went on a tour on the hop-on-hop-off bus and got off near Ground Zero. This was a very sobering and very emotional to see and you couldn't help but think of the poor victims who had needlessly lost their lives and how life had changed for the whole world following this. Then we went on a helicopter ride around the Statue of Liberty and the harbour. It was breath-taking, but I was crapping myself as I don't trust helicopters at all. We took the Staten Island ferry across the water and back again which I really enjoyed because at least it was free!

Next day was raining like you have never seen it in your life. We took the bus around uptown but couldn't see anything due to the rain and poor visibility. Gerr decided to get out of the rain and have her hair done whilst Trevor went shopping for clothes and CDs. Theresa and I went to Grand Central Station and upon arrival we were like two drowned rats from the torrential rain.

The station itself was a fantastic sight, with the hustle and bustle of life and all of the different tracks (in total, 69) taking people to all destinations across America, just like you see in the movies and moreover, the architecture of the building itself is out of this world and well worth the visit. Theresa and I had a good old drink as we watched the world go by, in the Grand Central Bar above the concourse, before heading back to our hotel, a little worse for the demon drink. That night we went to see the show, Jersey Boys, as it had just opened on Broadway. It was fantastic! All four of us loved the Four Seasons anyway and were so pleased and privileged to have seen the show before it came to Europe the following year.

It was still raining on the last day of our holiday, when we all went to the Empire State Building but it was zero visibility at the top and the rain was pouring through the top roof with sandbags placed all around the walkway to soak up the constant rain. We walked through Macy's and the girls had a good look around before heading back to our tiny hotel rooms to get ready for the flights back home. A nice non-grumpy taxi driver picked us up at the hotel and took us to the airport.

It had been an amazing holiday and one we shall never forget. Great places visited, great food and drink, great music, great weather overall (apart from New York and Hurricane Katrina) but we kept on laughing regardless. We met some wonderful people and characters, but most of all we loved the company of Trevor and Ger.

My account is only a brief snapshot of the tour and does not really cover all the many laughs and brilliant times we shared. Trevor and I never stopped laughing from the time we left until our return, and I felt so lucky to have such a great cousin. However, all good things must come to an end and having all embraced at the airport, we said our goodbyes and took our respective flights home. Our flight took off at 9pm USA time and we arrived in Birmingham, UK at 8.30am the following morning and were picked up by Theresa's ever-reliable brother, Barry.

2006 - Sardinia and meeting Rocco again by chance

Now then reader, do you remember that earlier in the book I spoke about my old school friend, Rocco Ambrico? Well, to bring you up to date, I had not seen Rocco since my late teens, as he had gone to Australia to play professional football in the late 60s / early 70s. Unfortunately, things did not work out for him regarding a football career and after two years 'down under' he went back to the village that he was born in called Tricarico in the Southern region of Italy, called Basilicata. It was here that Rocco met and married a local girl called Elana and went on to have two children, John Carlo and Stefania.

Theresa and I, as well as Ian and Elaine, fancied seeing the island of Sardinia and as it happens an Italian friend of ours called Maria Fazulo worked with Theresa as a health care assistant in the Royal Infirmary, gave us a contact number of a relative who had accommodation in Sardinia and would lease it out to us if they were not using it themselves.

On the particular day that Theresa booked the trip, I just happened to come home as Theresa was on the phone to the owners of the accommodation. Having agreed the date, Theresa asked the person concerned who to make the cheque out to and the person on the other end of the line answered Ambrico, to which Theresa repeated the spelling Ambrico aloud as she wrote it down.

Upon hearing Theresa saying the name, I asked her if I could speak to the person on the end of the line. Having introduced myself, I asked if she was in anyway related or knew of Rocco Ambrico to which she simply replied "yes, he is my brother-in-law!"

You could have knocked me down with a feather, as I had not seen or heard from Rocco for around 50 years and had I not come home at that precise moment of time and heard the conversation, I would probably never have seen Rocco again. As it turned out, Alison was married to Rocco's younger brother, Bruno, and unbeknownst to both Theresa and Maria for all those years, Maria's husband, the late Mario Fazulo, was Rocco's cousin (once again isn't it a small world and it is unbelievable how luck or fate plays its part in our all our lives).

Following the call, Alison provided Rocco's number in Italy, and we immediately made contact and picked up where we had left off all those years ago. The following year we visited Rocco and his family in his beautiful mountain village of Tricarico. Over the next decade, subsequent visits took place between us both with Rocco coming to visit us in England and us visiting him in Italy.

Tricarico, Italy

Theresa and I love to visit Tricarico, as the locals all take you to their hearts and just to sit drinking in the village square and watch the world go by is such a simple delight. Moreover, there are no tourists at all, and you have the feeling of being away from the rat race and all that goes with the stresses of modern life. It was also fantastic to catch up with Rocco and spend time alone which we did most days at his little allotment not far from where he lived, as following our hard work digging, planting, and tending the land, we would have a few beers and put the world to rights - very simple and happy days!

Rocco is also a real character and told me the story of the newly built Serviceman's Club that opened in his village a few years ago. Rocco apparently wanted to become a member of the club, but as it was only open to ex-servicemen, he decided to tell them that he was ex-navy. When put on the spot as to what branch, he replied, off-the-cuff, 'submarines' and when asked where he served, he replied "all over the world but mainly the Mediterranean!" Italians are very laid back and having only 8-10 members in the club they took his word and proof was not required as they were desperate to swell their numbers and would take anybody.

However, I was personally really embarrassed when he took me into the tiny club on my first visit and introduced me as his old shipmate, Dermot Kane, the submariner! Thank God no-one questioned me as very few in the village speak English and I speak little Italian. However, since then, whenever I text Rocco I always sign off as his old shipmate! Having met Rocco again, I was also reunited with his elder brother Joe and his lovely sister Angela back here in Leicester and over the years we have kept in touch with them periodically and enjoyed several Italian family celebrations in their company.

2007 - China

Growing up in Ireland, the thought of ever seeing other parts of the world was so far removed from reality that it never entered my mind that I would be privileged to visit so many places on this planet as I did later in my life. I can remember distinctly looking at a geography book in junior school and seeing pictures of the Great Wall of China and thinking "wouldn't it be great to actually see this wonder of the world", but then instantly telling myself "don't be stupid, this will never happen!" Anyway, moving forward to 2007, we had saved up for a trip of a lifetime to visit China for three weeks.

On the flight out to China, we became friendly with two other lovely couples namely Jan & Ray Higgins and Peter & Jane Leifer with whom we shared most of our time with whilst in China, and upon returning to the UK, we kept in touch with them and we meet up for a reunion annually. China proved to be mind-blowing for us both with its different cultures, history, smells, language and people.

We were lucky enough to see the huge world-famous site of the Terracotta Warriors with its thousands of warriors guarding their Emperor for time immemorial.

We also took a four-day cruise down the Yangtze River, which was incredible, with its beautiful green scenery and high cliffs on each side of the river. Moreover, as we passed each village we had a glimpse of the hard lives of the people living along the river who, despite their hardships, managed to wave at us as we passed them by. I have to say that the trip was fantastic, apart from our tiny cabins which contained a tiny bed (it was even small for us two little people) and a shower. I am sure you won't be shocked to find out that I somehow managed to flood the cabin on a couple of occasions but that's another story! The cruise ended up with our boat being pulled by natives wearing only loin cloths as they dragged us through the shallow waters of a gorge.

Another highlight was visiting Beijing and the massive Tiananmen Square, with its throngs of people, and Mao Tse Tung's Mausoleum that serves as his resting place since his death in 1976 and his preserved body has been on public display since this period. Following this, we made our way to the Forbidden City, with its history stretching back three millennia and was a totally different world for us to see.

Our tour included visiting several markets that sold any kind of animal that you could think of; the markets even had a stall that sold every kind of animal penises imaginable. What a sight!

Theresa and I on the Great Wall of China – note the wall stretching into the distance.

However, the thing I remember most is the trip to the Great Wall itself and when we arrived on the wall, both Theresa and I started to weep as we were both overcome with emotion at the wondrous sight of this mighty wall, on which you could drive a car along as it was so wide. Moreover, it stretched as far as the eye could see (it was actually 13,171 miles when first built in the Ming Dynasty and it's truly amazing!) For me, it took me straight back to Dublin when I had looked at the wall in the geography book, never thinking for a single moment that I would actually see it.

It was fascinating to learn about the building of the wall and how families would spend their whole lives living near the wall and would build a particular section of the wall (this would include women and children alike) until such time that they died either through old age or indeed being overworked, I suspect. When they did eventually pass away, each member of the family would be buried in the foundations of the wall which apparently was considered to be an honour by their Emperor.

Another fact about this mighty wall which you might not believe but is completely true I can assure you, is that the wall is held together by putting a portion of sticky rice in with each mix of mortar when it was originally built, and according to historians, this was the glue which has made the wall last so long and is still standing for us to see and enjoy today.

Anyway, going back to how Theresa and I felt seeing this amazing sight for the first time, we held each other very close and through our tears of happiness, we thought just how lucky and privileged we were to actually be standing on one of the wonders of the world and it is something that we shall never forget!

2008 - My surprise 60th birthday in Boston

I have always celebrated each decade of my life, as I think that it's important to acknowledge these major milestones in our lives as we reach them. With this in mind, I had decided to go back to Dublin in March 2008 to celebrate my 60th birthday and also see the Saint Patricks Day parade which I hadn't witnessed since my childhood back in Dublin. However, unbeknown to me, Theresa, Jonathan and Lilian had other ideas, namely, to take me on a surprise trip to the United States and see the St. Patricks Day parade in Boston! However, I had already contacted my cousin Trevor Kane in Dublin and asked if we could stop with him and he kindly said "of course" and so the trip was on… or so I thought!

Jonathan asked if Lil and himself could join us to celebrate my birthday and added that he would like to contribute to the trip by using up their air miles to take us to Dublin for very little cost. He also informed us that should we accept his offer, we would have to travel from Heathrow with them, as the air miles were in his name – all part of the ruse! Having agreed to his offer (as we were delighted that they could join us for the trip), we set off from his home several weeks later in a taxi to go to Heathrow Airport.

Now then reader, like most blokes, whenever, I am in a taxi I always ask the driver the same bloody questions; "What time did you start? Have you been busy? What time are you on till?" etc. It's pathetic really but we all do it, don't we boys? Anyway, this taxi driver appeared very ignorant and refused to engage with me and only grunted to my questions and so the remainder of the journey was mainly silent. As we got out of the taxi at the airport, I made reference to his ignorance, telling Jon, Theresa and Lil "what a miserable and ignorant old sod he was" without any of them replying, which I thought was a little odd! Little did I know but the poor taxi driver was aware it was a surprise and chose to keep quiet, rather than reveal the surprise on the way to the airport!

In the terminal, we had something to eat and drink and waited for our flight to commence boarding. At one point I made my way to the electronic flight board to look up our flight and as I started to put my glasses on Theresa apprehended me and asked me to take her to the toilets as she didn't want to get lost (this is normal for Theresa, as she could get lost in a telephone box, I am not kidding!) and so I thought nothing more about it as I escorted her to the loo. A little later, I looked out of the window in the waiting lounge and saw this massive plane and I thought it was very odd as we were only going to Ireland, however, I never gave it any further thought as we would probably have to walk to another part of the airport to catch our flight.

Just then, an announcement came over the speakers making a last call for the Thomson party (the flight was booked In Lil's name, Thomson) to come to the boarding gate as the gate was about to be closed. I was about to say "that's Lilian's name that's been called, what a coincidence" when Theresa grabbed me by the arm and pulled me towards the boarding gate in a panic and as we went through the gate, Theresa whispered out of the side of her mouth to the ticket collector "it's a surprise, he thinks he is going to Ireland." The person replied with a grin, "that's brilliant, but if you don't hurry up that's where you will end up!"

Now then reader, you might think how could I not know what was happening, but, hand-on-heart, I honestly did not have a clue, as when someone is leading on these trips I just sit back, relax and let them lead the way. On the plane, I was in totally shock as they told me where we were heading and it all started to make sense. The taxi driver had not wanted to give the game away, the flight board and Theresa wanting me to take her to the loo. I could only reply in a daze to myself over and over, "I'm going to Boston!"

Once there, Jon recommended that we all stay at the Lennox Hotel, where he had stayed many times, which was quite luxurious but not posh if you know what I mean, and it is probably the most friendly and best hotel we have ever stayed in. The staff were all lovely and the food and service were second to none and we would definitely recommend it, if you're ever in Boston.

We saw all the main sights including the Old State House, the bar from the TV series Cheers, and we visited several lovely restaurants, including the famous Oyster House, and we found this part of America to be very much like England, as the city itself maintains much of its early history when it was founded by the English Puritans who fled from England to pursue religious freedom.

The St. Patricks Day parade took place in South Boston and was amazing, with all the razzamatazz you would expect from the Americans with all manner of floats stretching back for miles. After the parade, we naturally headed for the pubs, which where all packed with young and old alike, many of whom were second, third and fourth generation Irish, who celebrated the day by drinking green lager, specially made for the day to honour St. Patrick and the Irish nation.

Now then, it was whilst we were at the parade that I received a call from Trevor Kane in Ireland. Now bearing in mind that he was in on the surprise, as Jon and Theresa had informed him of the Boston trip, would you believe he asked me outright and without a pause "are you still coming to Ireland Dermot?" Now then, I love him dearly but I was flabbergasted and lost for words as Trevor never ceases to amaze me.

St. Patricks Day in 'Southie' (South Boston)

Anyway, after three brilliant days in Boston we caught the train to spend some time in New York.

Jonathan and Lilian's engagement

Having arrived in New York, Jon had very generously treated his Mam and Dad by booking us into the Astoria Waldorf Hotel. We spent the following three days exploring and seeing the sights of New York, including Central Park and The Dakota building where my Beatle hero, John Lennon, was murdered by Mark Chapman on December 8th 1980. It was whilst we were in Central Park that Jon pulled off another surprise, as he got engaged to Lilian by proposing to her officially in a horse drawn carriage as they were being driven around the park, then off to Tiffany's on 5th Ave to buy the ring. It was a joyous occasion as we celebrated that night, even though Jon struggled to keep his wallet from collapsing after the cost of the ring! We continued our spree with a celebratory meal and then a visit to the Empire State Building at night, which was beautiful. The next day we went to Peter Lugers Steak House in Brooklyn, where Jon and Lil had been before, which was probably one of the best steaks I have ever tasted in my life. It had been a fantastic trip, thanks mainly to Jon and Lil, and another great memory to add to our list and I thank them both for sharing their time and love with us.

2010 - Mayhem on the ski slopes

In late December of 2010, we headed off on a ski trip with Liam, Donna and some of their friends including the Kerr Family members, Chris and Matt and their respective wives Lisa and Beth. This was to be our second attempt at skiing as the first time (where Jon and Lil joined the group) had been a bit of a disaster in Tignes, as we barely managed to ski on the little mounds of earth outside our hotel. Now then, following the flight and a couple of hours drive in the very thick snow, we finally arrived in the idyllic bustling ski resort of Morzine which is in the Alps region of South-East France.

The place was quite magical with the whole town covered in snow and looking like a picture postcard image of the perfect alpine village. We all stopped in a very large lodge which was manned by staff who cooked our meals, took us to locations in their minibus and generally took great care of us.

Over the next few days, both Theresa and I made great progress on the slopes and we felt like we had got the basics covered as by now I had learned how to stop and not crash into fellow skiers as I had done on my previous visit to Tignes. In the evenings it was great, with the whole party getting along supping beers and wine and singing our hearts out on the karaoke. Come New Year's Eve, we had a lovely meal cooked for us and following more karaoke, we celebrated seeing the New Year in with fellow revellers as the snow continued to fall silently outside our lodge whilst everyone hugged and kissed, happily welcoming in the coming year.

Anyway, the time went by very quickly, as you know when you are enjoying yourself, and on the day before we departed back to the UK, we went on the last skiing lesson with our instructor. However, the night prior to this, we had some rain and unbeknown to our instructor or indeed myself, this had caused some areas to have deep ice chambers / gulley's as the rain froze over at the bottom of the mountains. We started out on the trip which involved travelling over quite a distance onto several valleys and mountains and eventually completing a loop which would bring us back to our resort. All went well initially and by now (in my mind anyway), I felt like I was an Olympic skier as I gained more and more confidence with each traverse. However, with pride, there must come a fall and so it proved to be!

Dermot the Olympic skier

There was only fifteen minutes left of my last lesson, when the instructor stopped us on the top of the last mountain and gave us the instruction to get some speed up as we went into this ravine in order to get up the other side as it was so steep. "Leave this to me," I thought and so, like a madman, I took off with great speed thinking I was the best skier on two legs!

Down the ravine I went at breakneck speed, and it felt great, however, as I got nearer the bottom, I saw the thick ice chambers and I thought "oh shit" as I hit the first one and made it over – brilliant. I thought I was over the worst of it (wrong again) as there were lots more to come and as I hit the second one with the tip of my ski's, the skis stopped but I didn't and I went flying through the air (luckily, curling myself into a ball as I did so) before coming back down and hitting the ice snow full-on and then, would you believe, bouncing back into the air for a second time due to my speed. This time I landed and as I did, I felt my shoulder breaking and a lot of pain in the same area (however, I was so lucky not to have broken my back or neck, looking back).

As I lay on the freezing snow, Theresa was first on the scene as she was following me and saw it all. Now would you believe reader, her first thought was not about me, as she later told me, but her first thought was that she would have to drive up the motorway when we were back in the UK, as I was obviously not capable due to my shoulder injury. Bloody marvellous! You can't beat real love, can you?

Anyway, the instructor caught up with us and, using his walkie talkie, he requested the paramedics to attend to me on the mountain. Eventually, they arrived and put my shoulder in a temporary sling and then put me onto the snow skidoo stretcher before making their way back down the mountain. There was no room for Theresa on the skidoo and so she had to go to the back of the skidoo and put her legs akimbo on the edge of the vehicle and cling on for dear life as the skidoo swiftly made its way down from the mountain to the nearest emergency centre. Theresa was shitting herself and I have to say that the sight of her clinging on for dear life at the back made me laugh out loud, despite my pain. In the emergency centre, the first question the staff asked was "how are you going to pay for this?" and proceeded to ask for credit card and insurance details.

Having given the details, I was then given pain killers and a proper supporting sling, which eased my pain somewhat.

At the emergency centre, the staff had to cut off both my wedding and claddagh ring, as by now my arm and fingers had swollen up very badly. Skipping forward, regarding my rings being cut off, I had put them aside after returning home with the intention of taking them to a jewellers to have them repaired, when sadly both of these rings were stolen when burglars broke in whilst we were away in London celebrating with Jonathan, Liam and their respective families.

Liam and his lack of sympathy

The staff at our accommodation picked us up in the minibus and upon arrival, all of our friends gathered around to inspect my damage. At the same time, Liam arrived from the slopes and saw the crowd and also caught a glimpse of someone with a sling on. Thinking that his Mam had been injured, bless him, he ran to the bus, pushing everyone aside in order to get to his Mam. However, seeing me as the injured person he immediately turned to the crowd and informed them in a relieved manner that "it's only my Dad" and then proceeded to make his way into the lodge with his Mam on his arm. Who would have children I ask!

Back in England, I had further scans which revealed that there was more damage from the accident, as, apart from the broken shoulder, I had ripped the muscles and tendons on the back of my shoulder, which meant having physio and two months off work. To cut a long story short, over the next few weeks Theresa became my physio and pushing me to my limits whilst inflicting as much pain as possible and managed to get my arm working again without any long-term effects whatsoever, bless her. However, this was to be the end of my career as an Olympic skier!

Ironically, before I left to go on this trip, my colleague, my line manager and dear friend, Bridie Collins had said in jest "don't go breaking anything you old bugger!"

2011 - Our 40th anniversary

Yet another milestone in our lives was having reached our 40th anniversary having not killed Theresa yet! Joking apart, despite some ups and downs (mostly ups) over the years, we consider ourselves to be so very lucky as we have enjoyed the most wonderful life together.

The boys naturally wanted to celebrate with us and suggested we had a great big party. However, Theresa and I wanted on this occasion just to have the boys and their respective wives to celebrate privately in our own home. The boys said, "leave it to us" and so we did!

The boys informed us that they had arranged a surprise one weekend and gave us instructions that on this specific Saturday, Theresa was to go to church as normal and then join me and the rest of the boys at the Winstanley Pub after church. We had no idea what they had arranged on the night and why their respective wives were not joining us at the pub.

Having had a good few drinks at the Winno, we headed back to our house in anticipation, only to find the kitchen invaded by two female cooks who the boys had hired to cook a slap up meal for us all and serve us in our own home. How lucky are we? What great kids and what a lovely surprise by our lovely family. They are all brilliant!

The night was fantastic, with the beautiful meal being washed down with lots of champagne, wine and beers and all of us chatting, laughing and making the most of this special occasion. As the night progressed, we all sang along to old records from our era with Liam playing air guitar, the girls doing backing singing, whilst Jon, Jamie and I did the main singing and harmonies.

The night went by so fast and by 4am we were all on our last legs, particularly Jonathan, who couldn't even speak and basically went into a catatonic state! Donna and Lil were off their faces too (bless them), which is par for the course and to be perfectly honest we were all a bit worse for wear as the night concluded and we all headed to our beds. This was yet another marvellous occasion in our lives to add to our lifelong memories.

Celebrating with our boys on the night. Left to Right: Liam, Theresa, Jamie, myself and Jon

2011 - Disneyland with the family

Later that year, Theresa and I treated the whole family and flew them all out to help us celebrate our 40th anniversary in Disneyland, Florida, with the focus on our three grandkids at that time; Dylan, Evan and Imogen.

We stopped for the two weeks of the holiday at the most beautiful house in Kissimmee, with its own swimming pool which overlooked a golf course at the back. The kids all naturally loved the pool and spent as much time as possible in it. Dylan actually learnt to swim whilst on holiday thanks to daily lessons from both his uncles, Jon and Liam.

However, we also spent much of our time travelling to and from different locations, particularly Disneyland which was fabulous with its iconic fairy tale castle as you entered the resort. We had breakfast one morning at the resort, with all the major Disney characters present, including Micky Mouse, Donald Duck and Goofy and the kids loved every minute of having their heroes sharing breakfast and the joy on their faces was something I shall always remember. Over the weeks we saw all the major attractions including Sea World, where we were able to feed the fish and manta rays. There was also Animal Kingdom where we went on a safari and saw all the amazing animals you could imagine. It was really fantastic! We also celebrated both Immy's first birthday and Evans third birthday whilst we were there and it was lovely spending so much time with them all.

Theresa and Dylan in space

However, one of the funniest things was going to the space centre, where there was a replica of a spaceship and space control centre. It was just like the real thing! However, Theresa took the whole thing as being real and so we were given instructions by the staff regarding safety and following the command centres instructions to make a successful take off.

With this, we entered the rocket with our space helmets on and as we sat on our seats, Dylan, who was now pale with the thought of what was to happen, asked me nervously "are we really going into space, Grandad?" to which I gave him reassurances that we were not!

However, his looney Grandma was by now totally in control as she listened to the fictitious instructions coming from the control centre and followed their every word to the letter, as she pushed levers, pressed buttons and prepared herself for the take-off. Liam, Jon and I were in stitches with tears rolling down our faces, as we watched her fully concentrating on the task, as the simulator kicked in and the rocket fired its engines and began to rock pretending to take off. Theresa was completely in the moment, with the look of being frightened and yet in control at the same time. All too soon, the 'flight' was over and Theresa finally relaxed and I have to say that despite being a very intelligent woman, there are times when I feel that she is not the full shilling!

A ride in the Everglades

Another fantastic experience was all of us going on a fan-boat ride (you know, the one with the massive fan at the back of the engine which skims you over the water at great speed). It was an amazing thing to do as I had seen this many times on TV but never thought I would actually experience it. The driver took us through the Everglades, explaining the eco-system and showing us all the wildlife as we went along, including alligators. Back on land, the owner produced a small alligator about four foot in length, with its jaws closed with a strong elastic band, to stop it biting anyone and he then gave us all the chance to hold the animal as he informed us of the life cycle of the alligator, which was very informative. The kids loved the whole experience as they never thought they could be so near as to hold and touch such a creature.

On the day of our actual anniversary, we went to a place called the Crab Shack which is famous for its seafood, and it was here that I had to read out a funny poem about getting a dose of crabs, which was followed by the owners giving us an anniversary cake which we shared with all the other customers. It was a great end to a fantastic holiday which cost us a small fortune but nevertheless was worth every penny to have the family with us. However, bearing in mind how young the children were, I recently asked Evan what he remembered of the holiday and what he liked best, only to be told that he loved the coloured breakfast cereal 'Cheerios' only to be found in America at the time. What can I say?

Retirement

Theresa and I both retired on the very same day, the 28th February 2013. We both had separate leaving events with our respective teams and mine was set up by my late dear friend, Bridie Collins. Bless her, Bridie knew me better than myself and so she put on an Irish themed farewell with Irish flags and tricolour buntings all over the room. Moreover, she knew my obsession with boobs and so she got all the female staff to wear costumes with large, printed boobs on the front (it was very funny with no-one taking offence and everyone smiling and laughing at the spectacle).

Retirement picture with myself in the middle looking like a right plonker, dressed up to look like a leprechaun - it was great fun actually. Note the ladies in their Irish big boobs' costumes.

As I walked into the room with everyone clapping and one of my team playing Irish tunes on his mandolin, I was very moved by the whole set-up and the genuine love and affection shown to me by each of my colleagues and being so emotional, tears ran down my cheek as I also realised it was the end of my working life. The send-off was fantastic, and the generosity of my colleagues was overwhelming with cards and gifts galore.

However, as one chapter closes in your life, another one opens, and both Theresa and I were determined to embrace retirement by catching up with friends and relatives and seeing as much of the world as possible whilst living life to the full before our time runs out in this world. And so, with this in mind, we had arranged to go back to Ireland as our first retirement adventure.

Dublin

We arrived in Dublin on 15th March, as I particularly wanted to see the St. Patricks day parade on the 17th, as I had not celebrated St Patrick's Day in Ireland since I was a child. We stopped for the week with Trevor and Gerr in Raheny and on our first night, Trevor suggested that both he and I should pop around to his local pub (The Concorde) for a few jars. Having just retired and feeling fairly flush, Theresa gave me 500 euros to keep in my wallet, whilst reminding me, with a pointed finger, "to be careful not to lose it (I can't think why she reminded me of this as it's not as if I had ever lost anything in the past!).

We headed to the Concorde pub and over the next few hours, whilst chatting away and having the craic with my favourite cousin, we managed to consume a considerable amount of Guinness. At around midnight we made our way back to Trevor's house and went to bed feeling very satisfied with the night's proceedings.

The lost wallet

Following breakfast the next morning, I showered and got dressed for the day and it was then that I noticed that my wallet was missing from my pocket. I went into a sweaty panic as I searched through my coat pockets and all the garments I was wearing the previous night, but to no avail! I sat on the bed going over the previous night and racking my small brain as to where I could have lost the wallet. I then decided to take the bull by the horns and tell Theresa of my stupidity, yet again. Naturally, Theresa took it all in her stride! Trevor and I then took it on ourselves to retrace our route to and from the pub in case I had dropped the wallet on the way, but again without success.

The suspects

We then went into The Concorde and spoke to the landlord who informed me that nothing had been handed in, however speculation began with the landlord informing me of certain characters who frequented the pub but shall remain nameless (I have changed the names just giving other names for example) stating that, "if it was that fecker, Sean who found it you have got no chance of getting it back." He was then joined by a barman who cited a Mick as a "bloody arse hole who would rob anybody." Even the cleaner was called, who could only state that "she wouldn't trust anyone in here." Following this, and with a heavy heart, I headed to the police station and reported my lost wallet and was given a log number by the desk sergeant who told me that he didn't have much hope of me getting it back again!

Later that day, I cancelled my debit and credit cards with my bank whilst Theresa looked on with a face like thunder. The debate about the suspects continued with Trevor and his son Darren, who went through their own list of dodgy characters who frequented the pub whilst I remained in the doghouse for much of the day, feeling very guilty about my stupidity and the loss of the money. However, by the evening and after a few drinks, we were resigned to the fact that the wallet had gone.

However, to my embarrassment, shame and even amazement, the very next morning after I had showered, I put my hand into my suitcase which was lying at the bottom of the wardrobe, to pull out a pair of socks when, lo and behold, the very first thing I put my hand on was the bloody lost wallet! I was absolutely gobsmacked! To this day I don't know how it got there, I can only assume that I was pissed, and put it there for safety. I really can't remember. Nevertheless, feeling so stupid, I headed downstairs to tell the others of my find and not knowing what to say, I knocked on the downstairs door and holding the wallet in my hand and shaking it in the air without saying a word, just to indicate my lost, and now found, treasure. Trevor and Gerr started laughing whilst the air turned blue with Theresa telling me quite rightly with lots of expletives what a real idiot I am.

Later that day, Trevor rang The Concorde pub and told the landlord my story and apologised for any inconvenience I had caused and thanked them all for their input. With my wallet safely back in my pocket Trevor, Theresa and I headed in to see the St. Patricks Day parade, which we witnessed from the Daniel O'Connell statue at the bottom of O'Connell Street. It was fantastic and a big thrill to be there and following a good few drinks to celebrate our saint's day, we made our way back to Trevor's home where we saw ourselves briefly on TV with shots of us watching the parade on the late night news.

Northern Ireland

After a lovely week in Dublin with Trevor and Geradine, we headed for our first and only visit to Northern Ireland. We stopped for a week or so in a beautiful town called Ballycastle, which is situated by the sea and surrounded by mountains. We rented a house owned by a publican named Terence Bakewell and the pub itself (called The Bakewell, would you believe) was conveniently only a few doors down from us.

Theresa and I at the Giant's Causeway, dressed up for the summer!

Jonathan, Lil and a young Imogen joined us shortly after our arrival. They were followed a couple of days later by Liam, Donna and a very tiny baby Addison, who flew into George Best Airport in Belfast. As I picked them up at the airport, a snow blizzard started, and we had to make our way back to Ballycastle with great caution as the snow was coming down really heavy. Over the week we explored the beautiful coastline visiting towns, villages, castles, and harbours as well as crossing the famous Carrick rope bridge and driving over the beautiful snow-covered mountains which was absolutely breath-taking. However, the highlight was probably the Giants Causeway, with its amazing interlocking basalt columns and giant steps, made by mother nature herself - it's no wonder that it is one of the world wonders and a UNESCO world Heritage site.

Having my two boys and wives together with my young Granddaughter, Imogen and the newly born, Addison with us, made it a very special and memorable occasion. Theresa and I were over the moon to have them with us, as family means everything to us both.

2014 – "Spending The Kid's Inheritance" Tour

I could nearly write another book about this fantastic tour as it was so varied and exciting, with lots of wonderful experiences with people and places that we came across during the three-month period. However, not wishing to bore the reader, I have tried to condense it down to just some of the highlights listed below.

Friday 7th February 2014. The day had finally arrived for the start of 'Spending The Kids Inheritance' Tour, which we had been planning for months and was to take us to Singapore, New Zealand and Australia. The night before flying out from Heathrow, we stopped overnight at Liam's house which was not too far from the airport. After repacking our suitcases several times due to them being overweight, I managed somehow to break the luggage scales and therefore Theresa and I had a brief domestic… what a start to our holiday!

We kissed and waved goodbye to Donna and the kids, with Addison in tears (it was heart-breaking to leave him like that, but nevertheless we had to go), as Liam took us to the airport in very good time despite the London traffic, bless him. We quickly got through the check-in and security with the help of an airline agent and before we knew it, we were on our way to Singapore via an Airbus. The flight took approximately twelve hours and we both managed to get a little shut eye on the way.

Singapore

We arrived in Singapore at 7am and were met by our adopted son 'Singapore Joe', (our fourth adopted son) who we knew from his days at Loughborough University with our son, Liam. He was living back in Singapore, all grown up and married with four children and he was now a teacher by profession.

Joe had not changed one bit since we last saw him and following lots of hugs and back-slapping, he told us with a big smile that he had been waiting for his Leicester Mam and Dad to come to

Singapore for years so that he could repay us for the kindness we had shown him all those years ago (how lovely is that!).

Having dropped our bags off, we headed down to the quay, and following a tour of the area, we had a meal with Joe at a Persian restaurant, complete with a rather large belly dancer with massive assets, to entertain us as we ate. We eventually headed back at our hotel at 10.30pm as we were both knackered and needed to sleep.

The next morning Joe picked us up and took us for breakfast at his local market and we were joined there by his wife and children. He insisted on choosing the food which was cold curry and rice! Not wishing to insult Joe, I tried a couple of mouthfuls, but it was not to my taste. However, Theresa has a stomach of iron and wolfed it down like most foods that she has placed in front of her. Theresa then became my chief tester for the next three days in Singapore, as Joe got us to sample all kinds of local foods without telling us what was in the dishes, which we found out later included frogs' legs and all kinds of local exotic foods.

On one occasion, Joe got Theresa to try a dish which he said was wonderful for her skin. It was apparently tasteless according to Theresa and when she asked Joe what it was, he replied "Chicken Feet" – yummy, yummy, yummy! Now, not wishing to offend Joe or be discourteous in any way to him, the meal did not appeal to me as I am not good with foreign foods generally and so I politely declined the offer. Despite our differences in food tastes, Joe is one of the nicest men you could ever meet, and he laughed at my lack of appreciation for foreign foods and gladly our friendship is as strong as ever.

Later we had a good look around the market and briefly met his brother, before going to his apartment to meet his lovely mother who also thanked us for looking after Joe whilst he was in England.

Our adopted son, Singapore Joe with mum, Theresa in the beautiful eco house.

Over the next three days, Joe (who has a heart of gold) showed us all the famous sights of his beautiful city including the Eco Gardens, China Town, The Sentosa Universal Theme Park and the Singapore Night Zoo. We also went to the famous Raffles Hotel, to try the Singapore Slings and several beers. It was just like you see it in films and we felt privileged to see it whilst in Joe's company. It was not the cheapest place I have ever been, however, what a great time and experience we had. It was worth every penny.

Before leaving, we also went to the iconic Marina Bay Sands Hotel (that's the one with the ship on top of the three 57 floor hotels). The views of the city were fantastic, and it was well worth seeing, however, my wallet hated it as the bill for two small, bottled beers and one medium wine came to £36 would you believe – yes, you heard right, £36 bloody pounds! However, joking apart, it was worth it to be with Singapore Joe and meet his family whilst experiencing this beautiful city.

The Marina Bay Sands Hotel. Fantastic, but you need a big wallet!

Joe and his family had been so kind to us during our three day stop-over and it was somewhat sad to be leaving them. Joe kindly picked us up from the hotel and took us to the airport for our flight to New Zealand and after hugging and thanking him, we shed a few tears as we finally said goodbye, with the promise of keeping in touch with him.

New Zealand

12th February. We flew into the Southern Island arriving in Christchurch at 10.30am, New Zealand time. It took ages to get through customs as they went through all our baggage with a fine toothcomb as they don't risk anything coming into the country that might cause problems with disease and agriculture - quite right!

It didn't really help that one of our bags was virtually full with Jaffa Cakes, Paxo sage and onion stuffing and Bisto gravy granules, which we had brought with us from England as requested by both my cousin Jane and a friend of ours, Trevor Keohane. It was quite embarrassing getting them all out. They also went through our walking boots with a pen knife and thank goodness, they only found one single blade of grass which they disposed of!

I then collected our hire car which, unbeknownst to me, was a four-litre super-duper Ford Cougar (at least I think that's what it was called) which apparently is a boy racers dream - it was like shit off a shovel!

After we had freshened up, we took a walk around Christchurch. It was sad to see all of the damage caused by the earthquake that was still evident after three years, as little had been done to fix the lovely city and restore it to its former glory. Following a meal and several Monteith's crushed apple ciders (which I loved), we then headed back to the hotel to recover from jetlag with a good night's sleep.

13th February. Drove to Lyttleton, Governors Bay and back through Dyers Pass. In the evening we were picked up by Trevor Keohane (Trevor was at Coventry University with our eldest son, Jonathan) and taken for a dinner at his home. We had New Zealand lamb which was lovely, especially when made with the English Bisto gravy granules!

A great night was had whilst meeting his wife, Della and their children Kara and Connor, with plenty of good food and drink. Prior to leaving, we arranged to have a day out with Trevor the following day and stop overnight in his small 'man cave' at the bottom of his garden. It was perfect for two little people like us!

Lovely people - Trevor Keohane and his family.

"It's a very small world, isn't it?"

14th February. Had the day out with Trevor and he took us sight-seeing in Akaroa which is a small pretty town with French influence. Later we had lunch overlooking the beautiful bay with a few beers. It was all very relaxing and lovely to have Trevor (who is a lovely guy) to show us around.

As I write this book, I keep coming across coincidences, karma, fate or call it what you like, and this was evident again in the case of Trevor Keohane. You see Trevor, during his years in New Zealand, had come across many expats and on one particular occasion, whilst out and about, he had recognised an English accent and started to speak to the person concerned. Would you believe it, the person who he was speaking to turned out to be a great friend of mine called Robin Kay, who I worked with in a forensic nursing setting, prior to him and his wife Marie emigrating to New Zealand.

As they began to converse, Trevor naturally asked the other person where he had originated from and as soon as Leicester was mentioned, the links started to form and connections were made between the Kanes, Kays and Keohanes. Trevor explained that he had gone to university with my son, Jonathan, and consequently had met Jonathan's family and stopped at our house on several occasions. Conversely, Robin spoke of his relationship working with myself all those years ago. What are the odds of that? It really is a very small world, isn't it!

That night my old pal Robin and his lovely wife Marie joined us for the meal at Trevor's house and what a great night we had, catching up on our lives past and present via the odd beer and wine, and at the end of the night, we promised to visit Robin and Marie in Ashburton later on our travels (see section, Robin and Marie in Ashburton).

We said goodbye to Trevor and his family the next morning, ready to start our South Island adventure, with visits to Punakaiki Pancake Rocks via Arthurs Pass which took us over the mountains. Trevor suggested, as it was en route, that we should stop at a place called Sheffield and try the best pies in New Zealand. Trevor wasn't wrong, as within half an hour we were eating the best pies we have ever tasted in our lives. Thanks again, Trevor!

Sheffield pies, the best in the world! I had already devoured mine by the time this photo was taken.

Later, the drive to Punakaiki was breath-taking with stunning views over the mountains. We arrived late afternoon and took accommodation in a tavern and following a meal, we took an evening walk to the beach and watched the sunset. Life is great, it was beautiful!

My 65th birthday. Meeting new friends

On the 26th February, having left Oamaru, we headed towards Lake Tekapo, where Theresa hoped to find some really nice accommodation overlooking the lake to celebrate my 65th birthday, bless her! En route, we stopped off at two nice little towns namely Omarama and Twizel, and they were well worth the visit. Later in the afternoon we stopped to see the Mount Cook lookout which had breath-taking views of the mountain and the colour of Lake Pukaki, which stood at the bottom of the mountain, was unsurpassed for its vivid blue crystal-clear mineral-coloured waters. We were so lucky to experience this.

Having arrived at Lake Tekapo, we booked into the motel which was on the edge of the lake itself and the person on reception offered us a cabin overlooking the lake with a shared front balcony with wonderful views which we gladly accepted. A little later, a car pulled up with a couple in it who had booked into the cabin next door to us.

Having settled in, I opened a can of beer and headed out to the shared balcony to celebrate with a drink and to take in the beautiful views. As I walked onto the balcony, I found our new next-door neighbour sitting in a rocking chair enjoying the views.

I introduced myself and asked him if he would like to join me in a drink for my birthday as I hated drinking alone, to which he quickly replied "yes, of course" with a big friendly smile on his face. We were soon joined by our respective wives, and we spoke of our travels in New Zealand and to where we'd been and indeed where we were going.

This was the view taken from our cabin! Lake Tekapo with its blue crystal clear mineral coloured water and the mountains in the background. Nearly all the lakes in New Zealand are this colour. It's such a beautiful country.

It turned out that the lovely couple were Dutch and from the city of Groningen in the north of the Netherlands and went by the names of Reinder and Haijolien Groehewds. Theresa and I found both of their christian names very hard to pronounce, particularly Reinder's who I kept referring to and pronouncing as to a deer with antlers, until he firmly pointed out, probably feeling a little pissed off with me, that Reinder was actually pronounced 'Rander' and not as the 'deer' kind! Moreover, as for Haijolien, she asked us to call her

Haley as she said it would be much easier and to be fair, she was probably right!

We took to them both straight away as they appeared to be very down to earth, kind, and genuine people and we enjoyed their friendly company as we wound away the afternoon drinking and socialising. In the evening Theresa and I ate at the motel and following a few drinks went to bed as we were both tired from travelling. To be honest, when Reinder and Haley left the following morning, I thought we would never see them again, but you never know what will turn up in life and so fate took a hand once again later on our travels (See Kaikoura and the Dutch reunion).

Robin and Marie in Ashburton

28th February - We made our way towards Ashburton and stopped on the way at Timaru. It was pouring down with rain and so the visit was cut short. I can't remember much about the place apart from having yet another delicious Sheffield pie in a cafe in the town centre!

Having arrived early in the afternoon in Ashburton, we found a lovely little bar and had a few drinks whilst we waited to see Robin and Marie who were busy working. After about an hour, to my surprise, Marie walked into the bar. When I asked her how she knew where we there, she replied "it had to be you, as no one around here has a motor like the one you hired outside!" Now this is what happens when you're a trendy boy racer like myself!

Later, we were joined by Robin before heading back to their home for a meal. That evening, his next-door neighbour, a proper farmer, and his family, popped in to say hello and watch a live rugby match with a few cans of beers being drunk as we watched it. A lovely evening with great people.

The following day, we had a tour of their small holding. They were quite self-sufficient, with Marie growing the fruit and veg, whilst Robin kept bees and made lovely honey. Moreover, he makes his own cider from their orchards. It was like being back in the Good Life TV programme, with them keeping lambs and pigs for their meat, and chickens to provide fresh eggs daily.

Best of all, it was so nice to catch up with them both, particularly Robin, who I have a great respect for both as a nurse and lovely human being. We spoke a lot over a few beers about our time together in forensic nursing and of incidents and ex-colleagues.

The next morning, we said our sad goodbyes with lots of hugs and back slapping and Marie told us that she hoped to see us in the UK the following year to celebrate Robins 50th birthday.

Robin and Marie. Two beautiful people!

Kaikoura and the Dutch reunion

After we had said our goodbyes to Robin and Marie, we headed off towards Kaikoura, which was north of Christchurch, as we hoped to go whale watching from there.

Having arrived in Kaikoura, we booked into a small motel and the lady owner on reception introduced herself in a strong Kiwi accent as Dib, which translated to in English was actually Deb or Debbie! Having discussed that we would like to go whale watching, 'Dib' (I loved her Kiwi accent) rang and booked a trip for us the next day.

Later in the afternoon we headed into town to explore and following a good look around and having a meal, we made our way back to our motel in the evening. On our way back, I heard someone shouting loudly "are we having another drink?" and when we turned around to see who it was, it turned out to be Reinder and Haley, who were also staying in Kaikoura for a few nights. We were delighted and so pleased to see them again and they kindly invited us into their apartment for a drink or two. Moreover, after a good drink and catch up, they kindly asked us to come to their apartment the following evening for a meal.

The following morning, Dib (who must have been waiting up for us on the previous night) mentioned how late we had returned to the motel on the previous evening; it was only about 10pm! They mustn't do late nights in New Zealand it seems!

Theresa then went to mass and later we went to the Kiaro lookout and the seal colony, where we could go right up next to the seals. It was lovely to be so close to them. We then made our way to the whale watching centre, only to be told that our trip was disappointingly cancelled due to stormy weather at sea. We never did go whale watching, as the weather did not improve over the following two days, sadly.

In the evening, we went for a lovely meal with Reinder and Haley. They were so kind and generous to invite us and what a great night we had in their company as we discussed visiting each other in the future as we all got on so well. Reinder mentioned that they had some friends in England who they had visited several times. However, he added, somewhat disappointedly, that they had never bothered to visit them in Holland.

Later, at the end of the night, as we thanked them and said our last goodbyes, I made a promise to Reinder that we would visit them in Holland as soon as we could and with this, we shook hands as if to seal the deal. As we began to make our way back to our motel, we hoped that Dib wasn't watching or waiting up, as it was at least 11.30pm and we didn't want to be told off again as we felt like naughty children trying to avoid our mother!

Over the next few days, we based ourselves in Nelson and travelled around the area. We went to a beautiful beach called Kaiteriteri and later played a game of crazy golf which Theresa naturally won (she is so bloody competitive!). The following day, we went to Rabbit Island but, never came across a single feckin' rabbit would you believe!

The next morning, we headed northwards and went to Blenheim aircraft museum which was owned by Sir Peter Jackson, the film director. It was a great museum, with first world war planes manned by the mannequins from his film sets - so lifelike! Also, an amazing collection of classic cars, all well worth the visit. Later we headed to Picton where would catch the ferry the following morning. I returned my boy racing car, which was a little sad, as by now I had become quite attached to it. In the evening, we took a walk up the headland with great views of Picton harbour and later we had a few beverages in the harbour area as we watched the world go by.

Heading towards the North Island. View from the headland of a Picton ferry.

Wellington and the train to Auckland

It was a very smooth crossing and we arrived in Wellington at 2.30pm on 7th March. We booked into a Travelodge for two nights and were told by reception that it had great views of the harbour. It was on the 22nd floor and people looked like ants on the ground - so much for the views!

The next morning, we took a cable car to the top of the hill and walked back through the Botanical Gardens. Later we had a tour around the Parliament building, followed by a trip to the waterfront to see the dragon boat racing which proved to be a spectacle and very exciting to watch. We ended the day, would you believe, in an Irish bar with a good few drinks and a hearty meal. We then had an early night as we had to get the train at 7am the next morning to get to Auckland and see my lovely cousin Jane and her husband Nick.

The dragon boat race in Wellington.

Auckland with Nick and Jane Seymour

We caught the overlander train which took the scenic route through the middle of the North Island with just a few stops on the way. It took eleven hours to complete the trip, before we eventually arrived in Auckland for our two week stay.

Nick and Jane met us at the station and following hugs and kisses and a few tears from Jane (she a proper softy, just like her mum!) Nick drove us to their home via several sights of the city. Jane cooked us a lovely meal with all of her children present - Jordan, Connor and Ellie May, all beautiful kids, we love them! Despite our long journey and feeling knackered, a late night commenced as we all had a few 'sherberts' and chatted the night away. It was lovely to be with them all and once again I am so lucky to have such great relatives.

The next day we unpacked our belongings and eased into the day whilst talking to Jane about each other's lives since we last saw each other. It was so nice to have a place to unpack all your stuff and not have to rush around, as we had been doing since leaving England. After an evening meal we went to the local bay and had yoghurt ice cream. It was self-service with umpteen toppings, and I thought I had died and gone to heaven! I had one most days after this, whilst pointing out to the others that "bio yoghurt is very good for my immune system!"

Next day (11th March), Theresa and I caught a train into the city and went on a hop-on-hop-off tour. We stopped at Parnell Road, which is a road full of old wooden buildings which are very colonial and very elite. However, we had some trouble with the New Zealand accent of the guide, as he told us during his commentary that they had moved the wooden church from one side of the road to the other by being pulled by "a lot of bollocks!" We suspected that he actually meant bullocks, although it could have been people I guess!!

After the tour we went straight back home, as Theresa had been bitten on both calves and they were swelling up at a rate of knots. Back home I gave her some of my antibiotics which sorted her out after a couple of days. Even Theresa had to acknowledge my medical input by saying that "you do have your uses sometimes, don't you Derm?"

The next day, we chilled by taking the dogs for a walk, whilst looking around the area. We also went into the city in the evening with Nick and Jane for a fantastic meal at an Indonesian restaurant called the Moonsoon Poon. It was one of the nicest meals I have ever had, as the quality of the food and service was second to none. Nick was fast becoming my drinking mate, as following work we would have a few together and again when out and about we would do the same - top man, Nick! Later we walked around the city, which was lovely at night with everything lit up including its lovely waterfront. This turned out to be yet another late night as we were out until gone 10pm (I am not good at late nights, am I?)

Auckland waterfront.

The following day, we went back into the city to see the Sky Tower and watch people do a reverse bungy jump from the top. I don't know how anyone could have the nerve to do that! I also got Theresa to walk on the glass walkway at the top, as I am not good with heights and would probably shit myself if I had to walk on it. Later we walked around the harbour and went to the Maritime museum… and then headed for a pub!

In the evening, we video-called the family, including Jamie who had been in hospital with meningitis, unbeknown to us. Where was his mother when he needed her? We also spoke to Syd and Maureen (Theresa's aunt and uncle) and later to Barry, who was stopping with Theresa's Dad, Eric.

Eric, bless him, could not really comprehend that we were speaking from the other side of the world, as he kept on saying over and over, in complete wonderment that "it's just like you're speaking to me from next door!" Later, I naturally had a few drinks with my drinking partner, Nick, as I was really enjoying my new-found love of New Zealand cider, Monteiths.

Jane and Nick's next-door neighbour kindly offered us their 'Bach' for the weekend, which is their second home on a beach in a place called Mangawhai in the northern part of the island. Unfortunately, there was a cyclone forecast and the weather wasn't great for the couple of days we stopped there. However, we made the best of things by visiting nearby pubs for meals and the odd bevvy!

Apart from this, we were not deterred by the weather and had several walks on the beach and just about managed not to get blown over by the fierce winds. Due to the weather, we passed the time with Quizzes' each night, and it was great to spend quality time with my drinking mate Nick and cousin Jane.

The following morning, the wind had died down and would you believe the sun came out, and so we set out for a walk to the other side of the beach. After a lengthy walk, we decided to turn back as the sky was looking dodgy – but it was too late! The heavens poured down and we were all drenched to the feckin' skin. Despite this, we were all laughing at our predicament and were loving just being together no matter what the circumstances. Later in the afternoon, we returned to Jane's house with no damage to her house, or the kids thank God.

17th March - Paddy's Day! At dinner time, Jane took us to an Irish Pub in Newmarket called Doolan's. Connor and Ellie May joined us shortly afterwards and Nick turned up after work, but Jordan was missing in action as usual! The pub had a great atmosphere, and it was like being back in Ireland as we drank away. Later in the day they put on Irish dancing and I have to say they were brilliant!

In the evening, we headed back and having just arrived home, Nick got a call from the pub saying that I hadn't paid for the meals (what a bloody cheek)! We raced back to the pub and I showed the card I had paid with, but I could tell that they really didn't believe me. As I was one hundred percent sure I had paid, I did not agree to pay twice and gave them my details should they need further contact. It must have been right as they never rang back the next day!

No bad hangovers for me next day, but Nick took a sicky. Had a chilled day and in the evening, the four of us took a ferry to Devonport where we had a lovely meal followed by a nice long walk around the town before heading back to Jane's house, as the next day we were off to visit my old colleagues from forensic nursing and hopefully this would provide a break from us for Nick and Jane.

Out for a meal with Nick (my drinking partner) and my lovely cousin, Jane.

Forensic reunion

The next day we were picked up from Jane's house by my close friend and ex-colleague, Stuart Dysart, and he drove us to his home in Titarangi – don't you just love the names of places here - I can't help it, I love anything with a Tit in it!

We had come to visit Stuart, his wife Jo and daughter, the lovely Jenna, as well as some other ex-colleagues who I had worked with in a forensic nursing setting back in the late 90s, prior to them all emigrating to New Zealand.

Stuart had only just moved to this house and what a lovely place it was, with beautiful views across the valley complete with a hot tub and swimming pool. In the evening we were joined by my old pals Paddy, his wife Serena and Jason and his wife, Karen. It was fantastic to see them again and we caught up on each of our lives as we ate a delicious meal (NZ lamb) cooked to perfection by Stuart.

We then sat drinking and laughing the night away whilst watching the sky at night which was really beautiful, as they have little in the way of light pollution in New Zealand. It was also great to reminisce and recall some of the hair-raising moments of when we all worked together all those years ago.

Forensic reunion. Left to right: Jason Hammond and his wife, Karen. Paddy Modha, Stuart Dysart and myself.

The following day, Stuart and Jo took the day off and showed us around this beautiful part of the world, by visiting Piah Beach, Cornwallis Beach, Hula (where I had a lovely ice cream) and the visitors centre at Wiatakere, which had the most amazing views from the top of the mountain.

In the evening we used the pool and hot tub, and after a long hot day, it was so relaxing and once again the sky was so beautiful at night. I can't begin to tell you how much we enjoyed our short time spent with Stuart and Jo and it was sad to think we would leave them the following morning, as it was possible that we would not see them again due to them living on the other side of the world. Nevertheless, I was so grateful for this meeting and to renew our special friendship again.

Footnote: Stuart and Jo came back to the UK two years later for a short visit. I caught up with them both at a pub in Leicester with lots of our ex-colleague's present – happy days again! (see below).

2018 and reunited with Stuart again in the UK. Left to right: George Bogle, Stuart, unknown, Chubby Chauhan and myself.

Footnote: Sadly, George Bogle on the left of the picture passed away with Coronavirus in December 2020.

On 21st March, Stuart drove us back to Jane's house and we said our sad goodbyes. Later in the evening, we had a farewell BBQ, as this was going to be our last night with them. Their friends Sam and Paul came along and brought Sam's mum Pearl, who was a real character. We had a great night but felt somewhat sad that we were leaving the next morning.

Cousin Sue and husband, Derek

We managed to get everything packed and it was great not to have any Paxo or Bisto to carry around with us at last! Nick drove us to meet my cousin Sue Kearney (Uncle Danny's daughter) who lived about an hour away in a place called Drury. Sue and her husband Derek had recently moved into a new house and had arranged a combined housewarming / welcoming party for us, with all of their family, friends and neighbours and they had also kindly asked Jane and Nick to come too.

Sue had caterers in to provide a wonderful spread of hot roasts to eat, as we all mingled in her garden on top of a hill with marvellous views of Auckland whilst we drank the day away. Both Jane and Nick decided to leave fairly early, as they did not want to prolong their goodbyes any longer. We were all a bit tearful as we said our last farewells as we had all become very close during our time together over the last two weeks.

Apart from seeing Sue, it was also lovely to meet her daughters, Rachel and Louise (and their children) and also husband Derek for the first time, as they are all so welcoming and warm. Derek, a man over 6ft tall and of very muscular build, proved to be a gentle giant of a man with a big heart and they all seemed so happy together. The neighbours were all lovely and down to earth and we felt like we had known them all our lives. The day went so quickly with everyone having a great time, but it was yet another late night for an old fart like me. Nevertheless, I loved every minute of it!

Over the next few days, we were shown the sights by Sue and Derek, visiting Hunua waterfalls where I had a swim in the natural pool at the bottom of the waterfall. It was so nice and cooling as the weather was so hot. Later in the afternoon, we went for a long walk which gave us the opportunity to catch up with Sue and get to know Derek.

The following day we booked ourselves on a tour of Rotorua to see the sulphur springs and later went to the Maori Village of Whakarewarewa for a traditional Hangi meal, which is cooked in the ground via the hot springs - delicious! This was followed by traditional Maori singing and dancing.

The gentle giant, Derek, on the left, with Sue and myself.

Following our days out, we would spend the evenings in the hot tub (even Theresa liked it, as it was so dark, and no one could see her!) with a few beers whilst watching the stars in the clear dark sky with the city lights of Auckland in the distance - it was heaven!

On our last night spent with them, Sue had arranged a BBQ with her daughters and grandchildren, and I was in my element playing chase with the kids in the garden whilst the BBQ was being prepared. However, this also reminded me how much I missed my own grandchildren back in England.

It was a great night spent with them all but as usual the time went so quick and before we knew it, it was bedtime as we had to be up at 3am for our taxi to the airport. Sue saw us off in the morning and it was hard saying goodbye to her, as she said herself that she still gets upset even after 26 years down under.

Australia here we come!

26th March, off to Australia! Having checked in our baggage, we found that we were over the luggage weight limit, and it cost us another £65! Not only that, but she booked our seats and told us that as our seats were by the exit, we would have to assist in the case of emergency. We said yes to this, as we fancied the extra leg room for our little legs, but I didn't think she actually meant it!

Theresa and Dermot - cabin crew!

Bloody hell, how wrong could we be, as having boarded we were approached by the cabin crew who went through the emergency procedures in great detail on how to open the emergency door, get the life rafts down, usher the passengers outside and instruct them on how to slide down the chutes, etc!!

Feck it! I couldn't even reach the life rafts even if I wanted to as I am not tall enough! Moreover, they had the cheek to charge us for excess baggage whilst we were expected to act as cabin crew and do the work for them - fancy asking little people like us, it's not on you know!

Melbourne

Having arrived at our hotel, the Citigate in Flinders Street, we took a walk around the city, with its lovely quaint streets with great atmosphere and made even quainter by the passing of old trams as they rumbled by.

We then made our way to the river and found a lovely little bar with my favourite Monteith's crushed apple cider on the menu as we both sat watching the world go by.

The following day we went to the old Melbourne Gael (Jail) with 99% of the jail open to the public and it proved to be morbidly interesting with all the death masks of everyone executed over the years, which included the famous Ned Kelly. I also very secretly wrote my name on the wall in cell three, top floor of the jail, as I wanted to leave my mark as so many prisoners had in the past, so if you're ever in Melbourne, look it up!

Later that day we met up with the lovely, Margaret Blakeney, who is the mother of an ex-gap year student of Liam's called Stephen ('Crusty', due to his resemblance to Crusty The Clown from The Simpsons!) and who Liam took under his wing when Stephen was in England. Anyway, Margaret was going to be our host for our weeks stay in Melbourne and she very kindly lent us her second property, a flat which was normally used as a base for work by her husband, John.

She had very kindly arranged for us to see an Australian Football League game (Carlton, the Melbourne side) that evening. Despite being on crutches following a knee replacement operation a few weeks previous, she hobbled her way to the tram without complaint.

At the match we sat with her daughter, Megan, and both her and Margaret became very excited as the match progressed (as did we I might add) as apparently the whole family are massive fans. The match was brilliant and although Carlton lost by the odd point, the banter between the mixed crowd of opposing fans was friendly, sportsmanlike and second to none.

The following morning, we took a taxi to meet Margaret at her flat on St. Kilda Road. It was very beautiful and posh with its own concierge, pool, gym. How kind was it of them to lend their apartment to us? I don't know many people who would do that to total strangers but was no doubt due to the way Liam had looked after Stephen during his time working for him in Wimbledon.

Later, we took a trip to the dockland with its statues of famous Australians including Dame Edna, John Farnham but strangely, not one of Rolf Harris!

In the evening we met Margaret and John for a meal, and they introduced us to chicken parmigiana, which is a favourite dish of the Australian public apparently - I really loved it and it became my own personal favourite dish as we toured the rest of Australia!

Following the meal, for which we thanked them for their kindness, we arranged to meet them on the Sunday for a trip to Yarra Valley to do some wine tasting which Theresa was well and truly up for!

Yarra Valley with Margaret and John

The following day we were picked up, early morning, by John and Margaret and headed to Yarra Valley (the wine growing region) which was quite beautiful and very scenic. We had a great lunch with them, in order to line our stomachs, in readiness for the wine tasting and following this we visited two vineyards and tasted their delights before purchasing some of the goodies for John and Margaret. Naturally Theresa bought some Pinot Gris for herself! It was a great day out with our very kind Australian hosts.

Our very kind Melbourne hosts, John and Margaret Blakeney in the Yarra Valley.

Over the next few days, we took trams and visited and walked around the city and out-lying places including the Yarra River, Botanical Gardens, took the boat to Williams Town, St Kilda's

Beach for sunbathing and by now we were experts in finding our way about either on foot or on the trams.

Philip Island and the fairy penguins

The following day, Margaret picked us up with Stephen, who had by then returned from rowing with his team at the National Australian Rowing competition. It was great to have his company and spend time with him as he is a real character with a glint in his eye and a lovely human being.

The drive to Philip Island was very scenic and we stopped on the way at the 'Nobbies'. These are blow holes similar to the pancake rocks that we saw in New Zealand.

As we walked onto the boardwalk to see the rocks, there was a massive sign warning the public about snakes and how important it was to keep away from them. Theresa was sweating and wetting herself as snakes are her biggest phobia and to add to this, the sign went on to inform the public that if bitten by these snakes, there was no anti-venom! Needless to say, she did a quick walk to and from the Nobbies!

Later in the afternoon we visited a small fishing village where we had fish and chips before setting off to see the penguins in the evening. Just at dusk, the crowd started murmuring excitingly and before we knew it hundreds of penguins came out of the water and waddled across the beach towards their burrows, which took them past our viewing platform.

They were the most gorgeous things that you have ever seen on two legs! Standing between 8-10 inches tall (I think they are the smallest penguins in the world), fluffy and cute as you like. As they made their way to their burrows (some of them had to walk a mile on their little legs to their respective burrow), they would stop and look up at us for a few seconds, giving us eye-to-eye contact, which made them even more adorable. What a great sight and what a wonderful night!

Seeing the penguins was the one thing that Theresa wanted to see in Australia, and she had fulfilled her dreams in Melbourne thanks to Margaret and her kindness.

We got back late at night and said our fond farewells to Margaret and Stephen as we were catching the train to Sydney the following morning at 8am. We will never forget the kindness of this family and we hope to reciprocate this when they hopefully visit us in the UK.

Sydney

On the 2nd April, we set off on our 12-hour journey to Sydney by rail. The terrain along the route was very flat and bland and apart from stopping briefly at Wagga Wagga (I love the name, it's so Australian), the journey itself was uneventful. Having arrived in Sydney, we took a taxi to spend two nights at a Travelodge which was very expensive and to be honest, not the best of accommodation.

The next day we were picked up by Gill Becker who is the mother of another gap year student of Liam's, called Adam. Gill was very kind in putting us up for the rest of our stay in Sydney at her lovely home which was not far from Rose Bay. Over the next couple of weeks, we visited all the tourist spots either with the Beckers or on our own. This included visits to Bondi Beach, Darling Harbour, the Rocks, Manley Beach, and the Blue Mountains. However, the highlight for us both was to be the climb to the top of Sydney Harbour bridge.

Dermot's fear of heights

Prior to the climb, I walked with Theresa around the bottom of the bridge to inspect and evaluate the pylons and the height of the bridge itself, as I have always had a massive fear of heights. Having looked at the height, I was shitting myself and initially told Theresa that I didn't want to do the climb. However, as we walked back to the visitors' centre to book the climb for Theresa, I thought about my days as a nurse and how I had always encouraged my patients to face and overcome their fears and phobias using CBT. I decided there and then to give it a go, as I had two days to come to terms with my fear of heights before the actual climb.

With this in mind, I decided to use the proven methods of CBT (Cognitive Behavioural Therapy) on myself for the next 48 hours by taking control of my irrational thoughts and putting things into perspective, whilst using deep controlled breathing to bring my racing heart rate back to normal whenever I felt my fears getting the better of me.

It seemed to work as, come the day of the climb, I felt very positive with just a little touch of apprehension. The jolly group we climbed with comprised of all ages and sizes and the preparation took one and a half hours to complete before the actual ascent. We signed a medical questionnaire and then were breathalysed to ensure no-one was under the influence. Our glasses were fixed to our special suits and even our handkerchiefs were strapped around our wrists. We then practised going up and down steps with our safety harness fixed to ensure that you wouldn't get tangled up.

The climb began with us being hooked onto a safety wire which ran all the way to the very top. The guide stopped several times to point out the sights and inform us of the history of the area. Having reached the top, it was hard to describe the elation and joy that we felt regarding the experience. It was absolutely fantastic and what was more was that I felt that I had conquered my fear of heights.

Theresa and I on top of Sydney Harbour bridge – what an experience!

Needless to say, following the climb, we were both high on adrenalin as we headed for the nearest bar for a celebration drink, and we were still on a high later in the day as we headed back to tell the Becker family all about it. Many thanks to the Beckers for their hospitality on our wonderful and memorable stay in Sydney.

Barrier Reef and kissing toads

On 16th April, we took a flight from Sydney to Cairns. Having arrived in Cairns, we took the shuttle bus to the Rendezvous Villa resort which was to be our base for the week. Once we dropped off our bags, we quickly hopped onto a minibus which took us into Port Douglas town, which turned out to be very small with just one single street consisting of several shops together with few bars. Naturally we headed to the nearest bar!

Over the next couple of days, we visited the Daintree Rainforest, which is one of the oldest rainforests in the world and later we took a trip on a catamaran up to the Barrier Reef. Theresa was determined to have a go at snorkelling on the reef. Unfortunately, this didn't happen owing to her fear of water and the fact that she found it hard to wear and breathe in the snorkelling kit. However, she looked great in her tight wet suit! Nevertheless, I managed to swim with some turtles and we both enjoyed our lunch on a desert island that looked straight out of the Robinson Crusoe book.

Later in the week, we went into town to see the feeding of the enormous grouper fish which come up to the harbour restaurant to be fed at 5pm every day. Later in the evening we headed to the bar, which put on Cane Toad racing. I tried to persuade Theresa to have a go, but she was having none of it, stating that "I would sooner kiss you" as that's how much she hated the thought of kissing the lovely toads. Despite this, we had a fantastic night watching all the young girls closing their eyes and kissing our amphibious friends. It was great fun.

Darwin, hot days and the aborigines

After catching a flight from Cairns to Brisbane and a connecting flight to Darwin, we then spent the next seven days chilling, before our return to the UK. We loved Darwin from our first sighting, as it had a very friendly feel to it, whilst being the most relaxing place ever. The rainy season had just finished and so with the dry season just starting, the temperature was somewhat cooler at 33 degrees. We explored the small city and found a lovely lagoon where you could cool down and swim safely, as you were protected from the sharks by a barrier placed into the sea. We spent most days swimming and relaxing in this bay with its sandy beach and grassed areas.

We were lucky to be able to celebrate Anzac Day in Australia on 25th April. We were up at 5.30am for the Anzac service and found it amazing and very moving, with the whole of the city turning out to pay their respects, from the very young, right through to the very old. Later we took a tour bus around Darwin and hopped-off at several locations, including the Military museum, which was very interesting, as it informed us that Darwin had been bombed by the Japanese during the Second World War and the Australian's had actually suffered more casualties than the Americans had during the attack on Pearl Harbour.

One of the saddest sights in Darwin is the indigenous Aborigines, who appear to have little in the way of purpose in their lives. We saw them regularly roaming around the streets and parks like lost souls. They were often drunk, whilst sitting in groups in the park, swigging beer and passing the bottle around to each other and at night they could be found in their apartment blocks sitting in lines on the concrete floors in front of their apartment buildings, whilst sitting crossed-legged, drinking alcohol as they watched the world go by. We never saw them bothering anyone or become aggressive when drunk. However, it really appeared that they had lost their role and way of life since the coming of the white man and their complete change of culture and lifestyle. It was sad to see.

Later in the week, we took a guided tour which included a stop at several termite mounds, including one called the Twin Towers (two of them side by side) - they were massive, and it made us wonder how those little creatures could build such amazing structures.

Later that day, we called at the Florence Falls where I had a lovely swim to cool down. This was followed by a picnic and a river trip to see crocodiles. According to our guide, for every croc you see, there are another nine that you don't actually see or notice! Anyway, it wasn't long before we saw the biggest crocodile ever. His name was Nero and as our guide held out a pole with a whole chicken on its end, this huge croc leapt out of the water and grabbed the chicken before plummeting back down. What a sight it was, although I think most of us were shitting ourselves! Later we had prawns and champagne as we watched the sunset over Darwin, and this was followed by an almighty thunderstorm, in which we were soaked to the skin, but we felt very comfortable as it did cool us down.

On the 28th April we swam and chilled in the lagoon during the day, and in the evening took a taxi to Cullen Bay where Theresa had seafood and I chose a lovely steak, combined with a nice bottle of bubbly to wash it all down - lovely!

By 30th April, the holiday was nearing the end and so we took a last walk around Darwin before packing for the long trip home. We were looking forward to seeing all of the family again, as even though you can Skype them, it's not the same as seeing them physically face-to-face and having hugs and kisses.

Back in London, Jon picked us up at the airport, with a welcome home sign made by Immy - it was quite emotional. We were soon back at Liam's house to see all the others and give them lots of hugs and kisses and tell them of our wonderful adventure - what a holiday!

There is so much more that I could have written about our adventure down under. However, I don't want to bore the reader, nevertheless what a fantastic three months we had! Both Theresa and I felt so very lucky and privileged to have experienced the trip and to have gained so many new friends, and at the same time to have caught up with so many of our old colleagues and family members.

Footnote: I have to give Theresa full credit, once again, for helping me with dates, times and destinations for this chapter as she kept a diary account of the trip which proved very useful whilst writing about it (thank you, Trebor!).

Leaving my fingers in the car door

Having been retired for a couple of years, I did keep in touch by phone with several of my ex-colleagues and would meet up with them for a beer or a meal periodically. This would mainly be Bridie Collins, Amrat Chauhan and Alison Hirrell, as they had been my closest working friends. On this particular occasion, I had not seen them for some time due to Theresa and myself travelling to Australia and New Zealand. However, following a call to Bridie, I had arranged to meet up with them for an Indian meal at The Peoples Centre in Leicester.

On the night in question, Theresa and I were picked up by Alison and her husband Danny (incidentally, Danny's father had been a good friend of my own Dad!). During the journey, I was on a high, with the prospect of the food, seeing old friends and catching up on everything. I remember being in a hyper-state, talking incessantly about our recent trip down under and asking Alison about all of my ex-colleagues and the team in general.

As we arrived at the Peoples Centre, I attempted to get out of the car whilst still talking incessantly and not actually being self-aware. To this day, I swear that I don't know how this actually happened, but I slammed the car door behind me with some force, and whilst I continued to talk, I instantly felt this enormous pain in my hand as my friend Alison locked the door at the same time! I remember shouting out some unrepeatable expletives for Alison to open the "fu***ng door!" and after a few moments shock at hearing my language, she did.

Two of my fingers were completely flattened by the impact and blood spurted out from the tops of both fingers. Theresa was not happy to say the least, as she was very used to seeing my mishaps and was really looking forward to the Indian food as she had been informed that the Peoples Centre cooked the best and most authentic dishes in Leicester!

To cut a long story short, we ended up at the Leicester Royal Infirmary for the rest of the night, where I received treatment for this most unusual injury. The staff who treated me told me that they had never come across anyone who had got out of a car and yet, left the fingers behind - only the Irish can do such things! Even after five years, I still have little feeling in both of those fingers as a reminder of my stupidity.

2015 - our Dutch friend

Do you remember me telling you about the lovely Dutch couple that we met in New Zealand in 2014? Well, in 2015, following an invite from them, we decided to pay them a visit, as promised. We flew from Southend airport into the beautiful city of Groningen in the north of Holland, close to the Kropswolde area where they lived.

Reinder (pronounced Rander) and Haijolien (we call her Haley) were both at the airport to meet us with a welcoming smile, and after going through customs they took us on a quick car tour of the area they lived in, before we ended up at a pub close to their home. It was so nice to be in their company again and despite only meeting them fairly briefly in New Zealand the previous year, we felt like we had known them all of our lives.

Back at their house, we caught up on each other's lives and all that had happened to us since our last meeting the previous year and then they took us for a walk around the area where they lived. Their house setting was in a beautiful location with small lakes all around them and their back garden actually runs down to the lakeside, where they had their own private landing stage and boat - it was all very posh compared to us!

However, I have to say, that when I first met Reinder in New Zealand the previous year, he was so down to earth, telling me that he was a lorry driver by profession and gave no indication at all that he actually owned his own company, which built large car transport carriers! I think it's the measure of the man that he remained modest and unassuming despite his relative wealth and lifestyle, and I think that this is why I took to him from our very first meeting in 2014.

The following day we were taken to meet their lovely family - son Robert and wife Annette and their two beautiful grandchildren, Emma and Marit who lived close to them. Following this, they took us to meet their best friends Fenna and Gert, who put on a lunch for us, washed down with beer and wine and basically, we found them like so many Dutch people that we met, to be kind, warm and welcoming.

The next day, Reinder took us on his boat into Groningen city to spend the day sightseeing. As we walked around the market, Reinder asked me if I liked fish and I told him truthfully that I was not particularly fond of fish, other than that found in chip shops! Reinder has a wicked sense of humour and following my disclosure regarding fish, he began to pester me to try and eat raw fish as it was a tradition in Holland. After much badgering I finally gave in and both Theresa and I swallowed a whole raw herring straight down. Theresa took it all in her stride, but I felt sick just thinking about it, whilst Reinder couldn't stop laughing.

Can't believe I actually did this!

Later, we met up with Fenna and Gert again for a lovely Italian meal and spent the rest of the day drinking and getting to know them both. Apparently, Fenna and Haley had grown up together and so we heard all the stories about their childhood and affection they had for each other and their respective families.

We all got on so well and the day went too quickly, but before leaving us, Fenna and Gert promised to visit us in England as soon as they had the chance. The rest of the week was fantastic with sightseeing trips all around the north of Holland and even a trip into Germany.

I also remember, we went to an art gallery owned by the living painter Henk Helmantel and I was particularly taken with one of his paintings, showing a Bible with a vase placed on top of it. I know little or nothing about art, other than I either like it or not, however, I was taken with this painting, as some of the text in the Bible was magnified by the bottom of the vase which I thought was an amazing thing to capture the fine details in this painting. However, I didn't buy it and thought no more about it. The rest of the week went so fast and before we knew it, we were leaving our friends at the airport with the promise that they would keep in touch and visit us the following year.

Leaving our friends, Reinder and Haley at the airport following a great week spent in Groningen, Holland.

Skipping forward again to 2016, all four of our Dutch friends visited us in Leicester for four days and we had the privilege of showing them around and reciprocating the kindness they had shown to us in Holland.

I was very touched when they gave me a present of a framed copy of the painting by the aforementioned artist, Henk Helmantel that I loved so much and I couldn't actually believe that Haley had even remembered that I liked it from the previous year. Moreover, when Haley went to pick up the painting, the artist himself was present and so she got him to sign that it was authentic, and someone took a picture of him signing it with Haley in the background! The picture hangs proudly in my lounge with the certificate and photo stuck on the back and it reminds me daily of our lovely Dutch friends.

Going forward again to 2018, we spent another week in Holland and this time spent more time with Fenna and Gert at their second home, which was their country retreat, which helped them relieve the pressure of them both being GPs at their main home, which was the base of their surgery / practice. Their second home was also on a lake with its own mooring for their very posh launch, in which we spent much of the time exploring the area with them. It was a beautiful spot with wonderful views as we sat in their company, and I have to say that their hospitality was second to none.

Our Dutch friends, Gert and Fenna.

Whilst touring the area, we came across a pub / restaurant and pulled in for a meal and a beer around dinner time. As we entered the pub, we heard the voices of angels with beautiful harmonies drifting towards us. It was a touring choir practising for a concert at a local church that night! We were spellbound as we listened to their wonderful singing, and we soon struck up a conversation with them. They kindly invited us to the concert in the evening, which we gladly accepted. What a fantastic show they put on! I still have the video of it on my phone and periodically watch it to remind myself of the occasion.

Like all good things, they soon come to an end and before we knew it, we were heading back to England. However, my enduring memory of this trip is seeing Theresa in Gert's very large launch, acting like 'Lady Duck Muck' as we pulled into restaurants and pubs along the lakes, almost waving like the Queen with a big smile on her face. She told me afterwards she had always wanted to do that and feel what it's like to experience life at the top end. I have to say that all four of our Dutch friends are the most genuine, down to earth and generous people you could ever meet and we continue to keep in touch with them to this day.

Footnote: We are hopefully going to meet up with them in spring 2021 either in the Lake District in England or Portugal (subject to Covid) as it's both Reinder and Haley's, and our very own, 50th wedding anniversaries and we couldn't wish to celebrate with better friends.

2015

On our second visit to Tricarico, Rocco took us to visit his cousin's small holding, several miles away, and it was like going back in time as his cousin's husband made cheese by hand, whilst offering us their homegrown food to eat. The hospitality of his family is second to none and just being with them made you feel as if you were also part of their family, as they were all so down-to-earth, hardworking, and honest people.

We also visited his daughter-in-law's parents in Pulia, who had several fields full of cherry trees and spent some time cherry-picking with them. I think I ate as many as I picked as they were so delicious. Once again it was like being with your own family as they were so welcoming, kind and generous.

Rocco's cousins husband (Rocco Dicosmo) making the delicious cheese by hand in his kitchen.

During our visit we had a day out in the nearest city to Rocco called Matera, the caved biblical city built into the hillside with dwellings dug into the mountain rock to create cave homes, churches and shops. This is one of the oldest cities in the world and is now famous for the film by Mel Gibson called the 'The Passion Of The

Christ' and also the James Bond film 'No Time To Die' with Daniel Craig. It's a great place to visit if you get the chance, as it's unique and practically unchanged since Biblical times and it feels like you're stepping back two thousand years as you enter the city, looping your way from the very top of a steep valley and winding your way down to its city centre at the very bottom.

With my old shipmate, submariner Rocco on my last visit to Tricarico.

Another memorable visit was to stay overnight in one of the famous traditional Trullo Apulian houses, with the distinctive conical round roofs. It was so quaint and yet comfortable, and the lovely Italian wine consumed on the night ensured that we had a great night's sleep. We also visited the lovely town of Polignano-a-Mare, where Domenico Muddugno was born. He wrote the international hit song 'Volare' and in the town square is a twenty-foot statue of him. It's very impressive and such a beautiful place to visit if you ever have the chance.

We had a fantastic time, which was over too quickly, but hopefully it will not be too long until we visit again.

With Rocco and his family in Pulia.

Footnote: I love everything Italian. It's definitely my favourite place to visit in the world, hence so many visits including Lake Garda, Como, Rome, Venice, Verona, Dolomites, Amalfi Coast and so many other beautiful places, too numerous to mention. The country and landscape, food, culture, people, and history are all fantastic. Moreover, I also believe that the Irish and Italians are very similar in that they love family and having a good drink whilst celebrating life as they go along, and I think that is why I connected so well with Rocco and his family and long may this continue!

2016 - our 45th anniversary at Rules restaurant

During my lifetime I have had some pretty stupid ideas and I have to say that my idea of spending our 45th anniversary at the posh and expensive restaurant Rules, near Covent Garden, was perhaps the most stupid of all!

This beautiful, historical restaurant opened in 1798 which makes it the capital's oldest restaurant establishment and was frequented by the likes of Charles Dickens, Charlie Chaplin, Noel Coward, Buster Keaton, Laurel & Hardy and many other famous celebrities over the centuries. It also featured in several films over the years, including the James Bond film 'Spectre', starring Daniel Craig. Also, it was at Rules that Edward, the Prince Of Wales, would meet his famous mistress, Lillie Langtry, and to avoid being seen, the restaurant allowed them both to use a private side entrance to sneak into their own private dining room!

The building itself is beautiful, with oak panelling, plush red seating and a real feel of refinement throughout the building. I had booked the venue a year in advance to ensure we could hold this special occasion with our three boys and their respective partners, namely Lilian, Donna, and Fleur. We had selected a three-course dinner with the signature dish of the Rules restaurant being Beef Wellington as the main course.

The painful pay-out

We had our own private room with our own butler, as, would you feckin' believe, only parties of up to six people could be seated in the main part of the restaurant. And not just any private room by the way; the very room Edward and Lillie used! The food and service were second to none and the night was fantastic as we all downed bottles of wine and beers, amid all the chattering about our 45 years of marriage and the adventures we had together as well as reminiscing about our three boys growing up and the joys of having an extended family.

However, I was soon to sober up, as the butler brought me the bill for the night. I couldn't believe my eyes as it came to £1,400 pounds! Yes, £1,400. I nearly fainted on the spot as my credit card took a pounding and I was actually shaking as I put the card into the machine whilst trying to look like I was accustomed to such a lifestyle (it was definitely a bit different to my early life in Dublin). Joking apart, it was a wonderful one-off occasion that I had no regrets to pay for, as none of us will ever forget it as it gave us an insight as to how the other half live and it was a privilege to spend it with all of the people who I dearly love.

2016 - visiting old friends on the American west coast

I could write a lot about this visit to America, however, I will try to keep it fairly brief. Having spent a few days in San Francisco and seen all the sights including Alcatraz, where we met an ex-prisoner who signed the book he had written about his time in the prison for us. We decided to visit our old next door neighbour's Paul and Cathy Thomson, who now lived in America in a town called Los Altos near Silicon Valley.

We spent four fabulous days with them catching up, exploring the local area and laughing about old times in Leicester before departing for the rest of our adventure on the West Coast. However, before leaving, Cathy inquired if on the west coast route, we would be passing Carmel by the sea where, incidentally, the actor Clint Eastwood was mayor of the town in the 80's. The place is very wealthy, and we told Cathy, having looked at the prices to stop at the hotels in Carmel, that it was out of our budget range. Nevertheless, to our surprise Cathy offered to give us the keys to her second home in Carmel and naturally we bit her hand off for her very kind gesture!

Having left the Thomson's, we headed firstly to Yosemite with its towering cliffs and beautiful valleys for a few days, before making our way down the wonderful, beautiful coastline of the West Coast with the stunning Big Sur, whilst stopping on the way in Monterey Bay, Santa Barbara, Santa Monica, Oceanside, Randolph Hearst's amazing castle, and San Diego, before ending our trip in Las Vegas. However, one of the most enduring memories of the trip is our four-day stop in Carmel. It's a beautiful little town with lovely bars, restaurants, and a very beautiful beach. Most days we would explore the beautiful local area by car before returning in the evening to watch the spectacular sunsets from the beach. It was lovely just watching the sun slowly go down as we sipped several bottles of wine or champagne each evening, very happy in each other's company as we reflected on our lives and how lucky we have been. We shall always be indebted to Paul and Cathy for their generosity whilst giving us the opportunity to have such a wonderful, unforgettable time in Carmel.

Footnote: Sadly, several years later Cathy informed us that she and Paul had split up and gone their separate ways. It was so sad to hear the news as they were a beautiful couple and it shocked us at the time as they always appeared very happy for the 25 years they had been married (however who knows what goes on between people, it's just life).

Small world in San Diego and sad news in Las Vegas

Whilst in San Diego (which incidentally was really hot) we decided to visit the Old Town Museum and after a good look around we found that the heat was almost unbearable. With this, we saw a sign advertising a show with air conditioning in the building and thought we better go in to cool off.

As we entered the lovely cool auditorium, we came across a lady dressed in an old western style costume who pleasantly welcomed us into the museum with a very strong Welsh accent. I made some friendly reference to her distinctive accent, and she made enquires as to where we came from in the UK. Having replied Leicester, she said "Oh my daughter lived in Leicester a few years back". Now to cut a long story short, the conversation went on with the lady giving us more information about her daughter who had trained as a nurse and who also loved horses, Theresa's cogs were turning as she asked if her daughter's name was Sian, to which she replied "yes!" The lady was flabbergasted and could not believe the connection between Theresa and her daughter. It transpires that her daughter trained in Leicester to be a qualified nurse and Theresa had been her assessor and colleague during this period. The lady told us that she would be ringing her daughter that evening to tell her of the unbelievable coincidence. Once again, it's a very small world isn't it?

Having explored San Diego over the next few days, we made our way east to Las Vegas and stopped along the way in Flagstaff at a grubby hotel on Route 66 (which could be another story in itself) and also visited the Hoover Dam before entering Las Vegas. We had booked into the New York, New York hotel for the remaining five days of the trip before flying home. To say I disliked Las Vegas would be an understatement. I think even Theresa was disappointed as it was like Blackpool, but on steroids, however, it was nevertheless an experience and we felt privileged to have at least seen it.

However, after a couple of days we received a call from home, telling us that our brother-in-law, Joe O'Flynn, had sadly passed away. Now, Joe had been very unwell prior to us leaving the UK and we thought at the time when we visited him before departing on the trip, that it was possibly the last time that we would see him, nevertheless it still came as a big shock!

With this we decided to cut the trip short and fly back early to the UK to attend his funeral (our daughter-in-law Lilian kindly made all the flight arrangements for us back in the UK, bless her!). It was a very sad ending to our adventure on what was otherwise a marvellous trip. However, we did make it back in time for the funeral and to support Kate and her family. (R.I.P Joe O'Flynn, born 5th December 1946, died 27th September 2016. We really did have some great times together!)

2017 - my 70th

Looking back over my life and considering that I have an incurable lung problem (bronchiectasis), I never thought that I would actually live to the ripe old age of 70. Yet, here I was, still going strong and in pretty good health as far as I know at the time of writing. As I have always celebrated each decade of my life, I wanted to do the same for my 70th but keep it low key.

However, before I knew it, Trevor Kane and others in the Kane family wanted to help me celebrate and said they would be over from Ireland. Moreover, Alan O'Loughlin and his wife Theresa, along with the Casey clan and Sandra and Andre from France also said they would love to come and so it was on for a birthday bash at the Winno!

The Kane clan from Dublin started the visit in their usual style by booking into the wrong hotel. It was pandemonium as they had all made their way to the bar, when they were informed by the hotel staff of the booking error. Taxis were called and everyone was feckin' this and feckin' that as they boarded to go to the right hotel. However, they soon got over the problem and headed to the bar in their new accommodation and eased themselves into a good sup of the hard stuff. The following day I took them all for a tour of Leicester and naturally ended up in a pub would you believe!

The night itself was fantastic with all the people I loved attending, including Theresa's family and old friends with everyone having a laugh and a good drink to celebrate another milestone in my life. My three boys got up and performed a parody / piss take of me to the tune of three Beatles songs; Penny Lane, Here Comes The Sun and Hey Jude, complete with new words about my life and mishaps and everyone joining in on the chorus of "Na na na nana na na, nana na na, Hey Derm!" This was completed with life-sized cardboard cut outs of me as Superman, a leprechaun and a jockey placed on the stage with them as they performed. I can't tell you how happy it made me to have all my family and friends around me on such an occasion, especially when some of them had to travel from afar.

At closing time, most of the gang came back to my house where we put on the Irish records and sang our hearts out whilst having our fill of the demon drink. The night was made even more very special with Sandra and Andrea being with me and also having the company of new-found second cousin, Alan (Joan Behan / O'Loughlin son) and his wife Theresa present, as both couples made the effort to be there from France and Ireland respectfully. I feel so lucky to belong to such a great family and set of friends to share my life with.

My 70th… with a couple of friends!

Dermot and the Lindy Hop story

I think it was Christmas 2018 when my son Jamie gave us a Christmas present of dancing lessons (Jamie thought it was jive lessons) at his local community hall. Once Christmas was over, we attended our first lesson in early January. We had no idea what we were letting ourselves in for and upon arrival it transpires that we were learning to dance to Lindy Hop (neither of us had a clue what Lindy Hop meant or involved - it was actually inspired by the aviator Charles Lindbergh in 1927 and evolved from different dances including jazz, tap, 1920 Charleston, with elements of African, American and European partnered dance).

Anyone that knows me would know that I cannot dance to save my life and to say that I have two left feet would be an understatement! However, I was determined to give it a go and so I stuck with it for six or seven painful weeks under the gaze of a packed hall filled with very proficient dancers. With the passing of each week, I appeared to be getting worse not better and by the fifth week most of the regular crowd recognised us with most of the females having a look of dread on their faces as I was passed to each of them during the dances. Looking back, I could understand this as primarily they had all suffered from sore feet and very embarrassing moments as I did my best not to make a fool of myself during previous dances together. Sadly I failed badly every time.

The problem was that my feet wouldn't do what my brain was telling them to do. I naturally had a great sense of timing and rhythm and could follow the beat which all stemmed from my days in the band. Despite this, as I have said, my feet could never follow my brain's instructions and I found the whole bloody experience very frustrating. Nevertheless, everyone in the group was, on the surface at least, very pleasant, polite, and encouraging despite the mayhem I was causing on a weekly basis.

However, my reputation must have triggered some concern amongst the group as on one particular night, the lady organiser of the group approached me in the company of another slim looking lady who had the look of a dancer. This proved to be correct as she informed me that she was a specialist teacher of Lindy Hop and to quote her, she told me in no uncertain terms that she could "teach anybody to dance, no matter what ability they had to start with".

Moreover, she didn't mess about as she informed me there and then that she would prove this by taking me to an outside room to have private lessons with her.

Despite my protests and claims that I couldn't dance to save my life, she whisked me off and within minutes commenced to show me the basics steps and put me through my paces. It was a disaster from the start, with me stepping on her toes, using the wrong foot movements, and once again making a real idiot of myself! Despite her initial calmness and positiveness, she quickly waned and became very frustrated with my inability to grasp her advice or move with the faintest look of dancer and she began to raise her voice in her frustration, and huff in exasperation!

After approximately half an hour she was in a bit of a state and bluntly informed me that she could now understand why I had made the statement that I couldn't dance to save my life and she went on to say reluctantly and in a defeated tone that we should perhaps call it a day! It was all so embarrassing, but there again I had told her so! Nevertheless, I thanked the lady for her efforts and left the building with Theresa never to return and so ended my one and only attempt to learn to dance properly!

2018 - John Joseph (aka Jack) Kearney's grave

I would just like to talk briefly about a past relative. It was a hundred years since my relative John Kearney (Grandad's brother) had died in the First World War during the Battle of the Somme. He apparently died of shrapnel wounds, following a shell explosion and passed away at a clearing station (a front-line hospital) close to where he was mortally wounded. I had known little about John growing up, other than what had been told by my mother about his demise in the First World War.

I decided that, as no-one in the family had visited his grave for a hundred years and it being the 100th anniversary of the First World War, I would find out the exact location and pay him a visit to pay my respects and celebrate his short life (born 1896 and died 1917 aged 21).

We found the details of his grave through the War Graves Commission. Having done this, I asked my sons if they would also like to come and so Jonathan and Liam agreed, along with Theresa's brother Barry.

The journey to Belgium was relatively uneventful and the mood was mainly sombre. Having arrived at a small town called Diksmuide, which was fairly-near to the gravesite, we grabbed a couple of beers before retiring to bed. The next day we set off to find his place of rest and we had little in the way of problems finding it, as it was approximately within a half hour of leaving the town.

The Dozinghem Military Cemetary was close to the city of Poperinge, just off the main road. As we drove down the grass track from the main road with a mixture of anticipation, excitement and yet reverence, we spotted the woods on the left where the clearing station had once stood and there was an information block explaining the events that took place during the battle of the Somme.

The graveyard itself was beautifully kept but relatively small with just over 3,000 graves. As we made our way around each grave, looking for John's name, it was I who came across it first. I felt excited seeing it and yet a real sense of sadness overcame me.

As we all gathered around the grave, I took out my hip flask of whisky and made a toast to the memory of John saying that he was not forgotten by his family, and we were all proud of his sacrifice. I poured some of the whisky over his gravestone and then offered all present a good slug of the water of life in his honour.

John Kearney's grave & pouring a whisky on the headstone in his memory

We all stood there digesting the scene and thinking of all those who died in this foreign land far away from their loved ones. I felt very proud of John Kearney and proud to have shared this trip with my two sons. Later, back in our room, I remember telling my boys how lucky I have been in life, as my sons nor I had never had to experience war or the horrors of it and have had so many wonderful times with friends and family over the years, which was something that John never had the chance to experience.

The following day we made a trip to a family run museum nearby which was in essence a farm with the trenches on their land, untouched since the First World War. As we walked the trenches, we were aware that we were probably standing on many bodies who had perished during the Battle of the Somme, as due to horrendous shelling, many of the fallen were literally blown to bits and their bodies left were they had fallen. It really brought home the horrors of war and man's inhumanity to man. We also visited a museum in Dunkirk that explained the evacuation of the troops and the hardships they endured before the Germans took France. The whole trip was thought-provoking for me and it was a special occasion that I shall never forget.

My beautiful cousin Eileen Casey and her family

Since meeting the Casey / Jackson family back in the 1990s, Theresa and I kept in touch with my beautiful cousin Eileen Christina Casey (born 8th August 1941, died 15th August 2019) and her daughter Jane over the forthcoming years. We subsequently became very close to both of them and in September 2001, Jane and her future husband Nick decided to tie the knot and so Jane rang me and invited us both to her wedding. We felt so honoured and proud to be asked but Jane stipulated not to say anything to Eileen that we were coming as she wanted it to be a surprise to her mother.

When Eileen saw us on the morning of the wedding at Jane's house, she was overjoyed and kissed and hugged us both as she shed a few tears. Theresa helped Jane to get ready whilst Eileen and I caught up on family talk and reminisced about the past.

The wedding itself was a proper family do, with lots of laughter, booze and knees ups! At the end of the fabulous night, we were naturally all a bit worse for wear due to the demon drink and during the taxi ride back to Eileen's house she started to look for her keys. Unfortunately, she couldn't find them and having arrived at the house she began to look for a way to get in. Bless her, she found a very slightly opened small window in which she insisted on climbing into as I was too big to get through it. However, after much debate Theresa offered her services which was accepted.

We must have been a sight as we gave Theresa a bunk up and after some wiggling and a few laughter farts from her backside, she found that she couldn't get through the window! We were all killing ourselves laughing as we brought her back down.

Luckily enough, we spotted a young fit man innocently passing by and Eileen asked for his assistance. In a jiffy he disappeared through the window and quickly opened the door to let us in. Eileen was in fits of laughter and said she needed to go to the toilet or she would wet herself! It was one of the many happy times we spent in her company.

Smiles all around with Jane on her wedding day.

Eileen and I would ring each other every five or six weeks or if there was any significant family news to discuss. We would also pop down to Brentwood on occasions to see her. Eileen also came up to us with her girls, Sandra, Julie and Yvonne, who stopped overnight with us and we had a great time with them in the Winstanley pub over a few drinks.

Another occasion was on Janes 50th birthday bash on one of her many trips back from New Zealand to see her mum and family. Trevor Kane came over especially for the do as, like myself, he loved the craic and the company of the Casey clan. We also surprised Eileen at her 76th Birthday party when we attended, once again with our cousin, Trevor Kane.

Despite her poor health and pain, Eileen never complained and made the best of the occasion by laughing and joking and showing the love that she had for all her family and friends. I still have enduring memories and flashbacks of her in her yellow jacket and black and yellow top, laughing and having a great time with all her family over the years. However, shortly afterwards, she sadly passed away on 15th August 2019, surrounded by her loving family.

My lovely cousin Eileen as I always will remember her.

The funeral was a real celebration of her life as she herself had requested. Eileen gave instructions to the family, prior to her passing, to have a free bar for the night so that everyone could celebrate her life in the Irish way. This was done and all the family supported each other throughout the day, whilst telling their own tales about Eileen and her impact on their lives. Trevor Kane and Alan O'Loughlin and his lovely wife Theresa came over from Ireland and Alan's brother, Pascal, also attended from London to pay his respects.

We finished the night singing Irish songs (even me!) at the top of our voices in the Bardswell Social Club with everyone well-fed and watered with alcohol. It was a fitting tribute to our lovely late cousin with a send-off as she would have wanted. Theresa and I felt very privileged to have known her as she was a very special lady and cousin. We have so many happy memories of time spent with Eileen and her family, and she will always hold a special place in our hearts.

The Kangaroo, paint pot and toilet

In the summer of 2019, we decided to have an extension built at the front of our house, which would include another toilet in the new build. As the cost of the build was very high, I decided to do the footings myself in order to keep the costs down.

All went well initially as I swiftly dug the side footings for the drains. However, as I started to dig the main footings at the front of the house, I came across a whole section of concrete approximately twelve inches thick. After several hours of trying to chip away with my trusty Irishman's pickaxe and chisel and getting nowhere at all, I gave up, feeling knackered and cursing myself whilst wishing that I hadn't started the bloody project in the first place.

Theresa's nephew, Grant Hayward (a builder), came to the rescue and offered to lend me his Kango (a pneumatic drill). The following day he turned up with this bloody huge industrial drill which was nearly as big as my feckin' self! I am not kidding, as in height it just fitted under my chin and I could hardly pick the bloody thing up due to its colossal weight. However, not wishing to give up, I cracked on and after several hours, involving shouting and swearing at the machine and myself and falling over numerous times due to its weight, I finally got used to handling the beast.

I hope that you can visualise the next bit, as the only way I found to use the machine effectively was to start the beast and then jump up with both feet and land on the two footrests rods on either side of the machine and whilst standing completely upright literally hop about like a Kangaroo while trying to smash away at the concrete. I must have looked like a completely possessed insane Irishman to both my neighbours and people passing by, as I hopped about in a frenzy for the following two days. To make things worse, I had put my mobile phone in my front pocket before I started the job and after a day spent on the beast as a kangaroo I went to make a phone call only to find the feckin thing completely smashed to smithereens in my pocket!

Footnote: After getting a replacement phone, I then dropped this new phone in a pot of emulsion about 6 months later but managed to get it out quickly and got it working as I was sure that Theresa would kill me. Moreover, would you believe that as I was writing about this chapter in December 2022, I dropped the same phone down the toilet by accident and I have to say that that this time it was as dead as a dodo! I am a real prize plonker and not very good with phones as you can see!

2019 - Lapland

I have often talked about the generosity and kindness of our three lovely sons. Well, this small chapter is about my son Jonathan and his generosity which knows no bounds. Out of the blue, my son told myself and Theresa that he was taking us and his family on a trip to Lapland to see Santa with all expenses paid, bless him!! With the news, Theresa nearly wet herself with happiness, as she is still at heart a little girl when it comes to Christmas and Santa and she tends to whip herself, our three boys and all the grandchildren, up into a frenzy as we approach each Christmas period.

Came the day in mid-December, we all set off towards Gatwick airport in order to catch the flight. Immy and Alfie had no idea where they were going, and their faces were a picture when Jonathan showed them the sign stating the flight was heading for Lapland, beaming with delight as he gave them the news. Once landed, we headed off to the resort on a coach with all the adults and children singing and clapping the song 'we are on the search, for Santa and his elves' which was sung every thirty minutes or so! Once again, Theresa was in heaven as she joined in with great gusto whilst clapping and with a look of pure delight and happiness on her face.

Having arrived at our resort, we all gazed at our beautiful surroundings which resembled a magical land with the ground covered in thick snow and people pulling children on sledges, beautiful natural light, and glitz lighting around all of the Swiss type cabins, with the trees dusted with snow, giving you the impression that we were in fairyland (and it was)! Once we had settled in our cabins, we headed for the restaurant with both of the children being pulled on the sledges provided by the resort with big grins on their faces as they were being transported along.

Over the next three days we delighted in the festivities of being in Lapland and the Artic Circle whilst being asked to look out for any signs of Santa and his elves as we continued to tour the local area daily by coach, with the whole of the passengers singing and clapping along to the same song, as by now even the adults believed in Santa (even me!) We had many clues with different elves meeting us on our journey and giving us hints as to where we might find the 'big man' with the ruddy complexion and white beard dressed in his big red costume.

Apart from searching for Mr Claus, we had time to go sledge racing and I will never forget Alfie's face as he overtook us all in every race, whizzing past us whilst laughing and screaming with delight as he did so! Both Immy and Alfie loved every minute of the experience and as adults we were all transported back to our own childhoods. I could go on and bore you about every aspect of the trip as it was so fantastic, however, for me the four main things that I shall always treasure from this marvellous holiday are as follows:

Born to mush!

Part of the holiday was a chance for the adults to have a go at driving their own team of six huskies. My imagination ran riot at the thought of this, as I remember as a child seeing films and pictures of Arctic explorers or fur trappers in their fur skins driving their teams of huskies through the blinding snow whilst shouting "mush, mush" as they cracked their whips and drove them on, whilst facing all kinds of danger but were determined to conquer all adversities and become heroes.

As our coach pulled up to the huskie camp, I became very excited and my senses became more heightened as I could hear the sound of the huskies barking, yelping and howling in anticipation of doing what they were bred for, which is basically pulling sledges with their passengers and loads through the snow.

The organisers gave us all blue thermal all-in-one snowsuits and gloves to combat the cold on the husky run. However, in my mind and vivid imagination I was actually wearing trappers fur skin coat, trousers and fur skin boots and gloves and I suddenly felt like I had been reincarnated to a former life when I had been an explorer driving my team of huskies. I really did feel this at the time, honestly! My imagination continued to run riot as I introduced myself to each dog in the team giving them all a pat on the head whilst stroking their really thick fur and thinking of myself as their master at that moment in time. The dogs were so beautiful and loving in response to my stroking.

The dogs were now going mad in anticipation of what was to come, and they began yelping and pulling at the sledge and I naturally, being their master, had to put the brake on which is basically a piece of wood attached to the back runner which the driver put his foot to drive it into the snow in order to halt the sledge. My passengers, Theresa and Immy, were huddled together for warmth, underneath a fur blanket in the sledge as we took off at breakneck speed, which really surprised me as the dogs were so powerful and strong. Nevertheless, I quickly got the feel of the dogs and sledge before actually moving into the woods.

As we entered the dark woods, I put on my headband lamp to light the way. The wood itself was covered in virgin white snow and it was almost silent except for the sound of the dogs panting and their paws coming into contact with the snow and the very soft noise of the sledge runners gliding over the pristine white snow - it was eerily quiet on one hand but absolutely fantastic and completely enchanting on another!

The terrain changed quickly as we went deeper into the woods, and it became a little harder for the huskies to pull so I naturally started encouraging the dogs to pull harder by shouting "mush, mush" at the top of my voice. I was so engrossed in my work that I didn't hear Theresa and Immy pissing themselves with laughter in the sledge at my pathetic masterly orders to the dogs (apparently, they only say mush, mush in Hollywood films but I didn't know that did I?)

I can remember exactly the feeling of joy and happiness that I felt as we made our way swiftly through the woods, weaving either left or right, whilst touching the sledge brake to help navigate trees and bends in the difficult terrain. Some of our fellow sledge drivers became stuck on the odd occasion when their sledges had gone into a ditch. Not us I might add, with pride!

I continued to shout "mush mush" like a madman throughout the ride whilst Theresa and Immy were completely hysterical with laughter whilst snuggled together warmly in the sledge as we sped along. The ride was sadly over too soon and much to my regret, in what seemed like a blink of an eye, we had returned to the camp. Wow, what a ride! I was really on a high for the rest of the day as the experience was well beyond my expectations. I can honestly say that it had been one of the most exciting and exhilarating things I had ever done in my life and I still feel, looking back, that I had been an Artic explorer in a former life!

Me 'mushing' – what an experience!

Meeting the real Santa

Having recovered from the amazing husky adventure the day before, we resumed the search for Santa, and the elves gave us an indication which suggested that we might be meeting good old Santa as we had followed their clues. Sure enough, we arrived at a wonderful looking cabin in a wood clearing which potentially looked like it could be Santa's home and so it proved to be.

Prior to the trip to Lapland, Immy and Alfie had both written a letter to Santa with their requests for presents, subject to their good behaviour of course, and as with their family tradition, they had placed their letters in an open log fire and witnessed their precious letters being burnt and then the ashes of their letters rising up the chimney to make their way to Santa in Lapland.

Well, would you believe that as we entered the room, we saw Santa with the very same letters in his hand. How did he do that? What's more, Santa even recognised Immy and Alfie as he called each of them by name to come forward to meet him and discuss their requests, which naturally Santa approved of, as both of them had been very good! They even received one of the presents that they had requested on their lists.

Note: Santa's house in the background. Left to Right: Myself, Immy, Theresa, Alfie, Jon and Lil

It was quite magical, as Santa showed them both the letters he had received, and their faces were an absolute picture of astonishment, wonderment, perplexity and happiness. We were all nearly in tears as we watched the incident from the back of the room. Children's faces at Christmas are something else, especially when they meet THE Santa! It was one of the nicest things I have ever witnessed.

Theresa's love for Santa

By now Theresa was in bits for not only had she witnessed her own grandchildren receiving presents from the real Santa, but here she was herself in the presence of the great man. Somehow, she managed not to make a show of herself by not jumping up on Santa and snogging him, but instead she approached him and told him with loving eyes that she had "waited sixty years for this." At this point I was quite worried as I didn't know what Theresa was actually going to do next, believe me, it was more like a love scene from Romeo and Juliet! However, Theresa did manage to control herself and left the room with a glazed look on her face.

Alfie and 'Tricky Dicky'

One of the elves whom we encountered most days was the most mischievous elf of them all, named Tricky Dicky. Alfie loved him from the very first moment he saw him, mainly due to Tricky's naughty behaviour, which he carried out whilst shouting out at the top of his raspy sounding voice as he overturned sledges, furniture and anything else that was in his way as he created mayhem. Alfie loved all his antics and he quickly became his hero.

On one of the nights, Lil had requested a bedtime elf storyteller to come to our cabin prior to bedtime to read to the children. However, Lil was not allowed to stipulate a particular elf and you had to accept whichever elf you were given.

Come the evening there was a knock on the door and, low and behold, Tricky Dicky appeared, jumping and making loud silly noises as he entered our cabin without being invited in and immediately began turning the table over, scattering paper, disrupting everything! Tricky Dicky also made an attempt to hide at one stage but found it impossible as the lounge in the cabin was approximately 6ft by 6ft and so he decided to jump onto the fire place and stand there, still, pretending that no-one could see him. What a very naughty, mad elf he was! Alfie was spellbound as he witnessed the naughty antics of his hero, whilst poor old Immy laughed cautiously whilst also appearing to be a little shocked by his behaviour.

Tricky Dicky never did get around to reading the story apart from picking up the book and throwing it across the room saying it was rubbish, which Alfie found hilarious and then he went to the bathroom and squirted toothpaste all over the basin and floor. Tricky's continuous naughtiness had Alfie in stiches for the rest of the time he spent in our company. Immy, and particularly Alfie's laughter, is something that I shall never forget as I think there is nothing more beautiful than the sound of children laughing. What a memorable and fantastic holiday it turned out to be, so many thanks to both Jon and Lil for making it happen!

The infamous Tricky Dicky! As you can see, Alfie is absolutely mesmerised by his new hero!

2020/21 – a couple of years like no others

Having returned from our wonderful trip to Lapland in December 2019, Theresa and I were still on a high whilst getting over the trip, so, following Christmas period of festivities, it came as a shock when the Coronavirus pandemic hit the UK, with its first case reported in the UK on 28th February 2020. Little did we know at the time, of the impact that this deadly virus would have on all of our lives. Initially, I think we all thought that it was just going to be a short-lived virus but how wrong could we have been?

I could write another book regarding the virus and its effects on all our lives during this period, however, I have tried to condense it down as much as possible to give the reader a feel of how it was for us as a family and for society as a whole.

Initially, we were allowed to have four people in our homes and go out walking or shopping for essential goods, provided we took precautions by wearing protection masks and avoided any direct contact with members the public, family or friends. It was all so surreal if you went on a walk, for example, as the whole of society wore masks (not everyone by the way which is probably why it spread so fast) and people who you would normally talk to and pass the time of day on a walk, would now completely avoid you by crossing to the other side of the road. It was not normal behaviour for human beings and as it turned out, further down the line, a large proportion of the country suffered from mental health problems, not surprisingly, due to isolation and lack of social contact with fellow human beings.

By the time we hit April, protection masks and isolation were now part of all of our daily lives, as the pandemic was spreading fast and cases were growing by the day. With this, the Government ordered a series of complete lockdowns, apart from those involved working in essential services such as the police, fire service and NHS workers. The main thing missing from our lives from the start of lockdown was not having direct contact with our family, other than seeing them on video calls. Thank God for technology I say, as Jonathan very early on bought us a Facebook portal for video-calling, which was a life saver for us as we could at least see and talk to them all.

The first of the three lockdowns was a bit of a novelty and as the weather was really good at the time, Theresa and myself decided to make the best of things by having tiffin each day in the sunshine at around 3pm in the afternoon, which usually comprised of several glasses of gin and tonic and a few snacks to go with it.

As the whole of the country was in lockdown, my next door neighbour, Sundip Bhojani, who was not allowed to work at the time, also latched onto the tiffin period of the day and suggested hammering a large nail on our dividing fence with a long string attached to a carrier bag so that we could put beers into the bag and then swing it to and frow, to make a delivery to each other without having direct contact face-to-face. What a splendid idea I thought as it gave us the opportunity to continue to socialise and keep our spirit's up whilst not putting ourselves in danger of contracting the deadly virus! I also made use of a bell attached to my wall in the garden which I rang to inform Sundip of any fresh deliveries of beer.

Dermot takes on Joe Wicks

The Government also advised and encouraged the public to exercise daily at home and so Theresa and I, along with millions of others, started to exercise daily by watching, every morning on TV, overnight sensation Joe Wicks, who developed his own exercise programme for all ages. The women of the nation absolutely loved him as he is a very good looking, dark haired, fit and engaging guy. I personally don't know what they see in him!

As all my family know, I am not very good at co-ordinating my movements and I cannot dance to save my life (see earlier chapter regarding the Lindy Hop story if you want proof) and so I was no different in my attempt to emulate Joe 'good-looking' Wicks and his energetic morning physical exercises.

I was bloody hopeless as I tried to follow his every movement, but as usual, my hands, feet and body refused to follow my brain's instructions, resulting in myself looking like an 'octopus caught in a fishing net' whilst attempting to escape by thrashing about in panic with its many arms / tentacles against the net. Theresa used to video my pathetic attempts and send them to the family which had them all cringing, whilst pissing themselves with laughter at my every move, as their Dad embarrassed himself once again. Even I can't believe how bad I am!

Theresa and I were both classed as elderly and vulnerable due to our ages and also my lung condition, so Jamie and Fleur very kindly started to shop for us and it was so strange to see them delivering the shopping to our front door, but not being allowed to come in to see us. We sadly had to speak to them through from the other side of the window or door which again felt very unnatural.

With schools shutting down, it fell to parents to help home school their children, like Lil, which couldn't have been easy and Fleur, Liam and Donna who were all teachers, took to teaching their pupils via the internet whilst Jamie and Jon along with most of the country, started to work from home instead of their normal offices. The whole of the country, and indeed the whole world, was in turmoil and changing very quickly due to the Coronavirus and we all felt that life would never quite be the same again.

Having reached Christmas in the first year of the virus, this proved to be true, as it was to be the only Christmas that Theresa and I had spent alone in our 55 years of knowing each other. It was very lonely and very unnatural not to be surrounded by family and friends and all of the festivities that normally comes with this time of year. However, we made the best of it and thought of all those who had lost their loved ones due to the virus and considered ourselves to be lucky to be alive and healthy.

The Government of the day

Over the next couple of years, the Government of the day struggled to make the right decisions and tackle the Coronavirus pandemic as in between each lockdown there was indecision from one day to the next - the public really didn't know where they stood.

For example, they would relax the rules regarding social contact on one day only to have it rescinded a few days later and not only that, but the rules also differed throughout England, Wales, Scotland and Northern Ireland. The public really didn't know where they stood and it was total chaos!

I had some sympathy with the Government, as it was a world-wide pandemic problem and with the financial markets in total turmoil some very hard decisions had to be made. However, in my opinion, they made some very serious balls-ups, for example purchasing P.P.E. (personal protection equipment) which cost the taxpayer millions and millions of pounds for the health service, which turned out to be not fit for purpose, as the Government had not consulted the experts or those who actually used the equipment and whose lives depended on getting the right equipment in the NHS before they made the purchase. This is only one of their many cock ups which were so numerous to mention.

In my scepticism I suspected that during the pandemic, many businessmen and probably some MP's made a lot of money out of such 'deals'. I could be wrong of course!

Another much more serious blunder was their decision to send elderly patients who had contracted the virus, out of hospital and back to nursing homes, in order to free up beds within a hospital setting. Of course, these patients still had the active virus and so it spread quickly in the nursing homes resulting in 40% of elderly patients in nursing homes in England and Wales dying due to the virus spreading amongst its vulnerable population. It's so very sad and heart-breaking that the Government found life to be so cheap and expendable. I honestly think that upon reflection, the Government actually made this conscious decision, knowing that they were putting the most vulnerable of our society at risk. What kind of society is this I ask?

Apart from the Governments response to the pandemic, many of those in power at the time who actually made the rules regarding lockdown, proved to be the worst at keeping to their own rules. The then Prime Minister, Boris Johnson, and many of his other Cabinet members, held illegal parties and eventually were given a token fine by the police despite lying, time and time again, that they did not break any rules whatsoever. All this happened whilst many in the country had lost their loved ones to the virus in the community, care homes and hospitals as they were not allowed to visit them due to following the Government lockdown rules. The majority of the public had abided by the rules and by keeping the rules they had protected their fellow man. It was shameful of the Government!

By now I am sure that the reader must have spotted that I am a left wing socialist as my politics have always been towards the left and I make no apology for this. However, I still believe that democracy is still the best political system in the world despite its many failings. However, talking of failings, over the past four or so decades the gap between the rich and the poor has got wider and wider, and I firmly believe that there is enough wealth in this world for everyone to have a fair share. My wish for the future is that the wealth and power in this world should be more equally divided so that not a single person on this planet is short of food and all the basic requirements for life. I will get off my soapbox now!

Losing family and friends

Talking of losing loved ones, my own cousin, who was beautiful inside and out, Helen McLoughlin (born 15th April 1945, died 25th May 2020) was diagnosed with cancer and was admitted to hospital in 2020. Due to Covid we were not allowed to visit her prior to her sad passing. Moreover, only twenty people were allowed to attend the funeral and the normal send-off that Helen had requested on the last few days of her life (an Irish wake) was totally out of the question due to the rules. It was heart-breaking for Theresa and I, attending her funeral, not to be able to give support to her siblings and family members and not be able to continue the process of mourning in the Irish way at her wake. However, all of us were overcome with emotion and naturally, as human beings, we hugged each other for comfort.

The following year, another member of the family died, namely the lovely, kind Sydney John Ford (born 24th March 1925, died 9th January 2021) who was admitted to hospital due to breathing problems. At the age of 96, it was all so very confusing for him as he couldn't understand why no member of the family were visiting him, as he had totally forgotten about the current Covid rules. Sydney deteriorated fairly quickly after a short time in hospital and at the last minute, the family were contacted by the nursing staff who informed us that two members of his family would be allowed to visit to support him in his last hours. With the news, both Theresa and her brother Barry raced down to the LRI but sadly Uncle Syd passed away before they had arrived. It was devastating and so sad that he died alone!

Footnote: My friend and ex-colleague George Bogle died as a result of contracting the Coronavirus in 2020. RIP George, a giant of a man yet so gentle and kind in life.

At the time of writing, the official statistics for Coronavirus in the UK was 23.9 million cases and 210,000 deaths.

Breaking out to meet the family

The Covid rules kept on changing during 2020 and the Government declared that families of up to six people could meet in houses and open spaces. At this stage, Leicester was the only county in the country who were still in total lockdown and so by now Theresa and myself, and indeed all the family, were desperate to see each other face to face. And so, Jonathan had booked a glamping tent on a farm near the village of Market Bosworth to be near us and possibly meet us in a park in the area. However, on their way up to Leicester, the Government announced that lockdown in Leicester had now changed which meant that not only could we meet them but we would also be able to stay with them at the glamping site for three nights – what luck and we were so grateful that we were able to do this.

This was to be the first time that we had been away overnight since lockdown started which was roughly about a year ago. So, this led to us being able to meet up with other members of the family and the feeling of being able to do this was amazing after so, so long apart!

Liam and Donna then suggested that we could meet them in Canterbury for a week as they could swap their home in Wimbledon with their lovely friend and vicar, the Reverend Lindsay Collins the best-looking vicar in the world, who had married Liam and Donna back in the day. However, she now resided in Canterbury and her church was the cathedral!

We arrived in Canterbury at the same time as Liam and his family and I remember the joy we felt at seeing each other as Addison and Dawson raced across the road to greet us with tears in their eyes before giving us the biggest hugs you could possibly imagine from beautiful small children. It was quite overwhelming as all six of us hugged and kissed with the relief of being together, albeit temporary as the rules would change again! We had a fantastic time over the coming week but the main thing that we all felt was our love for one another as a family and for Theresa and I, this has been the most important aspect of our lives as we both feel like there is nothing more important than family even with all of its ups and downs!

2021 - our 50th anniversary

And so, to the 12th April 2021 and Theresa and I had now somehow reached our Golden Wedding anniversary (where did those years go?), but due to the Coronavirus pandemic, our plans to celebrate this special occasion had to be scaled down severely as the virus was still rife and the number of deaths continued to grow daily! However, as I said in earlier chapters, the Government rules regarding the lockdown had changed on a regular basis and so you could not meet indoor with others, but you could now meet outdoors with up to six people. This was a bit of a problem for us as we naturally wanted family and friends to help us celebrate this milestone in our lives.

Celebrating, videos and visitors

As we couldn't have any family sleeping in our house, Jon and Lil again booked Glamping on the same farm near Bosworth in Leicestershire, which would enable the family to visit us and help us celebrate our special day. Brilliant Jon - it's no wonder he is the brains of the family! Jon was joined shortly afterwards by Liam and family and so with the plan in place, we made arrangements for staggered parties of family and friends to see us on the day.

On the morning of our anniversary, Jon, Liam and Jamie came armed with a surprise. Because we couldn't have the party with all our friends and family, the boys decided to bring all those people to us in the form of a video. Prior to this, Jamie had been charged with the task of secretly looking at my phone and computer to obtain contact details of all of the people concerned that we wanted at our party and the boys reached out to them all and, would you believe it, they got over 80 video messages from all over the world including Iceland, New Zealand, Canada, Holland, Ireland and France. We were astonished to see all those people sending all their well wishes to us and we found it quite emotional and very moving. We never cease to be amazed at the lengths that our boys go to, to please their parents; we are so fortunate to have such great boys!

For the rest of the day, our next-door neighbour Dave Bassett kindly opened his garden as a temporary waiting room in case of overlap for numbers allowed in the garden. Theresa and I were on a high as Jamie, Fleur and Danny arrived for breakfast. Beer and wine became the order of the day even at breakfast. Just as Jamie, Fleur and family departed for home, Liam and his family arrived for lunch - it was running like clockwork! And so the day continued with drink, food and love in abundance. When Liam left to spend time in Jamie's garden, Jon, Lil, and his family arrived for tea - it was almost like a railway timetable!

The day continued in the same vein with friends and family arriving including Clair with Dylan and Evan and later, Theresa's siblings turned up to end the day with a bang. What a privilege to have them all with us on this special occasion.

Over the next week we continued to celebrate daily with all those we loved who popped in to see us, including Julie Kane and Kevin, Mick and Gill, and so many others… too numerous to mention.

To be honest, it was not what Theresa and I had originally planned. However, in many ways it was actually better, as with staggering the amount of people in the garden, it gave us the opportunity to spend more time with each individual as opposed to a large party gathering when you can only spend a few minutes with each person. What a wonderful time we had. However, shortly after this, something happened to turn our world upside-down.

2021 - the apple, and my close shave with death

Not only was it our 50th anniversary that year, but it was also Theresa's 70th birthday and I had made big plans to surprise her on her actual birthday, the 24th November. Unfortunately, best laid plans of mice and men, don't always go as planned as you will see in the following chapter.

I don't want to dwell too much on this chapter as it's both uncomfortable and painful emotionally to talk about. Nevertheless, my family all thought that I should write something on this chapter as it was yet another story in my life which thankfully turned out all right in the end.

In late November 2021, I ate an apple before retiring to bed for the night. I thought at the time that the apple was not ripe and so I discarded it into the bin. I awoke at about 4am with the most severe stomach-ache which at the time I put down to the un-ripened apple. Two days later the pain remained, in fact it was getting worse by the minute, but being a stubborn male, I still blamed the apple, thinking it would all pass through me. Wrong! An apple a day doesn't always keep the doctor away!

On the third day, I rang the NHS helpline as my stomach was so big, that I looked like a large pregnant woman and the pain was becoming almost unbearable. After answering all the questions with the NHS operator regarding my pain, I was directed to the Leicester Royal Infirmary. As Covid was still very prevalent in our lives, Theresa was not allowed to come into the hospital with me and so after twelve hours of waiting to see doctors and receive pain killers, I was eventually admitted to a ward and was put on morphine. After several days of tests and scans I was diagnosed as having an intestine blockage and an endocrine tumour. I was taken to surgery, but this was cancelled at the last minute.

The following day the surgery went ahead and during the operation they had to remove over 5 feet of my intestine due to the blockage at one end and the cancerous tumour at the other. Following the operation I went to intensive care, but unfortunately, after five days I had a coughing fit which resulted in the stitches bursting in my stomach and so I went back to theatre again to have another operation. A few days later, in intensive care, I was also diagnosed with peritonitis and to say that I was ill at the time would be a complete understatement!

I had nothing to eat for the three weeks I was in hospital other than fluids and nutrition via line feeds. My weight naturally plummeted down from 10 stone 8lb down to 8 stone 12lbs. I also developed a bed sore which was quite painful and to top it all, I was having hallucinations due to the morphine.

Looking back, I am so lucky not to have died and I remember clearly seeing myself in a mirror for the first time since being admitted to hospital and thinking I was not going to make it as I looked like the images you see of the poor souls in the concentration camps in world war two, looking so close to death whilst hanging on to life by a thread.

I also had a fleeting thought of ending it all after this incident but remember talking to myself and reminding myself not to be so selfish. I cried a lot during the nights in my room, as they seemed so long and the feelings of loneliness and despair were all too close to my state of mind at the time and I vaguely remember texting all my family and friends, telling them goodbye, as I really felt that my time was up. However, I can honestly and truthfully say that I was not frightened of the possibility of dying, even though I didn't want to leave this world prematurely.

Over the next three weeks I was visited daily by Theresa, bless her, as they started to let visitors back into the hospitals and following this, I had a first visit from someone other than Theresa, which was Jonathan (who came up to stay with Theresa the entire time I was in hospital), whilst I was hallucinating under the effects of morphine. I remember Jon's face was distorted as I spoke to him and I went on to tell him of a TV crew filming me daily on the ward and also bizarre sightings, such as seeing my two grandsons Dylan and Evans faces in rocks! It was bizarre and surreal for both Jonathan and me.

I can't tell you how much Theresa's visits meant to me, as the love for her and my family kept me going through these very dark days and nights. I looked forward so much to the sound of her familiar footsteps approaching my side room each day and my spirits rose with each visit as I held her in my arms and smelt her perfume whilst receiving her warm and lovely cuddles which seemed to make my world bright again. Moreover, her nursing skills were second to none as she daily cleaned me up, made me comfortable and put me back slowly on the road to recovery.

I could go on to write about some of the poor care I received in hospital, but I don't want to be negative about anyone, as the majority of the staff were brilliant despite their very heavy workload and the problems associated with Covid and the negative impact it was having on morale within the NHS. At the end of the day, I am so grateful for the skills of the surgeons and staff who managed to save my life and pull me through this very difficult episode in my life.

Escape committee and the getaway car

As I have previously said, I was so low at times in hospital and thought that I might never get out to see my home and family again, but there was a breakthrough with one of the consultants telling me that I was possibly being discharged over the next day or two. This appeared to be the green light for Theresa and the family as the next day Liam was up from London with the get-away car and Theresa came onto the ward ready to help me escape.

Theresa on the war path

The consultant told me prior, to Theresa's arrival, that I could go home that day, subject to the relevant discharge letter and forms being completed and take-home meds being available. However, Theresa was on full charge and in no mood for messing. When told she would have to wait for the paperwork and meds by the staff nurse, she informed her, in her own assertive way, that she was taking me home there and then and she would pick up the paperwork and meds later in the day! With this she had me up and walking off the ward and when asked by a nurse if I required a wheelchair, she told them point blank "No, he is walking himself without any aids!"

Outside the hospital, it was bitterly cold and I felt that I was going to freeze to death as I approached Liam's car with the engine running for the great escape. As I entered the vehicle I was crying with joy as I had made it out and would be seeing my lovely home and family soon. Liam, bless him, put his arms around me to give me support and reassurance with tears in his own eyes as I am sure this whole episode of my illness must have been very difficult for him and all of my beautiful family.

Upon arriving back home I hugged and kissed the brickwork of my house and continued to weep with joy and overwhelming happiness at being home at last, as I felt in my water that this was going to be the start of my recovery and so it proved to be the case, as within a couple of months I was back near to my normal weight thanks mainly to the best nurse in the world, the love of my life, Theresa.

Footnote: It must have been very hard for Theresa during this period as not only had she had to deal with the stress of it all, but she had also missed out on her 70th birthday celebrations. However, don't worry Theresa, I shall make it up to you in the near future!

2022 - Dylan in Dublin

Having recovered fairly quickly from my operation, I was determined to get on with my life again and keep a promise I had made to my eldest grandson, Dylan, regarding taking him back to Dublin when he was 18 years old, to see where I was born, have his first pint of Guinness in Ireland with his Grandad and meet some of his family in Ireland. Dylan celebrated his 18th birthday in May and so the trip was definitely on. Naturally, Jamie wanted to come with his son and Jonathan also said he would like to be with us and so we flew to Dublin in June of that year. My cousin Alan O'Loughlin and his wife Theresa had kindly offered to put us up for the four days in Dublin and the boys and myself were looking forward to spending some time with them both.

Prior to arriving in Dublin, I had made it quite clear to Alan that we would get a taxi from the airport to his house, as we didn't want to put him out, to which he initially agreed. However, being Irish, on the day in question he turned up to pick us up from the airport but he somehow managed to miss us coming out of arrivals. By the time he realised that he had missed us, we were already near his beautiful home - it was an Irish start to an Irish holiday!

Theresa and Alan proved to be the most welcoming and kindest hosts you could wish to find, with Theresa attending to our every whim and making us a hearty Irish breakfast each morning whilst

Alan tried to ply us with either food or alcohol at every opportunity. They also had a slightly out of tune piano (which incidentally Jamie tried to tune with limited success the following day) and a guitar in their home. As soon as we settled in, the boys asked their permission to use the instruments to which they appeared only too happy to say yes, in order to hear them played again. Very soon, their home was filled with music and singing from us and despite the noise and mayhem we brought, the both of them appeared happy to have us in their home and hear the racket we had caused.

Dylan's first pint in Dublin

The day of arrival was very hectic as Alan had kindly booked a tour for us at Glasnevin cemetery where most of the Irish patriots are buried. It was fascinating to see the graves and pay our respects to the likes of my hero Michael Collins, Grace and Joseph Mary Plunkett, Kevin Barry, Daniel O Connell, Charles Stewart Parnell and many other heroes too numerous to mention. It was all so very moving and very sobering as we made our way around the cemetery.

Alan then dropped us down to Rialto, just outside Bird Flanagan pub at the top of Rialto. By now, I was peppering for a pint with my grandson and so we swiftly made our way into the pub. I can't tell you the happiness and pride I felt as I downed my first pint of Guinness with my grandson, as I had not only kept my promise but following my tumour operation, which thankfully I had survived, I was still around to do it. I remember thinking how lucky I am and wishing hopefully that I may be around a little longer to see some of my other grandchildren following with me in Dylan's footsteps!

Dylan's first pint in Dublin with his family in Bird Flanagans pub, Rialto

After a couple of pints, we left and walked around Rialto where I gave them a tour of my old haunts, telling Dylan about my life and recounting some of my stories about my childhood, including the family in my Grandma's house, my own cottage where I was born, my school and the canal which is now filled in to make way for the tram service, The Luas, which runs along it. My mind was filled with lots of memories from my childhood as we strolled around the area - some of them tinged with sadness, but mostly good ones, as I felt so happy to be back on my home turf and to have my grandson with me.

Dylan and I outside 67 Rialto Cottages, where I was born. Where the feckin' hell does he get his height from?

Following this, we made our way towards Kilmainham Gaol, but before entering the prison, we enjoyed a couple of pints of Guinness in The Patriot pub nearby, which was very interesting with lots of memorabilia and photographs regarding Irish history (and by the way, a great pint of Guinness to boot) before making our way to the prison.

Kilmainham Gaol is a fascinating place which takes you on a journey through Irish history with stories of ordinary criminals held there alongside those who fought for independence over the years, including many of the heroes of the 1916 Easter Rising who were imprisoned and executed on the orders of the British Government. It was amazing and yet very sad at the same time to stand in the very same chapel that Joseph Mary Plunkett and Grace Gifford had been married in and spent a mere fifteen minutes together as a married couple (that's all the time that they were allowed by the guards) before Joseph was taken out to the courtyard and shot. Incidentally, the song 'Grace' is one of my favourite songs and I personally think it's one of the greatest love songs every written, given the subject matter of the song.

It was also very moving to see the courtyard again, where James Connolly had been shot in the chair, as he was unable to stand due to the wounds he had received during the rising. There never seems to be enough time in Kilmainham to see all you want and digest the history within, and our time sadly went all too quickly. However, at least Dylan had a brief snapshot of the history of Ireland.

Following this, we caught a taxi to The Hole In The Wall pub in Brownstown, where we met up with Alan and Theresa for a meal and a few drinks. The Hole In The Wall is interesting in itself, as it was built in 1650 as a coach house and as it was situated just outside the Phoenix Park walls, it became a place for political speeches - Daniel O'Connell apparently spoke there on occasions.

Later, the wall itself became the boundary for British troops stationed in the McKee Barracks from 1891 until 1922, which was within the Phoenix Park walls. The soldiers would apparently sneak out to the tavern for a pint, even though they were on duty. The landlord at the time was a publican named Levinus Doyle, who had the bright idea to put a hole in the wall to serve the soldiers without them leaving the boundary and hence the name - it could only happen in Ireland! The pub also boasts of having the longest bar in Europe which measures 100 metres in length. Having had our meal and downed several more pints of Guinness, we all headed back to Alan's house feeling very tired but contented with our first day in Dublin.

My animated cousin, Alan

Let me tell you about my cousin, Alan O'Loughlin. Alan is a very likeable 62 year old Dubliner, generous to a fault and short like myself in stature, slim built with a goatee beard and a twinkle in his eyes. He is a fairly quiet and reserved man normally but bright and intelligent when it comes to discussing anything you care to mention from world events to the history of Ireland. Moreover, Alan has a real passion and love for any kind of music, and I am sure he won't mind me saying that, despite the fact that he admits that he really can't sing or hit a note and even when he does sing, to quote Billy Connolly, he 'sounds like a goose farting in the fog!'

Nevertheless, I have never seen anyone whose demeanour changes completely when he hears music (especially when he has had a few pints), as he becomes completely uninhibited and doesn't care who is watching or listening to him whilst he dances around the room, singing at the top of his voice with his eyes closed whilst he is lost in the moment with melody, rhythm and the beat of the music. He is such a joy to watch and both myself and my boys love his company, as we have witnessed him on several occasions being completely engrossed in his beloved music.

I only really got to know Alan properly about four years ago when he and his lovely wife, Theresa, came over to Leicester to help me celebrate my 70th birthday and that was the first time I noticed his change in demeanour after a few pints and a singsong back at my house following my party. However, I am so pleased to have both of them in my life and it has been a real pleasure sharing their company over the last few years. (Read more about Alan in the following chapters).

Alan and Theresa in The Hole In The Wall pub. Note the Christmas decorations up... in June... the landlord left them up over lockdown to cheer everyone up!

Sightseeing in Dublin

The next morning, we caught a bus into Dublin centre to give Dylan a tour of the city and explained some of the history as we passed by many of the famous tourist sites including Trinity College, Temple Bar and Dublin Castle. However, the thing that fascinated Dylan the most was the GPO in O'Connell Street. He could not get over the bullet and shell holes left in the brickwork and the pillars from the time of the Easter Rising.

We had a good few Guinnesses in a pub along Grafton Street (I can't recall the name) before heading back towards the centre to meet up with my relatives in the James Connolly pub on the quay. We were first joined by Trevor and Gerry Kane who greeted us with big grins and massive hugs - it was so good to see them again! My cousins Mary and Anthony Kearney joined us shortly afterwards and finally in the evening Alan, Theresa and their daughter, Eadaoin also turned up. It was brilliant! With all the Kanes, Kearneys and O'Loughlins getting along famously; we had a right old session, with the demon drink flowing like water and I have to say that it felt so good and special to be in the company of my lovely cousins and family.

We were all half cut by the time we left and so we grabbed a taxi back to Alan's house. Back in his home, the drink flowed again, and Jamie and Dylan started playing songs as we all sang along. Alan, naturally after having a few jars, got up and danced around singing at the top of his voice whilst grinning from ear to ear as he did so. We had a grand session and it was all captured by his daughter, Eadaoin on her phone as she watched her Dad living in the moment, completely uninhibited!

Dylan's claddagh ring

The following morning, we were back in the city for Jamie to buy Dylan a claddagh ring for his birthday which would also be a memento of his trip to Ireland and a token of his father's love for him. After much searching through several shops and arcades he eventually found one that he really liked. After this we continued to explore the area and take in the sights, smells and character of Dublin city.

However, after a lengthy walk around the city it started to pour down with rain and so we headed up towards a pub, namely O'Donoghue's pub in Merrion Row. The pub serves a great pint of Guinness and is very famous for seeing the start of the legendary

Irish folk group The Dubliners, who played there regularly before they became world famous.

Dylan loved the music being played and the history and feel of the rough and ready pub with all the pictures of the group with world leaders, pop stars, football stars and even an American president. I think Dylan loved every minute of his time in the pub laughing and joking with his Dad, Grandad and Uncle Jon on this special occasion.

Session at the Halfway House

In the evening we headed towards Alan's local pub, The Halfway House, where we were due to meet up with the Kane and Kearney clans. The Kane clan consisted of Trevor, Gerry, Pat, Marcella, Helen and last but not least, was the lovely Geraldine. It was fabulous to see them all and I was totally surprised when my cousin Linda Kane (the queer one) and her partner Davy, turned up after travelling all the way from Wexford to see me. It was a lovely surprise. Later in the evening, Alan's son Eoghan also turned up to meet us and what a nice guy he is.

Gathering at the Halfway House! Left to right – myself, Geraldine, Helen, Jon, Dolores (Helen's daughter), Dylan, Jamie and Pat

My cousin Mona Kearney, who is so kind and with a heart of gold, also turned up, and she really made us laugh, as she arrived carrying a present for Dylan. Mona had totally forgotten that I had told her that Dylan was 18 years of age and she thought she would be seeing my grandson of approximately eight years old who would be a child in stature. Instead, she was greeted by a six-foot one inch, fully grown man! Her face was a picture as she looked up at him, then whispered in my ear, embarrassingly, that she had wrapped up a child's toy for him! Mona, who has not got a bad bone in her body, quickly gave the unopened present to another member of the family for their grandchildren before Dylan might spot her mistake. However, Dylan spotted it and was very touched that Mona had even thought to bring a present for him and so he took it all in his stride with a cheery grin.

Everyone was in great form as we all chatted and laughed the evening away. However, I began to feel fairly unwell as the evening wore on and by the time we left the pub and made our way back to Alan's, I was feeling really ill and a little irritable in mood. Back at his home, the drink was flowing, and music was blaring out as Theresa, was making sandwiches and cooking all sorts of food to keep us fed and soak up the booze. What a gem that woman is! Jamie and Dylan then started playing as we went into the early hours of the morning (Jamie actually had blisters on his fingers from playing so much).

My enduring memory of the night is one of both of my lovely cousins namely Alan and Pat Kane dancing and singing their hearts out in a duet (I can't remember what song they were singing) but I do remember that they were both singing in different keys, and it really did sound like 'geese farting in the fog!' However, it didn't matter a jot as they were smiling from ear to ear as they performed in their own uninhibited, unique style and everyone in the room loved every note and every minute of it. We were wetting ourselves with the antics and faces of both of them as they were both so funny!

I think it was about 4.45am when we all called it a day. I remember that Helen's daughter, Dolores, had remained sober for the night in order to give a lift home to Gerry, Geraldine and a very inebriated Pat. It was like a scene from Laurel and Hardy as he tried to enter her car but with each failed attempt he would turn around with a big grin on his face whilst mumbling to himself that it was the fault in the design of the vehicle (the doors and seat belts etc) that was preventing his entry. However, he was eventually helped in by others and he left looking happy but with a very tired and weary look on his face. I have to say that the craic had been mighty throughout the night and what a fantastic end to our holiday in Ireland it was!

Now then reader, I am sure that you have noticed that I have written extensively about stories that involve drinking alcohol. Well, I make no apologies for this and I would like the reader to know that generally speaking, I am a fairly moderate drinker. However, there has been occasions in my life when in the company of family and friends that I have let my hair down so to speak and have gone for the corner flag, if you know what I mean!

Alcohol can have a double edge to it, albeit good or bad. However, I have to say that whilst writing this book and recalling stories involving the demon drink, I can honestly say that alcohol has mostly enhanced such occasions and provided lots and lots of funny memories which I have happily recorded in my book.

Anyway, back to my story. The next day, after having a meal with our hosts and daughter Eadaoin, Alan kindly drove us to the airport. The whole trip had been amazing and unforgettable, and we found it sad saying goodbye to them all, as they had been the kindest and most generous hosts you could ever wish for. I hope to reciprocate their kindness sometime soon when they visit us in England.

Travelling back on the plane, I really felt very unwell and upon arrival back in England I suspected that I had contracted Covid. The following morning both Theresa and I took a test and, lo and behold, we both tested positive. Upon finding the results, Theresa made a declaration there and then, stating with a grin on her face, that most husbands bring back their wives a present from their travels, but in my case I had kindly brought her back the Covid virus... 'thanks very much, Dermot!' Sorry Theresa!

Footnote: Having both contracted the virus, unfortunately for Theresa, she had it worse than myself in terms of her symptoms. Nevertheless, all things must pass and so it proved to be as the case as the Coronavirus slowly subsided and our lives began to resume some kind of normality as we realised it was a virus that we would have to live with. It had certainly been a remarkable period in our lives, nevertheless, we came through stronger as human beings and more importantly stronger as a family.

2022 - Turkey

In August 2022 we had planned a three-week holiday with Liam and his family in the Mediterranean town of Kalkan in Turkey with its narrow-cobbled streets and quaint buildings and we were all really looking forward to spending time with each other in this beautiful location. However, it was to be a bitter-sweet holiday, as Liam and Donna had already accepted teaching jobs in Thailand for a period of two years and they were due to fly out shortly after their holiday with us. Unfortunately, they had to cut the holiday short by a week, as Liam had been appointed as Assistant Head and had to start earlier than planned.

Fortunately, and very happily for us as we didn't want to be alone when Liam and his crew departed, Jon and Lil asked to join us at the last minute, as they wanted to say goodbye to Liam, Donna and the kids, and also to kill two birds with one stone by also spending some time with ourselves when Liam and his family left.

We spent the first week with Liam's family swimming in the pool with the kids, eating out every night as the food was fantastic in each restaurant, exploring the mountains and visiting other towns in the local area. We also organised a trip to the spectacular gorge with a taxi driver called Hasan whom we had hired on our previous visit with Liam to Kalkan four years previously.

Every two days was a highlight for Liam and I, as we would look forward to a Turkish shave in the town with barbers Mohammed and Ali (brothers jointly named after the famous boxer would you believe). Each shave was an occasion in itself, as during the shave either one of them would shout up to the bar next door that two ice cold beers were required. Lo and behold, the two beers would be brought down to us and consumed with delight as the respective barber shaved us with an old-fashioned cutthroat razor, which left your face feeling like a baby's bottom when finished. Moreover, after the shave, you were given a total head, shoulder, and hand massage which left you feeling like a million dollars. We loved every minute of it as we felt like naughty children who had slipped out for a beer and a treat!

The first week slipped by very quickly before we were joined by Jon and family for the following couple of weeks. It was brilliant having both families together with the kids laughing and enjoying each other's company, mainly in the swimming pool, at our lovely villa, whilst the adults chatted and sipped their cold beers and wine. We also ate out most nights as the food was so good before exploring several of the friendly local bars to finish off the evening. Jon was quickly initiated into the Turkish shave club every two days, and he also became a big fan of the 'naughty boys' outings!

We decided as a family to hire a boat and skipper for the day and explore several of the islands and bays outside Kalkan. It was wonderful as we skipped from bay to bay, dropping anchor, before leaping into the warm waters to snorkel and gaze at the colourful fish and marine life. The kids particularly enjoyed having all their parents and grandparents together in the water including, would you believe, Theresa! It was lovely having the boat to ourselves as we could afford to be self-indulgent with the family and choose to do whatever we wanted.

The skipper and his mate made a delicious lunch with beer and wine to wash it down with as we bobbed gently up and down in one of the beautiful bays. On the way back, the children all took great delight in steering the boat, but I have to say that Alfie's face, as he took the wheel, was an absolute picture as he put full concentration into the task with a big grin from ear to ear! It was a fairly expensive day out but worth every single penny, as it was one of the last occasions that we all spent together with Liam and the family before they departed to Thailand and the memory of the occasion will last with us all for a long time to come.

Liam, Donna and the kids say goodbye

The time came for Liam and his family to depart and it was difficult for everyone concerned. It was early morning when their taxi arrived and by then, Donna was already on the verge of blubbing but was trying to hold on to her emotions so not to upset the kids and make their leaving as painless as possible for all concerned. We were all a bit choked up and a silence descended upon us as they quickly hugged us all before jumping into the taxi and speeding away before we really had time to digest what had happened.

In some ways having Liam and family leaving while we were still on holiday was made so much easier as we had the comfort and support of Jon and family with us for a further week and therefore this took our thoughts off Liam's family leaving to go to another country. As Liam had told us not to be sad or morose with their leaving, we carried out his wishes. As he pointed out, the two years were going to be an adventure for all concerned with the family having the excuse to visit Thailand for the holiday!

The following week continued with us taking trips to the mountains, visiting historical sites, eating out at beautiful restaurants and our continuing luxury shaves every two days. We also went back with Jon's crew to the spectacular gorge with its freezing waters that you have to wade through before you get to the gorge itself with its extremely high walls. However, the best part was hiring floating tyres near the forge for each of us and then floating miles down the Gorge River with Theresa and myself, Jon, Lil, Immy and Alfie all laughing our heads off whilst finding it exciting, relaxing and tranquil at the same time.

Our last trip was to watch a sunset a few miles from Kalkan, in a local village with its large sand dunes nearby. The sand was so fine and hot on our feet, but we had a lovely breeze to cool us down as we made our way towards the dunes. Having found a spot, we opened our beer, wine and picnic as we watched the sun slowly sinking in the sky and what a spectacular sight it was. I can honestly say I have never seen such a beautiful sunset in all of my days. It was so beautiful and awesome and made us all feel so very glad to be alive in this beautiful world and to be sharing the sight with each other in the company of Jon, Lilian and family. I shall never forget it.

Theresa and I watching the most beautiful sunset in Kalkan – hopefully lots more sunsets to come

All too soon our holiday was over, and it was time to return to the UK. It had been a beautiful holiday in a beautiful town and as it was Jon and Lil's first trip to Kalkan, I asked them what they thought. They both replied that "it was our first trip, but it won't be our last!" Theresa and I both loved being with the family on this amazing trip and we hope we have many more adventures and trips to come with them all.

Epilogue

As I reach the end of my story, I like to thank everyone who has contributed to this book, no matter how big or small their contribution. I particularly would like to thank Theresa and my three sons who have spent much of their time encouraging me to continue writing whilst also prompting or clarifying past events with me as I went along. I also want to thank Peter Goulding for his help, guidance and editing support on the book itself.

However, the biggest thanks must go to my eldest son Jonathan, who came up with the idea for the book in the first place and then saw the project through from the very start to the finish with me. I have to say that without his input, this book would probably never have been written, completed or indeed published. So, thanks again Jonathan, for persuading me to write it in the first place and add that it has been a very enjoyable experience and most therapeutic for me to write this book and reflect on my journey through life.

I want everyone who reads it to know that I have had a great life with wonderful happy times overall, but with some ups and downs naturally (but definitely far more ups than downs). However, to quote a wise man (my Dad) who told me many years ago, that there is 'no utopia' in life which has proved to be true!

Nevertheless, reflecting on my childhood in Ireland, which was quite hard, I could never see a future or had any real ambition or dreams to speak of. Moreover, I had little or no confidence in myself and being poorly educated, I was barely able to read or write when we left to live in England. However, despite this, life is amazing, and you never know what will turn up as you will have seen in this book.

Despite my deficits, I have always had purpose in my life and the ability to laugh at myself (I needed this as I made a show of myself so often!) and have always been a grafter and never workshy, whilst willing to give anything a go in life.

I also love the company of children and at heart, I am still very much a child myself. I have loved every minute playing with our beautiful grandchildren over the years, particularly playing the 'sheriff game' which I made up and gave me the chance to enter their world. The game involved me as sheriff, with the children as bank robbers. I would then chase them through the house or garden and upon arresting them put them in jail, only to have them escape again and repeat the process. It is fantastic fun with both the children and I laughing and giggling throughout the game! I sincerely hope in my heart that our grandchildren will remember and cherish these happy times spent together as they grow up to be adults.

I also love people generally and value friendships. I have been so lucky during my lifetime to have loyal friends for life such as Ian and Elaine Parkinson, Rocco Ambrico, Dave and Maz Williams, Bill and Julie Carpenter and Carey Maisey.

Also having wonderful large extended families in my life has helped me along the way with the Fords, Kanes and Kearneys and having special relationships and friendships with them all especially Trevor Kane, Eileen Casey, Joe Boy McLoughlin, Sheila McLoughlin, Nick and Jane Seymour, Alan and Theresa O' Loughlin, the Ford 'weakling brothers' (Barry, Trevor and Kelvin), Mona Kearney and Mary Doyle to name but a few.

I apologise if I have missed anyone out, but to be fair I am getting to be an old fart with poor memory and having met and loved so many people over the years, it's hard to give everyone a mention!

Love is the greatest gift of all

It has been a wonderful ride through life and hopefully there will be a few more adventures to come. However, I think that meeting Theresa was perhaps the luckiest thing that ever happened to me in my life, as she has stuck with me through thick and thin and guided me through the last 55 years. She is an extraordinarily bright woman and tougher than any person I have ever met and the love we have shared during our lives makes me realise how lucky I have been.

Moreover, Theresa gave me three wonderful boys, Jonathan, Liam and Jamie, who have all turned out to be fantastic human beings with values, principles and talents that have made both of us so proud. The boys and their lovely partners Lilian, Donna, Claire and Fleur have in turn given us seven wonderful grandchildren - Dylan,

Evan, Danny, Imogen, Alfie, Addison and Dawson - whom we adore.

Our beautiful grandchildren, left to right: Immy, Alfie, Danny, Dylan, Addison, Dawson and Evan

Although I am not religious at all and, in fact, I am an atheist, I do believe in a quote from the Bible that tells us that "love is the greatest gift of all" and I personally have been so lucky to have been gifted and surrounded by love of family and friends through most of my life and for this I feel so very, very grateful.

So, it's goodbye for now and thanks for taking the ride through my life with me. I sincerely hope that you have enjoyed the ride as much as I have!

Footnote: At the time of writing Theresa and I have booked to go to visit Liam and his family in Thailand in January 2023. Another adventure is on its way! Maybe there is another book left in me to write about the many stories that I have not got around to writing in this book - who knows?

Contemplating in Thailand....my next book perhaps?

Printed in Great Britain
by Amazon